THE BIGGEST GAME OF ALL

THE INSIDE STRATEGIES, TACTICS, AND TEMPERAMENTS THAT MAKE GREAT DEALMAKERS GREAT

LEO HINDERY, JR.

with LESLIE CAULEY

THE FREE PRESS

New York   London   Toronto   Sydney   Singapore

*f*P

THE FREE PRESS
A Division of Simon & Schuster, Inc.
1230 Avenue of the Americas
New York, NY 10020

THE FREE PRESS and colophon are trademarks
of Simon & Schuster, Inc.

For information regarding special discounts for bulk purchases,
please contact Simon & Schuster Special Sales at 1-800-456-6798
or business@simonandschuster.com

Manufactured in the United States of America

10   9   8   7   6   5   4   3   2   1

Library of Congress Cataloging-in-Publication Data

Hindery, Leo, 1947–
The biggest game of all : the inside strategies, tactics, and temperaments that make great
dealmakers great / Leo Hindery ; with Leslie Cauley.
p.   cm.
Includes index.
1. Negotiation in business. 2. Executives—United States. 3. Consolidation and merger of
corporations—United States. I. Cauley, Leslie, 1957– II. Title.

HD58.6 .H56 2003
658.4'052—dc21

2002034670

ISBN 0-7432-2900-2

To Ed Littlefield, Bill Daniels, and John Malone,
to whom I owe and dedicate
my business career

ACKNOWLEDGMENTS

The pathway of this book has been an evolving one—at all times, however, marked by a desire to write something that would have import and some legacy. Maybe one's second book is less intimidating. But the first one, I now know, is full of apprehension and concern—especially about writing something that later proves facile and of little consequence.

When Leslie Cauley and I first thought about this book, we concluded that we did not want to write just another "deal book," despite the fact that deals have permeated my career. Reprising deals, particularly notable ones, can be entertaining, especially for other deal junkies, but reprises alone afford no lessons. Also, there are always other deals in the offing. So there is no lasting literary import in simply augmenting the generally excellent financial reporting that transactions of the moment typically attract.

And so we decided that every chapter would contain specific lessons, of a sort. Lessons we hoped would help readers understand the impacts of some of the most significant business combinations and transactions of the last decade. Again, deals come and deals go, but why they happen, how they happen, and how the principals make decisions and interact can, I believe, be of importance to other business people, to educators, to students, and to others. At least I hope so.

Another perspective that caused this book to come into being is my belief that, since the mid-1970s, there has been a seismic shift in the visibility and relative importance of CEOs. At the same time mergers and acquisitions have come to distinguish American business and, in the process, the American economy. Prior to the 1970s, CEOs of significant companies were for the most part known mostly to other CEOs. The financial press focused primarily on companies, not on the men and women behind the scenes. Today, companies are routinely identified by their CEOs. Many are known just by their first names: Rupert (Murdoch), Barry (Diller), Jerry (Levin), Sumner (Redstone), Bill (Gates), and Carly (Fiorina) come to mind.

Unfortunately, during this same period there has been a dramatic deterioration in the ability of institutions and business practices to protect the interests of shareholders, investors, and employees. Directors, auditors, and analysts have all shown an ability to be compromised. WorldCom, Enron, Global Crossing, Adelphia, Arthur Andersen, and at least one top telecom analyst on Wall Street have recently emerged as poster children for how abusive these behaviors can become. I would also argue that the financial press dropped the ball by failing to adequately monitor and probe the activities of these and other companies. I suspect some reporters backed off precisely because these companies were large (read *formidable*) and, at least until recently, very respected companies.

As this is being written in the summer of 2002, the misadventures of unscrupulous CEOs have practically brought the U.S. economy and the financial exchanges to their knees. Hopefully, this shameful legacy will be short-lived. Given the growing importance of dealmaking and the ongoing elevation of CEOs in general, we had better figure out, if we can, how the good CEOs do it, and how we can emulate their practices. At stake is no less than the future of American business. If that's not enough incentive for change, I don't know what is.

It's been thirty-one years since I left Stanford business school to go to work for Ed Littlefield at Utah International. During that time, some truly remarkable people have shaped my career and contributed to my success, none more so than Ed. The generosity with which I was mentored by so many has defined my life and profoundly changed it. The employees with whom I worked at Utah International, InterMedia, TCI, and YES Network were (are) among the most extraordinary I have ever met. It was never what we did, but rather *how* we did it, and I hope that people will always remember that. At TCI, we first helped remake an industry, then helped define it, then made history by merging with AT&T. God, what an honor and gift it was to lead TCI, together with John Malone, on that incredible voyage.

There are some very special people without whom my career and life would not have been the same. I owe them more than I can ever express, but thankfully now I do at least get to acknowledge them. There was, again, Ed Littlefield of Utah International, who trusted me, taught me, and showed me just how wonderful it can be to work honestly and well in business. There was the late Bill Daniels, who gave me courage and his strong shoulder. There is John Malone, my partner and wonderful friend. There are my cherished cable industry pals and comrades, including, especially, Bill Bresnan, Steve Brett, Ann Carlsen, Brian Deevy, Grace de Latour, John Evans, Donne Fisher, Gerry Laybourne, David Mixner, Marc Nathanson, and Barbara Wood. There are my four great dealmeisters and allies: Len Baxt, Mark Coleman, David Klott, and Peter Zolintakis. There are my assistants and dear friends: Lisa Perreault, Carolyn Shanks, and Fran Hamlin. There is my family. And there is Leslie Cauley, my partner in this book.

Thank you all.

CONTENTS

THE
BIGGEST
GAME OF ALL

1

DEALMAKERS WHO MAKE
A DIFFERENCE

I WAS looking across the negotiating table and thinking to myself: *This stops right now.*

As CEO of AT&T Broadband, I had told the world a few weeks earlier that AT&T planned to buy MediaOne Group for $62.5 billion. Our offer blindsided Brian Roberts, the president of Comcast, who had announced his own plans to buy MediaOne just a month before that. Now Brian, who was seated across the table from me, was in a tough spot. He had to decide if he was going to stand down and lose MediaOne, or hang tough and fight us with a counter-offer.

The situation was tense, and growing more strained by the minute. Microsoft by then had already offered to help Brian if he decided to counter. A senior Microsoft executive, Greg Maffei, was waiting in an office a few floors down. Paul Allen, the software billionaire, had also offered financial assistance. Paul was in Seattle waiting for a call from his go-to guy, Bill Savoy, who was standing by in an office across the street. All Brian had to do was pick up the phone and call Greg or Bill (who would then call Paul) and I was dead meat.

Brian was edgy and probably a little embarrassed that we were trying to take MediaOne away from him, so he was liable to do anything. That scared the bejesus out of me. We couldn't afford *not* to buy MediaOne. The big cable TV operator was critical to AT&T's long-term business plans. But we couldn't afford to pay a stupid price, either. Though Brian had no way of knowing it, we had just announced our best—and only—offer for MediaOne. Unlike Microsoft and Paul, we didn't have the money for a bidding war. But we did have something they didn't have: Philadelphia.

Comcast, which is based in Philadelphia, had been trying for years to buy Lenfest Communications, which owned the cable systems in suburban Philadelphia. Gerry Lenfest, the company's founder and namesake, had always refused to sell. Luckily for me, AT&T owned 50 percent of Lenfest. To entice Brian to stand down on MediaOne, I decided to offer him Lenfest Communications. There was just one hitch: Lenfest wasn't mine to give away. Gerry still owned 50 percent and had veto rights over big deals affecting the company. I knew that Gerry would never sell his company to Brian. The two had competed for years, so there was a lot of bad blood. But right then I didn't care about that. All I cared about was holding on to MediaOne and getting Brian off my back.

I rolled the dice and made my move. I told Brian flat out that he could have Lenfest, and therefore the Philadelphia systems he'd wanted for so long, on one condition. He had to promise right then and there not to fight me on MediaOne. He had to agree to take Lenfest as a consolation prize and walk away. By then, Brian and I had been holed up for two days in AT&T's attorneys' offices haggling, so we were both exhausted. Brian considered my offer, then extended his hand to shake on the deal. My nightmare was finally over. MediaOne was ours.

I couldn't gloat right then, but in my stomach I knew I'd just hit the ball right out of the park. I'd managed to use a handful of relatively insignificant cable TV systems that technically weren't mine to give away to lock down one of the biggest and most important media deals of the century. I'd have to work things out with Gerry, of course, who still didn't have a clue. But that was just a cleanup detail. By the time it was all over, I'd make sure that everybody, including Gerry, walked away as huge winners. For a high-stakes dealmaker, that's about as good as it ever gets.

Dealmakers are found at every level of American business. But at the peak—the very peak—of the dealmaking universe are the ultimate wheeler-dealers. These are the dealmaking pros whose mere presence at a negotiating table is a sure sign that a big deal is about to go down—a deal from which they will most likely emerge as winners.

Pushing the dealmaking edge isn't for everybody. You have to be able to think fast, move fast, and bluff with impunity. You also have to have an iron stomach and an iron will. It doesn't hurt to have a sense of humor, which can come in handy on those occasions when everything blows up in your face. (And if you do enough deals, it does happen, believe me.) Much of the time, however, these super-dealmakers do succeed, often in spectacular fashion.

So who, exactly, are these business warriors? If you're breathing and live on planet Earth, they're hard to miss. Chances are you're already familiar with at least some of their handiwork.

There's Rupert Murdoch, the chairman of News Corp., which brought the world Fox Broadcasting, *The Simpsons,* Fox News, Fox Sports, and, overseas, BSkyB satellite TV. There's also Sumner Redstone, the chairman of Viacom, who turned MTV and VH1 into household names, then merged with CBS to produce a content-driven entertainment house that continues to push the borders of programming. Another dealmaking superstar is Gerald "Jerry" Levin, the former CEO of AOL Time Warner, the world's largest media company. AOL Time Warner is home to CNN, Home Box Office, *Time* magazine and, of course, Web giant AOL.

And then there is John F. Welch, Jr., the former CEO of General Electric. I consider Jack, as he is known to just about everybody, to be the finest CEO of the last century. During Jack's remarkable twenty-year run as CEO, the S&P 500 grew by a very respectable 15 percent return. Respectable, but puny by comparison to GE, whose shareholders during that same period enjoyed an astonishing 23 percent compounded annual growth rate. Jack Welch will be remembered for dozens of high-profile achievements: the growth rate, the introduction of the hugely innovative Six-Sigma approach to product defects; GE's management "college." But Jack's biggest accomplishment, bar none, was permeating GE with a dealmaking culture that will benefit the company for generations to come. At its core, GE still does a lot of relatively boring stuff. They still make locomotives, washing machines, and light bulbs. Yet, even as investors everywhere continue to chase the "next new thing," GE is still the yardstick by which other companies are measured. That's largely because of Jack's dealmaking credo.

Other members of this exclusive club include Mel Karmazin, the former CEO of CBS and current chief operating officer of Viacom; John Malone, the former chairman of Tele-Communications, Inc., and current chairman of Liberty Media; and Brian Roberts, the president of Comcast. All earned their dealmaking stripes the old-fashioned way: by making bold deals with bold moves intended to shake up the status quo. Mel engineered the blockbuster merger of CBS and Viacom, a marriage that would have been unthinkable just a few years ago. John dreamed up the groundbreaking merger between TCI and AT&T, a watershed event that kicked off a whole wave of consolidation in the cable and telecom industries. Brian grabbed headlines by making an unsolicited bid for AT&T Broadband in 2001, even as AT&T was attempting to spin off its cable and Internet assets in an initial public offering, or IPO. At the time AT&T Broadband was nearly twice Comcast's size. Talk about moxie.

Part of this group's notoriety stems from their collective style of dealmaking. It's big, it's bold—it's transforming. These dealmakers think way out of the box. (So far out, in fact, that at times it might seem as if they're on another planet.) Speed is their hallmark. They think fast, move fast, and pull the trigger on momentous deals faster than anyone—especially their competitors—would ever think possible. No committees here: These guys are singular Leaders with a capital L. They make decisions quickly, and with conviction. Sometimes they crash and burn spectacularly. Most times they soar, and in the process inspire us all to test our own wings.

Then there are the deals themselves. Like the men behind them, they're attention-grabbing. The deals put forth by this group tend to fire our imaginations and challenge our concepts about whole industries. These deals aren't neat and polite. They're big, loud, and often upset people, especially other CEOs. If you're a CEO and happen to bump up against one of these deals, either by design or by chance, you can almost count on having some sleepless nights. Just ask anybody who's ever tried to take on John Malone, Rupert Murdoch, or Sumner Redstone.

How to spot one of these transforming deals? You could start with what Potter Stewart, former Supreme Court justice, once said about pornography: You'll know it when you see it. Transforming deals have a tendency to jangle your senses. They have an aura about them that is almost palpable. They just *feel* different.

There are other, more worldly signs. Take regulators. What they say and how they say it can telegraph a lot about a deal's relative importance. Do they yawn? (Softball deal.) Or do they start hoisting red flags and talking tough immediately? (Tranforming deal.) Another indicator is the press. Does the national press—*The Wall Street Journal, The New York Times, Fortune, Forbes, Newsweek,* and cable and TV networks—pay attention? (Transforming deal.) Or do they refer to your deal in an abbreviated or, worse yet, humorous manner, or even take a pass altogether? (Softball deal.) Then there are the numbers themselves: They're huge. To qualify as a really big deal these days, you're usually talking about a transaction that is worth at least $5 billion or so. Anything less, at least in today's world, isn't a certified head-smacker. (As in slapping your forehead because you just can't believe that so-and-so is doing the deal you just heard about.)

The real telltale sign, of course, is the substance of the deal itself. Transforming deals tend to influence whole industries by their mere existence. Forget about closing one of these suckers, which can, in some cases, easily take a year or longer to accomplish. The mere *announcement* of a transforming deal tends to set off a chain reaction in the marketplace that can, in itself, lead to rather dramatic changes. When Bell Atlantic announced plans to buy Tele-Communications, Inc., in 1993, for example, cable and phone companies rushed to court one another. Almost overnight, companies that had practically ignored one another before suddenly couldn't say enough about how they might work together constructively going forward. Never mind that the Bell Atlantic–TCI deal would have taken a year to close, at least. Reaction to the deal was substantive and immediate. The Bell Atlantic–TCI deal ultimately died, but by then the seeds of a new way of thinking had already been planted.

Another measure of a deal's import is its impact. Size certainly counts. But size alone isn't the distinguishing factor. Daimler's acquisition of Chrysler, for example, was huge by any measure. So was Exxon's acquisition of Mobil, and Bell Atlantic's acquisition of Nynex. But did any of these transactions push the limits of our imagination, or cause us, as a society, to rethink the affected industries in new and exciting ways? Not really. At the end of the day, these marriages were all about making big, entrenched incumbents even bigger. The battle lines were fundamentally the same before these deals as after. The only thing that changed, really, was the relative size of the players. All the Goliaths just got a little bigger.

Now consider the Viacom-CBS deal. These two marriage partners were profoundly different on almost every level. Viacom was one of the most dynamic media companies on the planet; CBS was a traditional broad-caster with aging demographics and a mature radio business. In doing that deal, Sumner Redstone and Mel Karmazin were betting that the sum parts of Viacom and CBS—strategically, financially, and otherwise—were worth far more together than they were individually. It was a bold, even audacious, move that was fraught with risk. The early signs were most en-couraging. Soon after teaming up with Viacom, CBS starting seeing some gains in the prime-time ratings race. It also started making some head-way—slight but still there—in attracting younger viewers. To be sure, Viacom-CBS still got pounded along with the rest of the media world by the advertising dropoff in the aftermath of 9/11 and the general economic downturn. And Viacom's future management is something of a question mark, given Sumner's advancing years and Mel's short-term management contract, which expires in 2003. But these things will work themselves out over time. The point here is that Sumner and Mel had the foresight and courage to do the deal at all.

Same goes for AOL–Time Warner. Though a lot of CEOs had talked—for years—about buying AOL, Jerry was the only one who had the co-conuts to actually do it. The pairing wasn't without its risks. Time Warner and AOL hailed from opposite ends of the universe. One was an enter-tainment conglomerate; the other a maverick Web giant. One had a Holly-wood tradition that dated back decades. The other was a New Age kid still feeling its way around the Internet block. The day the merger was an-nounced, the old rules of engagement flew out the window; a new com-petitive dynamic was born. Like it or hate it, the AOL–Time Warner deal was that transforming. That's the sort of creative, over-the-top dealmak-ing that separates Sumner and Jerry from the rest of the pack.

That brings me to another basic characteristic of the *über*dealmaker: He has "vision." As a leadership characteristic, "vision" has become so overused that it's practically devoid of meaning. A lot of CEOs seem to think the label comes along with the title, like a company car or a golf club membership. But in my mind the meaning is clear. True visionaries antic-ipate; they don't just react. (Benjamin Franklin put it like this: "Genius is the ability to hold one's vision steady until it becomes reality.") Visionar-ies set their course according to their own mental image of the future, no matter how contrary that view might be to popular opinion. Nonvision-aries tend to let events of the day pull them along. It's a key difference, and one that gets overlooked a lot whenever the subject of "vision" gets raised.

Consider Bernie Ebbers, the former CEO of WorldCom. In the late 1990s, WorldCom was a growing telecommunications carrier on a tear to dominate the sector. Bernie rightly recognized that WorldCom's strategy and assets had some serious holes and set out to fill them. In short order he bought MCI, America's No. 2 long distance company—he had to wrestle it away from British Telecommunications, which had already announced plans to buy MCI—then turned around and laid plans to buy Sprint, the No. 3 player. In addition to having a solid base of long distance customers, Sprint had a growing wireless business and a very profitable local phone operation. Bernie figured the combination of all those assets would make WorldCom a particularly formidable competitor going forward. Sprint, a perennial No. 3 behind AT&T and MCI, quickly accepted his offer.

Enter BellSouth, the big Atlanta-based regional phone company. BellSouth had been eying Sprint for years but could never quite seem to pull the trigger. Once Bernie made his move, however, BellSouth scrambled and jumped in with a counter-bid. Like Bernie, BellSouth argued that a Sprint-BellSouth merger would leave both companies stronger. It also argued that the natural synergies between the two companies would accrue to the benefit of BellSouth shareholders. BellSouth said the deal was a hand-in-glove fit—strategically, managerially, and otherwise—on almost every level. So what happened? BellSouth got turned down flat, then turned on its heel and went home. Instead of hanging in there and fighting, BellSouth's CEO said, in essence, "Call me if you change your mind," and that was it. The BellSouth minidrama ended as quickly as it began.

Bernie ultimately wasn't successful in buying Sprint, either. Regulators later nixed the deal, claiming that a combination of America's No. 2 and No. 3 long distance companies was anticompetitive. But to this day Bernie will argue that the deal made a ton of sense strategically and should have been approved. And BellSouth? It later suggested that it was fortunate that its Sprint deal didn't work out, given the dramatic downturn in the telecom sector that followed. That is classic Visionary (Bernie) versus Nonvisionary (BellSouth) behavior. One sets his course according to an unflagging vision of the future. The other tends to get pulled along by events of the day.

Unfortunately, Bernie later got caught up in his own dealmaking web.

Bernie was ultimately forced out by his own board amid growing concern about WorldCom's finances. The second shoe dropped in June 2002, when WorldCom announced that it had hidden almost $4 billion in expenses—a figure that later ballooned to more than $7 billion—and posted bogus profits over a five-quarter period beginning in 2000. As this is being written, WorldCom has filed for bankruptcy, and the Securities and Exchange Commission is investigating the company for a variety of alleged offenses. Bernie's successor at WorldCom, John Sidgmore, is working on a restructuring plan, but the outlook isn't good. Unless John is particularly good at pulling rabbits out of his hat, WorldCom could be history by the time you are reading this. So could John, for that matter. The WorldCom board began searching for a new CEO in September 2002 after John let it be known that he no longer wanted the job. One can only wonder if things might have turned out different—for WorldCom and Bernie—if regulators had approved the Sprint deal. In buying Sprint, Bernie had hoped to turn WorldCom into a major player in wireless. After the Sprint deal died, however, Bernie gave up on that idea. The rest, as they say, is history.

BellSouth, to its credit, managed to avoid getting ravaged by the telecom meltdown. As of August 2002, BellSouth's stock price was basically unchanged from where it was five years earlier. That's not bad at all when you consider the fate of companies like WorldCom. But vision, as I said, isn't just about the short-term—or even the five-year—performance of your stock price. It's about looking into the future—years, or even decades—and having the guts to make big changes based on what you see. When Bell Atlantic and SBC Communications went on buying sprees a few years ago, BellSouth sat it out. BellSouth argued, as it had so many times before, that it couldn't—and wouldn't—expose its shareholders to undue financial risk. BellSouth also said it didn't need a merger partner to be successful going forward. It was big enough to go it alone.

True to form, BellSouth took a seat in the stands and watched . . . as Bell Atlantic and SBC made history and redefined the competitive landscape. In rapid succession, Bell Atlantic bought Nynex, the New York–based Bell, and then GTE. Not to be outdone, SBC snapped up Ameritech, the midwestern Bell, and Pacific Telesis, which provides phone service throughout California. By the time it was all over, SBC controlled the Midwest, Southwest, and California, and Bell Atlantic (now called Verizon) dominated the East Coast and large pockets in other parts of the country. The shopping spree left BellSouth, which formerly had bragging rights to being the biggest of the Bells, looking puny and badly in need of a growth plan. As this is being written, many people on Wall Street consider BellSouth takeover bait, even as the company continues to insist that it can go it alone.

Ivan Seidenberg, the CEO (and soon-to-be chairman) of Verizon, and Ed Whitacre, SBC's longstanding chairman and CEO, both deserve a lot of credit for having the foresight and courage to turn their regional companies into important national players. As of 2002, Ivan and Ed were still trolling hard for new acquisition targets. Verizon at one point contemplated teaming up with John Malone of Liberty Media (with me assisting on the side) to make a run at AT&T Broadband, AT&T's cable and Internet arm. They ultimately decided to take a pass, mainly because they didn't want the regulatory and political hassles that go along with trying to do a deal of that scale. SBC also considered making a run at AT&T on its own, but lost interest for similar reasons. No matter. Just the fact that Ivan and Ed contemplated those deals is confirmation of their creativity.

That's not to say that a CEO necessarily has to do big deals to achieve fame. Lee Iacocca, the former head of General Motors, is probably one of the best-known CEOs in history. Lee had a nice design sense for automobiles and tons of charisma, and he could certainly lead and inspire people. But Lee never did any business transactions of any significance. I also doubt that many people will be talking about Lee's contributions to his industry or to the world even a decade from now. That's not a criticism of Lee, mind you. But it is a strong reminder that fame, in and of itself, does not confer greatness or even importance. (Any time you need a reminder of this, just read *People* magazine.)

Sticking to a vision isn't necessarily easy. At times, in fact, it can be downright painful. Jerry Levin, the former chairman of AOL Time Warner, is a case in point. Shortly after the $165 billion AOL–Time Warner deal closed, the Internet boom went bust. Internet stock prices plunged. Jerry, who bought AOL near the top of the Internet bubble, took a lot of heat. In hindsight, critics said Jerry paid way too much for AOL. The company had to take a $54 billion noncash charge in the first quarter of 2002 to cover the plunge in AOL Time Warner's value. Even though it was a noncash charge, the perception that AOL was worthless hurt.

I don't know if Jerry paid too much for AOL, and I would argue that nobody else does, either. As this is being written, only God knows if Jerry overpaid. It will take the rest of us four or five years to find out. Regardless, the strategic logic of combining AOL and Time Warner is undeniable. Jerry, a longtime believer in the idea of convergence, figured the long-term benefits of buying AOL would far outweigh any short-term risks, including fluctuations in the marketplace. Bold? You bet. Risky? Of course. But if Jerry was right—and I believe that he was—AOL Time Warner will triumph once convergence turns real.

Jerry's vision has gotten him into hot water before. Back in the mid-1990s when cable TV stocks were in the tank, Jerry was under tremendous pressure to bail out of the cable TV business. "Jerry-bashing" on Wall Street (and even among some Time Warner executives) practically became a blood sport. Some analysts quietly began calling for his head. Jerry, to his eternal credit, refused to budge. He believed, in his heart and in his head, that cable was a powerful conduit for delivering all sorts of video and interactive services to consumers, including video-on-demand and Internet services. Jerry's optimism seemed like a bit of a stretch. At the time it was all some cable operators could do just to maintain halfway decent cable service.

Jerry was eventually proven right. Just as he had predicted, the cable industry got its act together and began attracting a slew of big new investors, including Microsoft. Convergence became the industry mantra. Wall Street joined in and pushed cable stocks to new highs. And Jerry? The guy whose head had once been on the chopping block was suddenly hailed as a hero.

It remains to be seen if Jerry will be hailed as a hero on the AOL–Time Warner deal. Jerry retired from AOL Time Warner in 2002 after thirty years with the company in all its various forms, the last ten as CEO. By the time Jerry left, cable stocks were again treading water and Internet stocks were, as I said, blasted. Investors are understandably upset. Though the ad market has lately been perking up, the short-term outlook is still rather dismal. All that said, I continue to believe that the AOL–Time Warner deal was smart strategically.

CEOs devise all sorts of clever cover-ups for their lack of vision and real convictions. When he was appointed CEO of IBM in 1993, Lou Gerstner attracted a lot of attention by saying that the last thing IBM needed was a "vision." Lou made that assertion at a time when IBM's shares were trading at historical lows and the longtime CEO whom Lou succeeded had just been pushed out. Lou was wrong, of course. If IBM ever needed a vision, it was right then. But Lou, who had never run a computer company in his life, much less a *Queen Mary* like IBM, didn't have one handy. So Lou did what most CEOs do who don't have a game plan: He said it didn't matter, and soldiered on. IBM eventually turned into a well-run organization under Lou, who retired in 2002. During his tenure, Lou cut more than a billion dollars of expenses from IBM's bloated structure and revived the company's tradition of treating customers well. He also took advantage of some opportunities created by the swelling popularity of the Internet. But I don't think you could say that Lou Gerstner was particularly prescient, and he certainly wasn't visionary.

My guess is that if you were to talk to any of the dinosaurs out there today—Bethlehem Steel, Xerox, Ford—they'd all tell you a version of what Lou so famously told his shareholders back in 1993. And the reason is quite simple: They don't have a vision handy, either. These are all big, substantial organizations. And they essentially have no vision. Some of them, such as IBM, are quite well run. Others, such as BellSouth, have been incredibly lucky. (BellSouth, which was created by the court-ordered breakup of AT&T in 1984, inherited its monopoly local phone business.) Most of them even have a strategy, or at least the semblance of one. But they have no vision. And to be a really successful, leading-edge company in the emerging world of New Media, you need both.

Hailing from the world of New Media, in and of itself, isn't enough. If that were the sole criterion, technology would surely win hands-down. Technology has become the lubricant of our society, and in the process it has become a fundamental part of our lives. Technology affects virtually every aspect of our existence, from the way we bank and shop to the way we socialize, look for jobs, and keep in touch with our families and friends. And yet, just try to name even a single successful dealmaker who has emerged from this community. Can't think of any? Neither can I. An industry that can produce microscopic computer chips, voice recognition technology, and encryption systems sophisticated enough to confuse the Kremlin *should* be able to triumph at the negotiating table. And yet, that is not the case.

Bill Gates of Microsoft, America's technology leader, is probably *the* most famous technology CEO in the world. Bill's genius, however, was never about dealmaking. It wasn't even about technology. Bill's genius was his laserlike ability to look into the future and envision a New World developing that embraced nonproprietary software standards. At a time when Apple was zealously guarding its proprietary software system, Bill smartly ran as hard and as fast as he could to license Microsoft's operating system to anybody and everybody. In the process, Bill ignited a computer revolution and secured Microsoft's—and his—place in history. And Apple? It chose to keep its operating system proprietary—and nearly killed the company.

Praise for Bill aside, let's be brutally honest here—the guy is no dealmaker. As of 2001, Microsoft's biggest business transaction consisted of investing $5 billion for a small stake in AT&T. And even that wasn't particularly well done. (See Chapter 5.) Other investments haven't fared so well, either. Trying to catch the Internet wave, Microsoft aggressively invested in an assortment of cable, telecom, and technology companies in the United States and abroad. When the Internet bubble burst, Microsoft got caught flat-footed like everybody else. In 2001, Microsoft was forced to write down more than $5 billion in bad investments, much of it related to cable, telecom, and the Internet. Microsoft, of course, is still an incredibly valuable company. But who knows what Microsoft might have looked like today if Bill had been able to leverage some of his famous smarts into prescient, forward-looking technology deals? What if Microsoft had bought Cisco Systems, Amazon, or AOL—or even all three—early on? Instead of just being a formidable software power, Microsoft today might be a media conglomerate leading the planet into a new Information Age. You can only wonder.

But taking Bill to task for not shining as a deal negotiator is like criticizing Tiger Woods because his bowling game isn't so great. Bill Gates is one of the true visionaries of our time. He is somebody we'll all be discussing not just a decade from now, but generations from now—and maybe for all time. His intellectual contributions have fundamentally and forever changed our lives, and in the process changed the world. That is, and always has been, the hallmark of a true visionary.

To be sure, a few technology stars did manage, at least for a while, to grow their businesses by acquisition. Most of them eventually bombed out. Cisco Systems, the hot maker of Internet networking gear, was classic. Using its soaring stock price as deal currency, Cisco acquired more than seventy companies between 1993 and 2000. By 2001, fully *half* of Cisco's revenues came from acquired technology or companies. That should have set off alarms—nobody can assimilate seventy companies in that short space of time. But it didn't. Wall Street was so enamored of Cisco's growth-by-acquisition strategy that it drove up Cisco's stock price even further. That, of course, just emboldened Cisco even more.

Then the Internet bubble went bust—and Cisco blew up like an over-inflated balloon. The company's lunar-bound stock price promptly went into a free fall, wiping tens of billions of dollars off Cisco's market value. Cisco's acquisition binge promptly screeched to a halt. As dazed investors tried to sort out what had just happened, Cisco got down to the difficult business of trying to sort through its bulging portfolio of new companies to figure out exactly how they all worked together. The short answer: A lot of them didn't. Cisco's famous nose for deals, so it seemed, was an illusion—just like the Internet bubble itself.

The high-speed Internet company controlled by AT&T, @Home, didn't do much better. Tom Jermoluk, @Home's CEO, decided to turn @Home into a bigger, better version of AOL. Never mind, apparently, that @Home was a *distribution* play that was never intended to be a content-driven company. In 1999, @Home acquired Excite, a big Web portal akin to Yahoo!, for $7 billion. @Home also bought Blue Mountain, an electronic greeting card company, for $780 million, including $350 million in cash. I was on the @Home board during this time (from 1997 to 1999) and frequently butted heads with Tom about the company's strategic direction. Out of twelve directors, I was the only one who voted against the Excite and Blue Mountain acquisitions. Tom basically ignored my concerns, and who could blame him? The more @Home invested in other Internet start-ups, the more Wall Street cheered. Investors eventually pushed @Home's stock price to near the $200 mark. It was a heady time for a company whose shares had started trading just two years earlier for $10.50 apiece.

By fall 2001, the party was over. Ravaged by the Internet bust, @Home's expected revenues from Excite never materialized. Service quality deteriorated under AT&T, which committed an extra $3 billion to take control of @Home on the belief that it could provide a handy platform for high-speed and interactive services. @Home's other cable benefactors, who sold @Home exclusively, soon started talking about withdrawing their support. In fall 2001, @Home finally threw in the towel. It filed for bankruptcy and began auctioning off its assets. And Excite? By then, @Home had been trying for months to literally give the portal to anyone who would take it. (And when I say "literally" I mean just that: @Home had figured out it would cost a couple of hundred million dollars to shut down Excite and was willing to give it away to avoid incurring those costs.) As for Blue Mountain, @Home did manage to sell that—for $35 million, about 5 percent of the original purchase price. So much for creating the next AOL.

The dealmaking report card for the U.S. telecom sector was even worse. Global Crossing, where I briefly served as interim CEO in mid-2000, spent billions of dollars to construct an international fiber-optic telecommunications network in the belief that demand for transport capacity would far outstrip availability. Unfortunately, a lot of other carriers had the same idea. It soon became apparent that the market was, in fact, being flooded with millions of miles of fiber-optic capacity that weren't being used. Prices for fiber-optic capacity plummeted. So did the fortunes of Global, which eventually filed for bankruptcy court protection.

Global might have been one of the more notable telecom flameouts, but it was by no means the only one. Winstar, an acquisition-prone wireless upstart, essentially got a $700 million loan from Lucent, a big U.S. equipment provider, to get its business going. Then Winstar went belly up, leaving Lucent to eat its $700 million in so-called vendor financing. Lucent wound up writing off most of Winstar's loan, then got hit again and again as other small carriers flamed out—taking Lucent equipment and contracts with them. Lucent's management got blindsided by the telecom meltdown. Trying to right itself, Lucent's management cut costs to the bone. More than half of Lucent's employees were let go or resigned in less than six months—and still the reductions continued. Nortel, the big Canadian telecom equipment maker, also got socked. It announced a $19 billion write-off in 2001, one of the biggest in corporate history. Those moves, for the telecom sector, were only the canaries in the coal mine.

Carrier after carrier crashed and burned. Billions in investors' money went straight down the tubes. In the thirty-six months ending December 2000, a breathtaking $1.24 *trillion* was lent to telecom carriers of all sizes for plant and infrastructure development. (And that didn't even include the billions of dollars of vendor financing that were extended to technology start-ups such as Winstar that eventually went under.) Roughly 30 percent of the growth in the U.S. economy—jobs and capital—during this remarkable three-year period was due to companies in this sector. When the sector went under, so did those investment dollars. Hundreds of thousands of people lost their jobs.

By the time September 2001 rolled around, the economy was already flirting with a recession, and 9/11 tipped the scale. After the attacks, there seemed to be little doubt that America was in a full-tilt recession. The airline, hotel, and tourism industries got pounded. Tens of thousands of employees were almost immediately laid off. Congress had to come to the rescue with a large economic aid package. Within weeks the United States retaliated by unleashing bombs, and then troops, on Afghanistan, the country where the terrorists who had planned these awful attacks were believed to be hiding. As if all that wasn't enough, an anthrax scare soon followed. Several people died from exposure to the deadly disease. Fear gripped the nation.

Corporate America blinked hard. The New York Stock Exchange, which was closed on the day of the attacks, reopened a few days later. When the opening bell rang, the Dow headed straight for a cliff and jumped off, finishing down a gut-wrenching 700 points for the day. The steep drop in the stock market caused all of us to catch our collective breath and wonder what the next day would look like. And the day after that, and the day after that. A lot of CEOs, quite understandably, were positively reeling. So were investors. Many saw their portfolios, along with their retirement incomes and life savings, plummet in value. Even seasoned investors were shaken. It was a painful, uneasy period for our country and for the world we live in.

But America's dealmaking giants, to the man, held their ground. On the same day the newspapers were talking about America's gloomy economic outlook, Rupert Murdoch was still in there pounding on GM's door trying to buy DirecTV. Brian Roberts of Comcast was still running hard after AT&T Broadband, and John Malone, being John Malone, was still figuring out new ways to conquer the world. Times might have been uncertain, but these titans of business were, in fact, still very certain of their respective places in the world. And even the horrific events of September 11, and all the awful implications of that singularly devastating day, couldn't shake their fundamental beliefs and hopes about the future.

And that, in a nutshell, is why I'm such a fan of Rupert, Brian, John, and the others. It's not because they're famous. It's not because they are influential. It's not even because they are successful. Quite the opposite: They're successful, influential, famous—and *different*—precisely because they have a clear-eyed vision of the future. They have an indelible road map in their brains of how they want to get there and they stay the course. They don't panic when the stock market tanks. They don't wring their hands when the economy takes a dive, or even when a global response to terrorism threatens. They don't lose their cool, period. Instead, they do what great business leaders should do—they *lead*. And that, at the end of the day, is what being a successful CEO in today's global environment is all about.

As a dealmaking veteran myself, I've had the honor and pleasure of spending time with all of these remarkable executives. Sometimes we've been on the same side of the negotiating table; other times not. But I've learned an awful lot from each of them over the years, which is one reason I decided to write this book. My hope is that somewhere in here you'll find something relevant to your own life and career, or maybe both. And maybe, just maybe, even a little bit of inspiration as you navigate your own chosen path in life. With that in mind, I'd like to offer some brief observations about the people to whom this book is dedicated, America's true dealmaking giants.

Rupert Murdoch, Chairman, News Corp.: (Okay, so he's not American-born. But he is Australian, which is close enough.) I hear young executives all the time talk about "Rupert," even though most have never even met him. It's that kind of suggested familiarity that defines this small but influential group of CEOs, and Rupert is right at the head of the pack.

Rupert has one of the most formidable creative minds on the planet. He is also one of the most long-reaching deal guys you'll ever meet in your life. His sense of continuity is remarkable. Rupert is building something for the generations that haven't even been born yet. Because of that, he is willing to take huge risks and suffer tremendous downturns, all for the sake of the out years. Rupert is allowed to be the visionary of the sort he is—commanding, forward-looking, and stunningly creative—because he controls News Corp. Otherwise, he could have been fired three or four times by now. Every time his stock price took a serious dive, he might have been whacked.

Rupert is a certified genius when it comes to programming and marketing. That's why so many people fear him. As of 2002, Rupert's satellite TV ventures in Europe, Asia, Latin America, and Australia reached more than 85 million homes. As he looks to expand even further into the United States, cable television operators are rightly worried. Cable operators complain that Rupert plays dirty in the market—favoring his own content over that of others is the biggest complaint. But that's just a lot of bunk. The real reason cable operators don't want Rupert to come into the U.S. market is that nobody wants to compete against him. The guy is just that good, and everybody knows it.

Rupert spent more than a year trying to buy DirecTV, the big domestic satellite TV company controlled by General Motors, only to get outdone at the last minute by his archrival, Charlie Ergen of EchoStar, another satellite TV provider. DirecTV prospered under GM. But in the hands of a true programming master like Rupert, DirecTV might really take off at the expense of traditional cable TV operators. (Bingo: This is the real reason cable operators fret about Rupert.) Though Rupert lost the first round to Charlie, don't count him out just yet. As this is being written in the fall of 2002, regulators have turned down EchoStar's bid to buy DirecTV, paving the way for Rupert to swoop back in and buy the company. So stay tuned.

Sumner Redstone, Chairman, Viacom: Sumner's ability to peer into the future and set strategies, then execute brilliantly, continues to amaze. He may be in his seventies, but Sumner is one of the quickest son of a guns you'll ever meet. His willpower is also legendary: Sumner famously survived a hotel fire by literally hanging by one hand off the third-story ledge until he could be rescued.

In business (as on that ledge), Sumner has demonstrated an enormous amount of courage. He had the temerity to combine Viacom, his longtime baby and one of the most vibrant media empires on the planet, with the blue-haired lady of broadcast, CBS. The $37 billion merger recast the competitive landscape and pushed the boundaries of our thinking about the role of traditional broadcasters in the emerging world of New Media. The union, not insignificantly, left Sumner (and his No. 2, Mel Karmazin—see below) in charge of a stunning collection of assets: Blockbuster, Paramount Pictures, Simon & Schuster (Free Press, the publisher of this book, is a unit of Simon & Schuster), radio and TV stations, outdoor billboard advertising, and, of course, CBS. Not bad for a guy who started out with a string of movie theaters.

Mel Karmazin, Chief Operating Officer, Viacom: Mel merged himself right to the top of the media world. He engineered the merger of his former company, Infinity Broadcasting, into CBS, then became CBS's CEO. That would have been a career-capping transaction for many guys— but not Mel. Right after he did the CBS deal, Mel proceeded to up the ante by proposing to Sumner that they merge CBS into Viacom.

Some critics considered the marriage a stretch. CBS, after all, was a traditional broadcaster with seriously aging demographics. The network was known for such TV classics as *60 Minutes, On the Road with Charles Kuralt,* and Walter Cronkite, the famous CBS news anchor. Viacom, in contrast, was anything but classic. It had urban edge all over the place. Viacom's stable of (new) cable classics include MTV, VH1, and Nickelodeon. Many also doubted that Sumner, who is the heart and soul of Viacom, would ever be willing to share power with anyone, much less the grande dame of traditional broadcasters.

To be sure, Mel and Sumner had their run-ins. Whenever you get two large personalities like that in the same room conflicts are bound to occur. But I also think it's fair to say that Sumner and Mel had an enormous amount of respect for each other's talents and contributions. In any event, how Sumner and Mel fare as a management team is almost beside the point. What does matter is this: Their shared vision of the future is what brought Viacom and CBS together. The combination, at one time considered unthinkable, not only profoundly changed the two companies, it altered the direction of an entire industry.

Gerald "Jerry" Levin, (former) Chairman, AOL Time Warner: Jerry engineered the $165 billion merger of his company, Time Warner, with America Online. The deal, breathtaking in its size and scope, radically redefined the competitive landscape. It also made Time Warner the biggest mountain in that landscape. (This media mountain range, it goes without saying, also includes Mount Viacom and News Corp.)

This deal, at the time, was counter-intuitive. Up until the day the deal was announced, AOL was the cable industry's chief nemesis. AOL has basically declared war on cable operators over the "open access" issue. That is the notion that cable TV operators should be forced to provide access to their systems at greatly reduced fees. AOL argued that such access was necessary in order for AOL and others of its ilk to exist going forward. Cable operators balked and promptly labeled open access nothing more than "forced access" designed to enrich AOL and cripple them. AOL refused to take no for an answer and turned to the government for help. Cable operators stood firm, but in truth many were quite worried.

Enter Jerry Levin. Once the AOL–Time Warner merger was announced, AOL did the equivalent of an about-face on the issue of open access. Almost overnight, the issue that seemed to define AOL's very existence became a nonstarter. Once it switched sides and became a cable TV operator itself, AOL, so it seemed, no longer wanted to discuss open access, much less broach the issue with regulators. A lot of smaller players tried to carry on the fight. But absent a well-funded mouthpiece like AOL, the issue largely faded away. Cable executives, of course, couldn't have been happier. So not only did Time Warner end up with a formidable Internet partner, it vaporized, in one fell swoop, an issue that gravely concerned Jerry. And AOL? It finally got what it wanted—a powerful foothold in the cable TV (distribution) and "content" world.

Jerry, as I mentioned, took a lot of heat for this deal once the Internet market soured. It will be up to his successor, Dick Parsons, who was Jerry's No. 2 for six years, to make the merger sing. Dick is a master at constituency building, a talent that should come in very handy now that AOL Time Warner is the size of Delaware. Like his longtime mentor, Dick's a big believer in the power of convergence. He's also not afraid to pull the trigger on deals. So stay tuned.

John Malone, Chairman, Liberty Media: John is one of the great dealmakers of all time. He's also a visionary in the purest sense of the word. In the early 1990s John foresaw a world of five hundred channels, a world where interactive television influences all that we are and all that we do. Though John might have been a little early in his predictions— some would say a lot early—his bold pronouncements continue to be borne out by technological developments. It's not a matter of "if" interactive TV arrives, but merely when. John, as usual, called it early, and called it right.

John, the former chairman of Tele-Communications Inc. (TCI), was already a giant in the cable industry by the time he asked me to become president of TCI in February 1997. A little more than a year later we announced plans to sell TCI to AT&T for $48 billion, setting off a chain reaction in the cable world that wouldn't settle out for several years. Our original plan called for AT&T to use the cable TV lines to offer local phone service across America. Though things didn't exactly work out as planned, the deal forever changed perceptions about the cable TV business. It also changed, fundamentally and forever, a great American icon, AT&T.

John has a reputation for being quite intimidating at the negotiating table. And for good reason: He is. Over the past twenty-five years, John has negotiated literally hundreds of deals—with bankers, cable operators, TV networks, and regulators. As a result, complex financial arrangements are second nature to him. John is a master at using his intellect like a fist to batter you into submission. He's also a master at outmaneuvering people, often on several levels simultaneously. It's not that John's trying to be coy; that's just the way his brain works. John used to say that doing a deal is like three-dimensional chess. If you're not playing four to five moves ahead on different planes at all times, you're going to lose. And John rarely loses. Just ask anyone who's ever sat on the other side of a negotiating table from him.

Brian Roberts, President, Comcast: Dealmakers at this level have an uncanny ability to peer into the future and act decisively when opportunities arise. No obvious opportunities out there? No problem. Like human tsunamis, when these guys get you in their path, things just have a way of happening. Or blowing up.

Consider Brian Roberts, the youthful president of Comcast, and his father, Ralph, Comcast's founder and chairman. The Robertses made an unsolicited bid to buy AT&T Broadband in the summer of 2001 for $58 billion. Their surprise move followed weeks of talks with AT&T that went nowhere. Brian timed his move to upset AT&T Broadband's plans to make an initial public offering, or IPO, of its stock to the public. (AT&T was publicly traded; AT&T Broadband, under the plan in effect at the time, would have traded as a separate stock.) An IPO is the first public sale of a company's stock to the public. It's considered a very big event in the life of any organization, much less a high-profile brute like AT&T Broadband. Brian's trump move forced AT&T to delay its IPO, setting off a long wait-

and-see period with the AT&T board. Brian's bravado eventually paid off, netting him AT&T Broadband—and a place in my Dealmaking Hall of Fame. Once the deal closes, Brian and his father will control the biggest cable television company in America, not bad for a father-son team from Philadelphia.

"Ted" Turner, Founder, Turner Broadcasting: Ted was once quoted as saying, "This is America. You can do anything here." And boy, has he.

Ted has only done two or three big deals over the course of his remarkable career. His biggest was selling Turner Broadcasting to Time Warner. But Ted's prescient vision of a twenty-four-hour news network—CNN—changed our perceptions about news, the global village, and the roles of media and technology in our day-to-day lives. He foresaw a world developing that nobody else did. And after a while, thanks to some prodding by Ted, the world finally caught up to Ted's magnificent vision.

As a CEO, no one was better than Ted. He had a clear-eyed vision of the future, set out a differentiating strategy for his company, and executed brilliantly on that strategy. Ted is an eloquent reminder that, as a CEO, you can't just have strategy and vision; you also have to be able to execute well. That is a basic, and perennial, prerequisite to success. Ted did all that and more with his company, and in the process he profoundly changed the world. That makes Ted, in my opinion, one of the most important media visionaries of our time.

Jack Welch, (former) Chairman, General Electric: Few people know it, but Jack's nomination in 1980 as GE's chairman and CEO almost didn't happen. Walter "Dave" Dance, a much-respected GE vice chairman, was actually in line to get the job, at least on a transition basis. GE planned to have Dave lead the company for a few years before handing the reins over to Jack, allowing Jack, just forty-five at the time, to get some more seasoning before taking over the top job.

But Dave got passed over at the last minute, in no small part because, of all things, he (supposedly) fudged on his golf scores. Ed Littlefield, a former member of GE's Nominating Committee, was my longtime friend and mentor. Ed told me—and the story was later confirmed by another GE executive—that some GE directors had observed Dave trimming his golf scores during outings to Augusta and elsewhere. Ed, who passed away in September 2001 at the age of eighty-seven, said nobody ever confronted Dave directly. But when the time came to consider him for the CEO's job, the Nominating Committee decided to take a pass on Dave and go directly to Jack. Ed said the directors figured that if Dave would cut corners on golf, he might not be the best guy to lead GE, where golf and the integrity of the game are integral parts of the senior corporate culture. Other factors, no doubt, also figured into the directors' final decision.

I have no idea if Dave trimmed his golf scores or not. It's possible the GE directors were simply mistaken; it's also possible they were right. But what is certain is this: The unintended consequence of this episode is that Jack Welch became GE's CEO a lot earlier than he would have otherwise. That event, in retrospect, profoundly affected the direction of GE at a critical time in its history. As for Dave Dance, he served admirably and well until his retirement. (For more on unintended consequences, see Chapter 8.)

Jack did not do a lot of major deals himself—only three, really, and two of them he probably could have done without (the aborted deal to merge GE with Honeywell being one of them). But Jack did something far greater during his extraordinary tenure as CEO: He instilled GE with a successful dealmaking culture. Thanks to Jack, GE today routinely does more than a hundred deals a year. And it does most of those deals quite well, as evidenced by Jack's remarkable legacy of shareholder return. During Jack's twenty-year run as CEO, GE shareholders enjoyed a remarkable 23 percent compounded annual growth rate. During that same period, the S&P 500 squeaked out a very respectable (but still puny-looking by comparison) 15 percent return. Some of these performance statistics later came under close scrutiny on Wall Street. But no matter. The managerial and cultural gifts that Jack left behind will continue to benefit GE and, indeed, Corporate America, for generations to come. Given that we live in a world where you have to do at least a deal or two a year to remain competitive, those are truly priceless gifts.

B efore Jack came along and helped popularize the idea of growth by acquisition, Corporate America rarely resorted to dealmaking as an actual growth strategy. Deals that did get done tended to be strictly insular:

Widget makers would only buy other widget makers, and so on. That's how giants like U.S. Steel and General Motors became giants. Companies didn't think to look outside their immediate areas of business for new opportunities. It just wasn't done. By the late 1980s, however, the limitations of this approach were painfully apparent. Companies started bumping up against the legally allowable limit on "concentration," meaning they had bought so many companies in their own industry that they were in danger of forming monopolies. That, of course, is a big red flag for the Justice Department's antitrust division. All of a sudden, companies with a grow-by-acquisition strategy had little choice but to look beyond their core businesses for new opportunities.

Some companies, elated at the thought of pushing beyond the borders of their own industries, rushed into deals that later turned out to be fatally flawed. (AT&T's purchase of NCR, a former cash register business, comes to mind.) Others sat on their hands and did nothing. (Think Bell-South.) A few companies, however, recognized the paradigm shift for what it was—an invitation to think way outside the box—and executed brilliantly. The fact that Jack was able to turn around such a whale is even more remarkable when you consider that GE had a hundred years of history—and habits—firmly entrenched by the time he took over as CEO in 1981.

What does Jack have in common with Sumner, Jerry, John, and all the others I've been talking about? To be sure, they don't look alike, weren't educated alike, and have varying business objectives. Their early vocations in life—Jerry Levin was a biblical scholar, Sumner Redstone was a lawyer, and Jack Welch was a chemical engineer—are also all over the map. But what they do have in common, to borrow a phrase from Sumner, is a real passion to win. These men are hugely successful because they are willing to work harder than anyone else and subordinate their egos (to a point, at least) to their respective strategies. As a result, they almost always outsmart the other guy. In addition to pushing the high end of the IQ range, they are without exception self-confident and stunningly clever. Most important, these are some of the quickest and most spontaneous individuals you'll ever meet in your life.

Jack Welch aside, all of these deal revolutionaries hail from the media world. No surprise there. To crib an observation from F. Scott Fitzgerald, successful media executives today really are different from the rest of the crowd.

Media types are wired differently. They talk different, act different, and sometimes even dress different. They tend to lean to the brassy side. They sometimes upset people with the things they say and the manner in which they say them. (Think Ted Turner.) They also capture our imagination and inspire our dreams. (Again, think Ted Turner.) How else do you account for the fact that the press seems to hang on every word that John Malone utters? Or the fact that Rupert Murdoch can send ripples through a room packed with A-listers just by showing up? These are all larger-than-life figures with larger-than-life personalities—and aspirations to match.

Corporate upbringing has a lot to do with it. Media organizations, with their sometimes-quirky cultures, tend to be frantic, spontaneous, and unrehearsed places. As a result, they tend to attract people who flourish in that type of environment—which is to say people who know how to react spontaneously to a spontaneous world. Managers who rise to the top of a media organization tend to get a lot of practice negotiating . . . everything. As a result, the art of debate—some might say intimidation— becomes second nature. Almost by necessity, they learn how to think fast, move fast, and make decisions with conviction. And they certainly don't fret about upsetting the status quo. People who are raised in a bureaucratic or regulated environment, by comparison, are seldom good at acting decisively. They also tend to not be so great at coming up with creative solutions to problems. It's just not in their blood. Try throwing these characters into a real crisis, and most of them fold like a house of cards.

In the aftermath of 9/11, fear gripped the nation. Americans, quite understandably, were skittish about flying. Passenger traffic plunged along with the confidence of the nation as a whole. Airline executives were rattled—and boy, did it show. In appearances before the press, the airline CEOs were almost herdlike in their responses. No creative solutions would be forthcoming from this bunch. They were reactive across the board. Within a week, most announced massive layoffs and cut way back on their flight schedules. One thing they didn't touch was fares. They said they were already low enough. The message to America was clear: We're in trouble and we don't know what to do.

The sole exception was Herb Kelleher, chairman of Southwest Airlines. Herb, who's been upsetting the status quo in the airline industry for years with his cut-rate, no-frills airline, was inspiring. And he had just what the flying public needed right then—a calming voice. In public statements, Herb came across as calm, collected, and firmly in control of his company. Southwest didn't announce layoffs or even schedule cutbacks. Quite the contrary, Southwest continued flying its planes while beefing up security in a measured and controlled way. Given the extraordinary circumstances, Southwest also said it would consider reducing fares to help entice people to start flying again. It was exactly the right message to send to America's jittery flying public—and to Wall Street. While other airline stocks initially plunged more than 50 percent, Southwest's shares slid just 20 percent. His handling of the crisis was, by every measure, a triumph.

Herb Kelleher is far more the exception than the rule in the airline industry. But you see that kind of creativity and gritty resolve all the time in the media world. Go to Viacom: There are eccentric, creative, and spontaneous people walking the halls there every day. That's no accident. People at every level of Viacom are rewarded for decisiveness, for thinking out loud, for being willing to make a bold or even risky move. That's not to say Viacom's efforts are all successful. Some flame out in spectacular fashion. But people at Viacom also know that, provided they've been thoughtful in their approach, they can push the edge with impunity. And push hard they do.

The obvious rejoinder to all this is that the media tends to cover themselves—and these CEOs—a lot more closely than they do other, inherently less interesting industries. (Heavy industries come to mind.) But that would be far too simplistic. The fact is, the businesses represented by these media executives wield a lot of influence over our lives. Consider these statistics from Jupiter Media Metrix, a research firm in New York City: As of the end of 2001, 73 million homes were hooked up to cable TV; about 18 million subscribed to satellite TV. More than 71 million homes had a personal computer. Of those, about 52 million subscribed to some sort of dial-up Internet service, such as AOL. About 10 million subscribed to high-speed Internet services, also known as broadband. (The bulk of these—about 7 million—favored cable modems.) Jupiter Media Metrix expects the total number of online households to top 86 million by 2006. For Sumner, Rupert, and the rest, that's a lot of eyeballs, a lot of opportunity—and a lot of impact on our lives.

Jack Welch, as far as I can tell, has far more Viacom in him than GE. Jack's immediate predecessor, Reg Jones, was regarded as one of the top CEOs in the country, and rightly so. In the face of runaway inflation and a busted stock market, Reg, to his eternal credit, managed to make GE deliver impressively for its investors. Then Jack came along—and all the old rules went right out the window. Jack, by his own description, was a total misfit. He was brash, outspoken, and impatient. He despised bureaucracy and eschewed convention. Jack was, in fact, the antithesis of the prototypical GE CEO. Up until then, GE CEOs tended to be quite capable. But they also tended to be quite conservative, rather scripted, and decidedly risk-averse. Until Jack slipped into the driver's seat, GE was mostly known as a barometer of the U.S. economy. GE didn't have a dealmaking culture. Though it was a training ground for managers and one of the yardsticks of corporate excellence, before Jack showed up, GE was basically the U.S. Steel of global conglomerates.

The ability to make decisions quickly—for which Jack was famous—is perhaps the key characteristic that successful dealmakers share. Jack never fired anybody for mistakes, unless you happened to make a lot of them. But he'd crush you for nondecisions. And rightly so. Decisions are the lubricant that keeps organizations moving. If a CEO can't or won't make decisions, and make them quickly, everything gets bogged down. Human nature being what it is, nothing gets done and no decisions get made down the line because everybody is waiting for the CEO to make his or her move.

Decision-making by committee is not a substitute for the real thing. It never has been. And it never will be. Committees by their very nature appeal to the lowest common denominator, hardly a way to achieve brilliant results. (The way to find out the IQ of any committee, so the saying goes, is to get the IQ of the dimmest bulb in the bunch, then divide by the number of members in the committee.) For brilliant outcomes you need seasoned leadership that can think fast, move fast, and make decisions quickly and with conviction. It's like racing a car: It's all about your reaction time. Can you make it through that hole? What's ahead? If the car in front of you drifts to the left, should you follow? Or should you pull hard to the right and attempt to pass? Timing is all the more important when you consider that dealmaking time frames tend to be measured in days or even hours, not weeks and months. That sort of rapid-fire living requires a very different set of reflexes.

Old-line companies, for the most part, just aren't equipped to deal with that kind of spontaneity—and that kind of personal responsibility. Look at AT&T. It was an American icon with a long history of excellence—and for most of that time it penalized people at every level for making mistakes. That's one reason decision-making by committee developed as a way of life at AT&T. Nobody ever wanted the burden of taking responsibility for an actual decision, lest they be proven wrong later. It was far safer, and far more career-enhancing, to simply walk the path of least resistance. (With apologies to Ivan Seidenberg of Verizon and Ed Whitacre of SBC, who were obviously born on another planet and separated at birth.)

I got a taste of AT&T's risk-aversion during my short tenure as CEO of AT&T Broadband. It was clear to me that AT&T execs were far more comfortable devising and debating possible options than actually making a decision. AT&T managers up and down the line were more than happy to draft out memos and produce "decks"—documents that can be used with overhead projectors—to give us all something to talk about at our next meeting. (And there was *always* a next meeting.) But ask for an outright decision? Not a chance. It didn't matter if the topic was a simple branding issue or a more complicated budgeting question. Nobody could seem to make a decision—and I mean nobody. AT&T's liberal use of outside consultants only slowed the decision-making process even more.

This paralysis extended to lower-level meetings as well as to top-level executive meetings. The AT&T board, for example, debated the question of whether to issue a new "tracking" stock for AT&T's cable TV and Internet assets for more than a year—a year!—before deciding to just break up the company into a couple of big pieces. Never mind that a tracking stock, which permits investors to monitor the performance of specific assets, could have been issued in a matter of months, while a breakup would take much longer. (As this is being written, in 2002, AT&T is still in the process of breaking up the company.) In the fast-paced world of telecom, where a day's indecision can burn you forever, AT&T's inability to move quickly was akin to Nero fiddling as Rome burned. And AT&T investors paid mightily because of it—over and over again.

That you can pull the trigger on a deal, of course, doesn't mean that you should. Even Jack Welch had a couple of notable failures. GE's ill-fated attempt to buy Honeywell in 2001 for $45 billion died amid stiff op-position from European regulators. GE's 1986 acquisition of Kidder, Peabody, the big Wall Street firm, was also quite ill-advised, a fact that Jack himself admitted later. Honeywell and Kidder, of course, were far more the exception than the rule for GE. But the point is this: Even the best-laid merger plans by the best-trained merger specialists can go badly off track if you're not careful. Recent history is littered with examples of smart companies making not-so-smart acquisitions. And that a merger is between two like-minded companies doesn't necessarily help. Look at Daimler and Chrysler, the two big auto giants. Their marriage has been challenging since day one. Likewise, Quaker Oats' acquisition of Snapple, the fruit drink maker, was supposed to provide a neat complement to its Gatorade division. It didn't. The proposed merger between Lucent and Alcatel, the big French telecom equipment maker, bit the dust over "so-cial" issues—which is Wall Street shorthand for saying that the two CEOs couldn't agree on who got the bigger title and office.

The jury is still out on some of the biggest mergers of recent years. The big Bell mergers that dominated the headlines in the mid-1990s seem to have worked out pretty well for the most part. The real proof will come ten years from now, by which time it should be clear if "bigger" Bells really did translate into "better" Bells from regulatory, consumer, and fi-nancial standpoints. It's difficult to gauge the success of oil giants Exxon and Mobil, one of the largest mergers in U.S. history. Call me in a few years when the energy rush is over and I'll tell you if the two companies really came together crisply and well. Even then it would be difficult to put Exxon-Mobil in the same category as AOL Time Warner. Exxon-Mobile does one thing. AOL Time Warner does about twenty things. And forget about GE. That company does so many things they can hardly cram it all into the annual report.

Even under the best of circumstances, big mergers can be fractious and difficult. It takes a Jack Welch–type personality to run these big honkers. And even Jack had a lot of help from a whole cast of extremely capable senior managers. Mike Armstrong arrived at AT&T in 1997 with the unenviable mission of turning AT&T into a New Media company. He failed, and no wonder. The 1984 breakup of Ma Bell ended the company's monopoly status—but not its entrenched culture. Not by a long shot, in fact. To nobody's surprise except maybe Mike's, AT&T's corporate culture refused to yield. By the time AT&T started to get carved up in 2000, it was still a bureaucratic *Queen Mary* that refused to budge. As most of us know from experience, old habits die hard. And they don't die any harder than they do at a hundred-year-old company with a proud heritage.

GM is another case in point. Like AT&T, GM for years regarded its stiff resistance to change almost as a point of pride. (At GM, the inside joke for years was: "We not only shoot the messenger, we bayonet the stretcher carrier.") Not exactly an environment that inspires creative, out-of-the-box thinking—and it sure showed in GM's tired car designs. Trying to put a little pizzazz back in its cars, GM in 2001 brought in Robert Lutz as the new head of design and production. Bob, a certified car design whiz, was pushing seventy at the time. GM had to waive its retirement policy, which requires executives to step down when they reach sixty-five, to get him. By bringing in Bob, GM hoped to send the message to Wall Street that it was serious about jazzing up its car designs.

All GM's move said to me was that it didn't have a clue how to fix things on its own. Even more startling, Bob's appointment left the impression that GM didn't have anybody inside its own ranks who was capable of taking on that big job. That begged an even bigger and ultimately far more important question: Why not? Don't get me wrong—Bob Lutz is a tremendous talent, and GM was lucky to get him. But the fact that one of the largest car makers in the world couldn't fill such a coveted and important spot from within its own design ranks spoke volumes about the quality and effectiveness of GM's own management planning process, or lack thereof. In any event, I look forward to seeing his new designs, which are expected to hit the market in a few years. By then, perhaps, GM will finally have the *next* Bob Lutz in training.

As you've probably already figured out by now I have some strong opinions about business and how it should be conducted. I also have some fairly strong opinions about the rarefied world of dealmaking and the top negotiators who dominate the game. You are certainly entitled to wonder why my opinions are even worth considering. Only you can be the judge of that, of course. But before you can form an opinion, you'll need to know a little bit more about me, so read on.

THE MAKING OF A DEALMAKER

I learned my way around the negotiating table the same way a lot of people do—by trial and error. I was also fortunate to cross paths early on in my career with some incredibly capable, gracious, and generous people. For that, and to these people, I will always be grateful.

I graduated from Stanford's business school in 1971. My first job right out of school was with Utah International, a very large mining company based in San Francisco. Ed Littlefield, the firm's CEO, hired me to be his assistant. I didn't know it right then, but it would turn out to be one of the luckiest breaks of my life.

My starting salary at Utah International was $15,600—which was $600 more than the median salary of Stanford MBAs that year. Ed made sure of that. I found out later that he had called Stanford to find out what the median salary for graduating MBAs was likely to be that year—$15,000—then he tacked on an additional $600 to make sure that I would be above the average. That was just the kind of generous guy he was.

Back then, Ed was considered one of the top CEOs in the country. He was the chairman of The Business Council and sat on the boards of General Electric, Chrysler, and Wells Fargo, among others. As Ed's assistant, I had a direct line into all these companies. I used to help him prepare for board meetings. After a while, I learned a lot about all the companies, as well as the broader business issues that dominated the era. I've always told people that I spent two years in business school at Stanford and an additional two years in business school with Ed, because that's what it felt like. I learned a ton by just watching and listening to him.

Ed was a firm taskmaster. But he could also be incredibly patient. On one occasion I fielded a call from a reporter from *Business Week*. The reporter was doing a story on the environmental effects of strip mining and wanted to talk to Ed about Utah International's coal mine in Farmington, New Mexico. The mine had always been somewhat controversial. In addition to being the largest surface mine in the world, it was located on a Navajo Indian reservation. Like many Indian reservations, this particular reservation was severely depressed. Many residents lived in abject poverty;

unemployment and alcoholism rates were sky high. The local terrain was also quite harsh. In a flippant moment, I cracked that "there were only two trees on the property when we showed up, anyway, and one of them was dead." My comment was incredibly insensitive and inappropriate—and it showed up in *BusinessWeek* the very next week.

I was mortified. I was also afraid I was going to get fired. That Monday morning when the issue hit the stands, I ran to our mailroom to collect every issue of *BusinessWeek* we had. I prayed that Ed hadn't yet seen the story, as I wanted to explain what had happened before he read it. As soon as Ed arrived for work, I went straight into his office with a copy of the magazine to deliver the bad news. Ed heard me out, then uttered a single sentence: "Well, there's a lesson for you." (And boy, was it.) Ed never brought up the matter again.

After two years of my shadowing Ed, he decided that I was ready to try my hand at management. Ed sent me out to run the Farmington, New Mexico, mine, the same one that I had so crassly joked about to the *BusinessWeek* reporter. The mine was situated in the desolate Four Corners area, which is where Utah, Colorado, Arizona, and New Mexico meet. I had no experience running a mine, mind you. But that didn't seem to bother Ed. I guess he thought—and he was right—that I'd work seven days a week to avoid disappointing him. So off I went to New Mexico to learn the mining business. I was twenty-five. I looked so young I grew a mustache to look a little older.

The experience opened up my eyes and ears—as well as my heart—to some real truths about business and people. One of the biggest lessons I learned is a variation on what Woody Allen, the great American comic, once said: Eighty percent of life is just showing up. Among other things, I learned that you can't understand the ins and outs of a business by simply looking over the balance sheet, or by talking to managers on the phone, or by trading memos with executives in the field. The only way to truly know a business is to show up—every single day. Then you have to be willing to talk to people, ask questions, and open your heart and ears enough so that you really hear what people are saying. That's not to say you're always going to like the answers. But you have to be willing to at least listen.

I also developed a healthy respect for the employee lunchroom. To understand any company, eat lunch in the cafeteria with the workers—not their bosses. The company cafeteria is essentially a bigger version of the water cooler, and it's the nexus of any company. You also have to make it clear to everybody that you are engaged, interested, and really care about the events that affect their lives. It also doesn't hurt to check your pride at the door. And last but certainly not least, have a sense of humor. Mistakes happen. Learn from them and move on. These lessons would stick with me for a lifetime.

I already had a pretty healthy respect for workers in general by the time I showed up in New Mexico. As a boy growing up in Northwest Washington, I'd spent time as a manual laborer on local farms. If it grew, I picked it. I'd also worked a variety of jobs starting in grade school. Over the years, I'd worked as a newsboy, a grocery store bagger, and, later, a laborer in the merchant marine and in the local shipyard. But my time in New Mexico would remind me—every single day—how critically important the rank and file is to the long-term success of an enterprise. Managers have a special role to play, as well. But the men and women who show up for work day after day after day are the people who keep the trains running on time, so to speak. They are the reason—*the only reason*—you have a business at all. Managers who forget that do so at their own peril. This lesson, too, would stick with me for a lifetime.

After I had spent two years in New Mexico, Ed brought me back to headquarters to be one of Utah International's corporate development managers. That same group today would be called "mergers and acquisitions." The psychological difference was key. Back in the 1970s, you see, people didn't do big mergers to change their businesses. They looked for ways to expand and develop the "core" business, which is to say they looked for ways to add to the basic business, but they did *not* look for ways to dramatically change it. That simply wasn't done, at least not back then.

My first deal target was a big one: Peabody Coal Co., a major competitor. We spent four months trying to buy Peabody in a friendly transaction (again, the only kind that got done in those days) for about $500 million. The deal was memorable for two reasons. First, it was my very first deal, which always sticks with you. Second, I got a big promotion right in the middle of it. Ed decided to put me in charge of Utah International's entire corporate development group. I was twenty-seven. Ed wasn't troubled by my utter lack of deal experience, even though he probably should have been. I guess he just knew in his gut and in his heart that I could never let him down. Ed, as usual, was right on the screws.

In retrospect, Ed knew something else about me that I was only beginning to appreciate. I absolutely loved the dealmaking game. Even though I only had one big deal under my belt, I had the bug. I loved the process of wheeling and dealing and playing the intellectual equivalent of 3-D chess at the negotiating table. I gravitated to the almost athletic nature of trying to wear down the other side at the negotiating table, both mentally and physically, as you pounded out deal terms day after day after day. There was no question: I was hooked.

I spent the next twelve months working on a number of big deals for Ed, including one worth $650 million for a mining project in Brazil. Then, in the fall of 1976, I worked on my biggest deal to date: the sale of Utah International to General Electric for $2.25 billion. Ed, who was still chairman and CEO of the company, decided to sell because he thought it was in the best long-term interest of shareholders. Ed stayed on as CEO of Utah International for a year, then stepped aside but kept the chairman's title. When Ed retired, I left to go looking for my next great adventure.

It would take a while.

I spent the next several years casting around trying to find a corporate home as gratifying as Utah International had been. Nothing seemed to mesh. During that time, I wound up working with a lot of people I didn't particularly enjoy, doing things I didn't particularly like. It was a bleak period of my life. I felt aimless and without direction. I have since come to refer to this period of my life as my "wilderness" years because that's what it felt like. Ed, who by then had become a father figure to me, remained a steady source of calm and advice in my life. Other than Ed, however, there were few bright spots.

In 1985 I landed a job as chief financial officer and head of planning and development of The Chronicle Publishing Co. The company owned publishing, broadcast, and cable properties. It was headquartered in San Francisco, one of my favorite cities in the world. In addition to being in a location that I happened to like a lot, the job gave me my first introduction to a business that definitely intrigued me: cable TV. Chronicle at the time owned a mishmash of businesses, including a low-level (read "lowlife") movie production company. We soon decided to sell off the movie company and all the other extraneous businesses so we could focus on the core assets—broadcasting, newspapers, and cable. I knew next to nothing about the media business, but decided as CFO I needed to. So, heeding my own lessons from New Mexico, I hit the road to learn more about the cable and broadcasting world. Thus began a wonderful, magical journey that would change my life forever.

One of my first calls went to Bill Daniels, the chairman of Daniels & Associates, a big cable brokerage firm in Denver. Bill, a former Navy pilot, got his start in cable in the 1950s. He was in the insurance business at the time, and he happened to be driving through Denver on a Friday night and stopped at a bar. The placed was packed with people watching the Friday night boxing matches, which were being piped in via cable TV. Brian Deevy, Bill's longtime associate, said Bill decided that night to get into the cable business—and never looked back.

Bill started out in rural cable in Colorado and Wyoming. Before long, he fashioned himself into a cable "broker," which is the cable industry's equivalent of an investment banker. One of his early clients was Tele-Communications, Inc. At the time TCI was just starting out. With Bill's help, TCI eventually developed into the biggest cable TV operator in America. Bill's reputation grew along with TCI's fortunes. By the time I put in a call to Bill in 1985, he was already a legend in the cable industry.

Bill didn't know me at all, of course. But he took my call anyway and patiently listened to my spiel. I told Bill I wanted to learn more about the cable business and asked for his help. In retrospect, this was the equivalent of a first-year college student calling up Albert Einstein for math tutoring. But nonetheless, that's what I did. Bill was as gracious as he could be and agreed to meet with me to discuss the matter further. I flew out to Denver to meet him. During that first meeting, Bill insisted that I meet a friend of his—John Malone. John at the time was the president and CEO of TCI and a titan in the industry himself. I, of course, was thrilled, and jumped at the chance to meet him.

When I got back to San Francisco, I called up John straightaway. John, who had already been briefed by Bill, agreed to meet with me. Once more, I headed back out to Denver—and once again a titan of the cable industry patiently listened to me explain how I wanted to become more involved in the cable television industry. John listened to my pitch, then asked me to step out into the hall. There on the wall was a big map of the United States. It was covered with little pins that identified the location of TCI's cable systems. "Which ones do you want?" John asked rather casually. I almost couldn't believe my ears. John Malone, the most influential cable television operator in America, had just issued me a personal invitation to join the cable club. John, of course, was dead serious. It was the start of what would become a warm, lasting, and, at times, complicated friendship.

Throughout 1986 and into 1987, I began spending more and more time talking to Bill and John about the cable business. The more I learned about the cable business, the more I liked it. As a mainstream business enterprise, cable still hadn't hit its stride. This was before the days of high-speed Internet access, e-mail, and digital cable. But it was clear that the business was evolving quickly and well, and had a lot of upside financial potential going forward. I was hooked. I soon landed a deal that would have let Chronicle take a 40 percent stake in a new cable TV network devoted to nature, animals, and the great outdoors for just $6 million. I made an impassioned pitch to the Chronicle board, but in the end, against my recommendation, the company took a pass. John Malone didn't make the same mistake. After Chronicle passed, he jumped on the deal. (Too bad for Chronicle. The network, you see, was Discovery, which went on to become a monster success. As of 2002, John's stake in Discovery, which has since ratcheted up to 50 percent, was worth more than $6 billion.)

By December 1987, I was aching to start my own cable business. But I had a big problem: I couldn't afford it. I had a wife and young daughter to support—and just $20,000 in the bank. Bill, who by then had become a very close friend, called me up one night as I was racking my brain trying to figure out what to do. As he had done so many times before, Bill patiently listened to me. When I had finished, Bill asked me just one question: If I did start this business, he said, how long did I think I could hold out financially on my own? April, I told him. That was just four months away. Bill considered my answer. Then he said something that would, once more, change my life forever: Bill told me that if things didn't work out by April, I could come to Daniels & Associates and work for him. So I had a job waiting for me. But give it a try, Bill urged me. You'll regret it if you don't.

I never had to take Bill up on his kind and generous offer. But just the fact that I knew I had a job waiting if things didn't work out gave me the strength and courage I needed to give it a go. I started my own cable company, InterMedia Partners, with a couple of other partners in January 1988—and never looked back.

InterMedia was a resounding success. I started out hoping to raise $100 million. The response was overwhelming. I eventually cobbled together $192 million from thirteen investors, including $40 million from my new friend and business partner, John Malone. Other investors included the Bank of New York, Chrysler Pension, GE Capital, Sumitomo, and New York Life Insurance Company. By the time I sold InterMedia a decade later, it was the ninth-largest cable operator in America with 1.4 million customers. All of my investors, including John Malone, were repaid handsomely. As for that $20,000, thanks to InterMedia's more than 40 percent compounded annual return, it eventually turned into a tidy nest egg worth more than $100 million.

That brings me to another lesson I learned at Utah International, one that has been reinforced again and again and again over the years. The relative success of any deal always depends on who happens to be sitting on the other side of the table. When you get smart, experienced dealmakers like Rupert Murdoch, John Malone, and, if I may be so bold, Leo Hindery, in the same room, nobody is going to get steamrolled. That's just a fact. But stack up Rupert, John, or me against an inexperienced or poor dealmaker and the picture changes dramatically. Heads will roll—and chances are they won't be ours.

2

WHY PEOPLE DO BIG DEALS

J.P. MORGAN, the great American financier, once said that a man usually has two reasons for doing something: a good reason, and the real reason. The same is true for CEOs involved in big mergers.

No big merger ever gets announced without a lot of thought beforehand about how it will be explained and justified to the public. These explanations are considered crucial to gaining the approval of investors, the financial market, customers, and employees. Getting a green light from Wall Street, in particular, is essential. No matter how forcefully a company might argue that a merger is crucial to its future, most CEOs will only tolerate so much damage to their stock prices before they back down. So it's really important to get your message out forcefully, and thoughtfully, on day one.

Most big deals are about one thing and one thing only: improvement. Listen to any company explain why it wants to merge with another, no matter how big or how small the transaction, and the takeaway is always "improvement"—of opportunities, the bottom line, and corporate life in general. All of these motivators, in turn, are attempts to improve the shape of what I like to think of as the "triangle" of business. That's a made-up term. But it's also illustrative. The three sides of the triangle are the three elements that define, more or less, all businesses: product, technology, and distribution. "Product," for purposes of the triangle, is whatever you happen to sell, be it cable programming, fruit drinks, or luxury automobiles. "Technology" is just what the dictionary says it is—the methods

37

and processes by which business and society solve their technical problems and meet their larger needs and desires. "Distribution" is the delivery vehicle you use to get your product into the hands of buyers. If you're a bank, you can do that through branch offices; if you're a media company, you use your cable television or broadcast networks.

Most CEOs in America grew up on one side of the triangle. For years, there wasn't much incentive to venture too far away from familiar territory, so nobody did. Most CEOs are pack animals, anyway, so they were content to stick with what they knew. The predictable result: Distribution companies tended to stay in the distribution business, technology companies tended to focus strictly on technology, and product companies spent all their time looking for the next great widget. By the 1990s, however, some of the more clever CEOs started taking off the blinders . . . and they really liked what they saw.

Bell Atlantic, the big regional phone company (now called Verizon), is a good example. Like all the regional Bells, Bell Atlantic for years pretty much stuck to what it knew: local phone service. In 1993, Ray Smith, Bell Atlantic's wonderfully capable CEO, decided there was life beyond local phone service. He rightly concluded that Bell Atlantic's vaunted local phone network, if upgraded with new electronics and other advanced technology, could be used to ship all sorts of new services to the home, such as e-mail, high-speed Internet services, and, over time, movies on demand and other video services.

Ray rocked the telecom world that fall by declaring his intention to buy Tele-Communications, Inc., the big cable TV company headed by John Malone. Ray argued that the acquisition would not only expand Bell Atlantic's distribution network (side 3), but also give the company an attractive new revenue stream from a brand-new product, cable TV (side 1). Over time Bell Atlantic planned to seriously upgrade TCI's aging cable network, a veritable Model T at the time, with expensive new technology (side 2) to make it the equivalent of a high-performance sports car. The proposed merger later blew up amid disagreements between Ray and John over price and other issues. But by then Ray's novel way of looking at the Bells' hundred-year-old networks had radically changed the thinking in the telecom and cable industries. Ray's idea today seems logical, even common sense. But at the time it was quite revolutionary.

As more and more CEOs started following Ray's lead and taking the blinders off, a curious things happened to the triangle. The three distinct sides that before had never touched, except at the very outer edges, began to amalgamate and consolidate. Then the whole thing went into a full-tilt spin, resulting in a constantly rotating circle. After a while, it was impossible to see where distribution ended and technology began, or where content started and distribution began. What we wound up with, of course, was convergence, which in its perfect state is a seamless melding of product, technology, and distribution. To be sure, the term "convergence" gets a little (even a lot) overused these days. But whatever you choose to call it, one thing's for sure: It's a prime motivator behind a lot of deals these days.

Once a CEO gives himself or herself permission to branch out beyond his or her industry, imagination takes over. Ideas percolate. Combinations that you never would have contemplated in a million years all of a sudden seem possible, even practical. It's sort of like playing charades. Once you get going, you tend not to care how you might look—you just want to win. It's the same for CEOs on a creative bender. Once you allow yourself the freedom to think the unthinkable, all sorts of clever ideas and combinations suddenly occur to you. That's exactly how an AOL Time Warner evolves or an AT&T-TCI. It's also behind some slightly less brilliant combinations, like Hewlett-Packard-Compaq and AT&T-NCR. Obviously, some CEOs are more artful at doing this than others. But that's the general idea.

Public explanations for deals are only part of the story. A lot of the time, complicated human motivations are also at work. These are the "secret" deal drivers, so to speak, that most CEOs don't like to talk about. But everybody knows they exist. Ego, for example, can be a powerful driver in some transactions. Some CEOs do deals simply to cover up the fact that they don't have a clue how to run their business. (I call this the "Shell Game" tactic.) Some do deals out of sheer panic. Others do deals for what may be the basest motivation of all: greed.

One of the greatest fears of a CEO is that somebody will come along and buy his or her company and kick him or her out. The acquirer becomes the CEO, and you're just flat out of luck. CEOs rarely talk about this fear publicly. But trust me on this—it is deep-seated and very real. Most CEOs spend their entire careers trying to get the CEO's title. The prospect of having to relinquish that title or, worse yet, having somebody yank it away is terrifying to a lot of CEOs. (All of which makes Mel Karmazin of CBS and Ivan Seidenberg of Verizon, both of whom surrendered their CEO titles for the greater good of their respective companies, seem all the more remarkable.) This anxiety can cause some CEOs, especially those who are already on shaky ground or who feel a need to prove something, to make some truly bad calls.

AT&T is a prime example. Mike Armstrong, AT&T's CEO, should have been far more open to Comcast's offer for AT&T Broadband in the summer of 2001 when it was first lobbed. (AT&T Broadband was the cable and Internet arm of AT&T.) The deal made a lot of sense on a lot of levels. Comcast was one of the top cable operators in the country. Its operating profit margins and cash flow growth, two key indicators of a cable company's financial health, were among the best in the business. That was in no small part due to Comcast's crack operating-management team, which was led by Steve Burke, a former Disney executive who Mike himself once tried to recruit. Comcast's president, Brian Roberts, grew up in the cable business and was quickly emerging as one of the great leaders of the cable TV industry. His father, Ralph, Comcast's founder and chairman, was regarded as an industry pioneer.

Mike turned Brian's offer down flat. One stated reason was money, and perhaps rightly so. Comcast's opening bid was good but not great, and it certainly had room for improvement. Mike also made much of the fact that Brian and Ralph, who together controlled Comcast, would also have voting control over the combined company. Both reasons were valid, and certainly merited more discussion by both sides.

But at the end of the day, I don't think price or control were the real reasons Mike turned Brian down. The reason was ego. After initially hailing Mike's arrival at AT&T in 1997, Wall Street had begun to turn on him. By then, AT&T had spent more than $100 billion on Mike's phone-over-cable effort, but still had little to show for it. Making matters even worse, AT&T's basic cable business was suffering badly. Cash flow was way down. The operating profit margins were downright pitiful in comparison to Comcast and other big cable operators. Dan Somers, Broadband's CEO, had little credibility in the cable industry or on Wall Street. Mike couldn't say a lot about that. After all, Mike was the one who had put him in the job. By the time Comcast showed up on AT&T's doorstep, Mike was constantly defending himself and his cable strategy on Wall Street. Adding insult to injury, Comcast made it clear that it intended to radically slow, if not kill, Mike's phone-over-cable plan if it was successful in buying Broadband.

I suspect it was all too much for Mike's ego to take. At the time, Mike was relatively close to retirement. He probably didn't cherish the idea of leaving on a down note like that. I suspect Mike wanted to prove to the world, and maybe to himself, that he was capable of running AT&T well, and to good effect for shareholders. Mike had just announced plans to spin off Broadband as a separate company and had made it clear he intended to personally run it for a few years before retiring. His hope, I suspect, was that things would turn around and he could retire with his head held high. If Mike accepted Comcast's offer, however, he was never going to get that chance.

After he turned Brian down, Mike started working the phones trying to drum up competing offers. He called Disney, AOL Time Warner, Microsoft, and a couple of others. Mike made it clear to everybody that he was part of the package. He would agree to sell Broadband only if he could run it, just as he had planned, for a couple of years. Needless to say, that suggestion went over like a lead balloon. Mike kept dialing for dollars throughout the summer of 2001.

Then 9/11 happened, and all bets were off. The New York Stock Exchange was closed for several days right after the attacks. When it reopened the following Monday, it plummeted almost 700 points. Comcast's share price got slammed along with that of virtually every other company. Because its bid for AT&T Broadband was composed entirely of Comcast common stock, the value of Brian's offer plunged right along with the stock market. The haircut shaved more than 20 percent off the value of Brian's bid. The capital markets, which had been edgy to begin with because of softness in the U.S. economy, dried up almost overnight. So did a lot of merger talks.

Suffice it to say, no competing offers for AT&T Broadband emerged during this period. AT&T later set up a "bidders" room at its lawyers' offices at AT&T in hopes of enticing other companies to step forward with competing bids. Despite heated press reports to the contrary, talks with AOL Time Warner went nowhere. Cox Communications, an Atlanta-based cable operator that also owns a lot of TV stations, came forward with an offer. But it quickly bogged down over the same control issues that the

Roberts offer had. (Cox is controlled by the Cox sisters of Atlanta, who were unwilling to give up their control to get a deal done with AT&T.) Federal television cross-ownership rules, which don't permit cable companies to own broadcast TV and cable properties in the same market, were also a problem. Brian, to his credit, hung in there. He even sweetened his offer just a shade.

In December 2001, Mike faced up to reality. He agreed to sell Broadband to Comcast for $47 billion in stock and the assumption of $20 billion in debt. Brian and his dad, as expected, retained voting control. As part of the deal, Mike Armstrong will leave AT&T and join Comcast as chairman. He'll remain in that position through spring 2005, though the title will be downgraded to nonexecutive chairman in 2004. Titles aside, however, Brian, Ralph, and Steve Burke, Comcast's cable operations chief, will continue to run the show.

I was sorry that Mike didn't come to his senses a lot earlier. If he had done that, it would have given AT&T shareholders some certainty at a time when AT&T and our nation as a whole needed it the most. In retrospect, Mike was fortunate that Brian didn't pull the plug and walk away as so many others did in a variety of deals right after 9/11.

The Shell Game is a deal motive that might not seem so obvious at first glance. And it's certainly not a motive that you'll ever get a CEO to own up to publicly. But in some deals—some of the highest profile deals—it's a bigger factor than you might think. As with the classic version, where the unwary mark can't figure out which shell hides the pea, confusion is the tip-off.

When some CEOs can't manage a business to expectations, one way to divert attention is to impress everybody by doing a big, complicated deal. The aim, however misguided, is to make sure Wall Street is so confused that investors are forced to stop beating up on you. These types of deals typically don't fit into any easy, neat category. So there usually is no apples-to-apples comparisons for Wall Street to fall back on. Investors, instead, are forced to wait it out and see what happens. That, of course, is precisely the goal—to buy time. Another variation of this type of transaction is the panic deal. In these cases, the CEO doesn't have a clue how to fix whatever might be ailing his or her company. The company's share value is so blasted that the CEO is willing to try almost anything to elevate it.

The merger between Hewlett-Packard and Compaq Computer was

classic. At the time the deal was announced, Carly Fiorina, H-P's CEO, was under a lot of pressure from Wall Street. H-P, like a lot of technology companies, was feeling the pain of the Internet bust. Adding to H-P's woes, the company had a lot of exposure to the fractious personal computer business. Fierce price wars had sent PC prices and profit margins through the floor. H-P was positively reeling. Carly didn't seem to have a clue how to fix things. How embarrassing. When she'd arrived just two years earlier, Carly seemed to have all the answers. She even had the H-P board buy her a $40 million Gulfstream Jet so she could take her "Travels with Carly" lecture tour on the road to get the word out that Carly was on the case. Carly also launched a $200 million ad campaign featuring—you guessed it—Carly talking about H-P's legacy.

As it turned out, Carly didn't know much about H-P's legacy. Even worse, she didn't have a clue how to get the company back on track. Within two years of her appointment, H-P's stock price was off by nearly 50 percent. Under Carly's leadership, H-P had managed not only to substantially underperform the S&P 500 but to trail such competitors as IBM and Sun Microsystems. Press reports that had been so favorable suddenly painted Carly as an out-of-touch CEO struggling to stay afloat. Before long, rumors started circulating on Wall Street that Carly was about to get booted. Then, just like clockwork, Carly did what a lot of panicky CEOs do when they find themselves in a tough spot—she nailed a big deal. H-P announced that it was buying Compaq for $25 billion to create a PC Goliath.

I've seen a lot of really awful deals over the years, but few were as intuitively screwed up as that one. Both companies were already bleeding badly from overexposure to PCs. In buying Compaq, H-P wouldn't get one more capability, one more channel of distribution, or one more advantage that it didn't have already. What it would get was a bigger piece of the faltering PC business. Compaq was America's No. 2 PC maker; H-P was No. 3. It was like merging two buggy-whip makers. There was no question that their combined market share and clout would be a lot bigger, but so what? The PC business was a dog, and getting worse with each passing quarter. There were also questions about whether regulators would let the deal go through. The deal, after all, would combine the No. 2 and No. 3 PC makers. Carly brushed aside all these concerns at the time, saying investors shouldn't worry.

Investors worried. Shares of both companies plunged, knocking almost $5 billion off the value of the deal right off the bat. Within a few days, H-P's shares were down more than 20 percent and still falling off a cliff. Compaq's shares were right behind. The Hewlett and Packard families, which owned big blocks of H-P stock, were also worried. They later vowed to vote against the deal, saying it would leave H-P too exposed to the troubled PC market.

Walter Hewlett, the son of H-P's cofounder and an H-P board member, soon emerged as the chief opponent of the deal. Walter considered the proposed merger a costly and irresponsible gamble. He was also concerned that the merger would dilute H-P's interests in the profitable imaging and printing business, a core strength of the company. Carly, stung by the public criticism, pushed back hard. She accused Walter of being out of touch with reality. Walter returned fire, saying Carly stood to personally reap millions if the deal went through. And on and on. It was a really awful spectacle to watch. I liked and admired Walter's father (H-P cofounder Bill Hewlett) a lot. If he hadn't been already dead, I know all of this would have just killed him.

For the record, I personally agreed with Walter. He was right on the screws: Carly didn't know how to manage H-P or the wonderful assets, including the dedicated workforce, that she inherited. Before the Compaq deal was announced, Carly had planned to buy the consulting group of PricewaterhouseCoopers for $18 billion in stock. When the CEO of H-P even thinks about buying a consulting business she might as well take out an ad proclaiming that she doesn't understand the tradition, ethos, and mentality of the place. H-P grew up as an instrumentation business. It developed proprietary technology, and for years did everything better or differently than everybody else. And consulting? It's a business with no assets other than people. And people, of course, unlike patents, come and go. Trying to merge PricewaterhouseCoopers and H-P would be the equivalent of trying to herd cats. It just wouldn't work. But it was sure to blindside the capital markets, which is exactly what happened. As soon as the Pricewaterhouse deal was announced, H-P shares fell through the floor. Carly tried to push back. But in the end she was forced by the market to abandon the deal. (In 2002, IBM announced plans to buy PricewaterhouseCoopers for $3.5 billion.)

Carly eventually won her proxy fight to buy Compaq. But the victory was a hollow one. In her campaign to save the deal, Carly managed to inflict wounds on H-P that were so deep and so ugly that they could take years to heal. I hope for the greater good of H-P that the company can regroup and come back strong. But strong companies need strong leaders. By the day of the final vote, Carly had already lost the confidence of Wall Street and her own employees. All you had to do was look at the badly split vote to see that—slightly more than 50 percent favored the deal, while slightly less than 50 percent didn't. So while Carly won the battle, she clearly lost the war.

No CEO can flag the market on big holes he needs to fill in his strategy, and then not fill them. Consider the saga of Bernie Ebbers, the CEO of WorldCom. Bernie spent most of the 1990s building WorldCom, his Clinton, Mississippi–based telecom carrier, into America's fourth-largest long distance company. In 1998 Bernie bought MCI, pushing WorldCom into the No. 2 spot right behind market leader AT&T. Hoping to up the ante, Bernie announced plans to buy Sprint in October 1999. The company was best-known as America's No. 3 long distance company. But Sprint also had an incredibly strong wireless business. As a bonus, it also had a growing market presence in "personal communications services," a next-generation wireless technology that enables all sorts of digital enhancements, including e-mail, interactive applications, and wireless access to the Internet.

Bernie for years had argued that he didn't need a wireless business to be successful. But by 1999, Bernie knew that he'd missed the boat on wireless, which had turned white-hot. Bernie admitted as much to Wall Street, which in itself was a big step considering he'd been dissing wireless for a lot of years up until then. According to Bernie, Sprint was just the antidote he needed: Not only would he get a ton of new long distance customers, he'd also expand his distribution network and layer on a lot of technology muscle in the form of wireless capability. WorldCom would also pick up Sprint's local phone operations in Florida, North Carolina, and more than a dozen other states. (Though Bernie wasn't particularly interested in the local phone business, he was very interested in the cash that those operations generated.) Bernie made it clear that he needed to move fast. The regional Bells were inching ever closer to getting into the long distance business. Since WorldCom had only a long distance business at the time, it stood to suffer the most once the Bells busted into that market.

You had to give Bernie credit for coming clean on his strategic weaknesses. But his timing was somewhat problematic. Regulators hadn't yet passed on the Sprint deal, so there was a risk they'd turn it down. Hoping to preclude that possibility, Bernie told the world—over and over again— that Sprint was WorldCom's only salvation. He also predicted rather darkly that WorldCom would have serious difficulties going forward if regulators didn't approve the deal. Oopsie. That stark admission, even if it was true, was a huge blunder. Upon hearing that, some investors looked around and said, "Gee, Bernie, that's an interesting tale of woe you just told us. We didn't know that." When regulators later nixed the deal, Bernie had nowhere to hide. He was Dead Man Walking on Wall Street. There was nothing Bernie could do or say to regain investor confidence, and WorldCom's shares suffered accordingly. WorldCom, as I said, has since filed for bankruptcy.

Ivan Boesky, the famous Wall Street investor, once made the observation that "greed is healthy." I don't agree with that, but I do know that greed can be a powerful deal motivator. Not a good one, mind you, but a powerful one. The greed for stock options, as a deal motivator, is particularly insidious. Over the years, stock options have become the cocaine of executive compensation. People used to say that cocaine will make you feel like a new man—and the first thing that new man will want is more cocaine. Much the same can be said of stock options. Once an executive gets hooked, there's usually no looking back.

When I started my career in the early 1970s, it was uncommon for more than 10 percent of an executive's compensation to be anything but salary. Stock options, which were conceived as a way to give executives an incentive to stick around, were generally set up to vest over five- or ten-year periods. Today it's just the opposite. Top executives today typically make millions on the backside in options, and much more modest amounts in salary. Executives routinely expect stock options to be part of their regular compensation package, and in larger and larger quantities. They also expect their options to vest over relatively short periods—sometimes in just months.

I'd be less than honest if I didn't say that I have personally earned a ton of money off stock options in recent years. And I continue to use stock options as a tool to reward my own executives. I've even been accused by some people of being a little too generous when it comes to awarding stock option grants. I don't think that's true. My employees, some of whom have been with me for years, are a talented bunch who work incredibly hard to deliver results for shareholders. As far as I'm concerned, they deserve—and earn—every appropriate financial incentive that I can secure for them. So I make no apologies for rewarding them well.

But all that said, I do believe that the general trend of awarding people gobs of stock options in place of regular salary is a truly awful development. Short vesting periods only compound the problem. The lure of stock option wealth sometimes blinds people. It can also cause them to do things that you wouldn't, or couldn't, anticipate. Sprint's experience in the ill-fated WorldCom deal is a case in point. To be sure, stock options were never the driver of this deal. The deal, as I said, was about shoring up Bernie's stable of telecommunications assets. By the time it was all over, however, stock options had assumed a starring role that nobody ever anticipated.

After Sprint and WorldCom announced plans to merge in 1999, they decided to send a message to regulators and to Wall Street that shareholders overwhelmingly supported the deal. The two companies, as promised, held shareholder votes on the same day in April 2000. The merger, as expected, was overwhelmingly approved. That was the good news. The bad news was that regulators hadn't yet had a chance to weigh in with their opinion. Even worse, Sprint's shareholder vote triggered a clause in the company's stock option plan that caused all stock options, including those held by senior management, to vest immediately.

Oops. As soon as the vote went through, Sprint employees up and down the line starting making a mad dash to cash out. The exodus was ugly. More than twenty-five executives at the vice president and above level resigned. Whole departments at Sprint were decimated. Executive headhunters, sensing blood in the water, only added to Sprint's misery by cherry-picking those who were left. Just when Sprint thought things couldn't get any worse . . . they did. Regulators turned down the WorldCom-Sprint merger, arguing that the combination of the No. 2 (WorldCom) and No. 3 (Sprint) long distance companies would be anticompetitive. Sprint was devastated. It also had a lot of explaining to do. The stock options debacle only added to Sprint's embarrassment. Sprint was later hit with several lawsuits related to its handling of the stock options matter.

Options, of course, derive their value from the underlying price of the stock. But that's only one reason why most CEOs are obsessed with stock prices. Stock prices, after all, are the yardstick by which they tend to get measured—by their own boards, individual investors, and Wall Street. "Popping" the stock is another obsession. The term is Wall Street parlance for any action that causes a short-term surge in the stock price. Even though most CEOs won't admit it publicly, popping the stock is a huge deal motivator. If I've heard it once I've heard it a hundred times in board-rooms: "Will this [deal or action] pop my stock?" And believe me, when-ever somebody asks that question in that setting he or she wants an answer—and it better be a resounding "yes."

Wall Street knows the drill, and actively participates. The night before any big transaction is announced, a company will typically brief a few fa-vored analysts. The underlying premise of these confidential meetings is crystal clear to everybody: "How do we tell this story to pop our stock?" People don't usually say it that explicitly (though some do). But that is the underlying assumption of these conversations. Analysts are generally happy to oblige. When the deal finally gets announced the next day, the analysts look incredibly clued in and the companies can count on a nice boost in the market. So it's a win-win for everybody, you might say. Crass? Perhaps. But a lot of CEOs feel they don't have much of a choice, especially given the increasing importance investors put on short-term stock per-formance (not to mention the desire to keep their own stock options above water).

It wasn't like that years ago. When Ed Littlefield, Utah International's CEO, decided to sell the company to General Electric back in 1976, Ed stood on a stage and talked about the transaction in ten- and twenty-year horizons. He talked about what these two companies would look like a decade or more hence. Today, you get up in front of an audience and talk about the expected impact in the weeks and months ahead. And the whole time you're talking, some joker with a handheld computer is even clocking your real-time stock movement. Unbelievable.

Part of the problem is that today's shareholder base is so transient. A lot of investors have also come to expect results almost immediately. To be sure, you still have a lot of individual investors who buy stocks with the idea of holding on to them for years. But a lot of money in the market to-day is allocated by fund managers and institutional investors who have really short-term horizons, sometimes just a few months. Making matters even worse, professional investors compete against one another for one-

year (at most) performance statistics. When I first looked at AT&T's shareholder base in 1997, the average shareholder held the stock for about four
years. As of 2002, the average AT&T share was held for just three *months*.
By definition, that meant AT&T was getting a whole new shareholder base
every three months. That puts a lot of pressure on fund managers, and by
association CEOs, to produce short-term stock gains by whatever means
necessary. The unfortunate result: Some CEOs wind up doing deals they
shouldn't just to pop the stock.

Wall Street deserves a lot of the blame. To be sure, Wall Street is full of
smart women and men with a lot of good ideas about business and the
economy in general. But investment trends come and go on Wall Street.
You can find yourself in a free fall real fast if you latch on to the wrong one
at the wrong time. Take revenue growth. In the late 1990s, Wall Street
couldn't heap enough praise on companies that emphasized aggressive
revenue growth and delivered on its targets. Enron, the big energy-trading
company, to its credit (and later, to its discredit), read the market brilliantly.
It delivered spectacularly, at least for a while. Enron, for years a dowdy
natural gas company from Houston, morphed itself into an energy-trading
machine and took off from there. Quarter after quarter, Enron posted unbelievable (literally, as it turned out) revenue growth figures. Wall Street
cheered the company's new direction and sent Enron's stock price soaring
to record highs. By 2001, Enron was America's seventh-largest company
by revenue, and a certified darling on Wall Street. Enron rivals that insisted on hewing to a more traditional way of doing business were dis-
missed as out of step with the times. Enron, it was clear, was the gold
standard of the energy business.

Enron was the gold standard all right—fool's gold, that is. By fall
2001, Enron's accounting methods and Byzantine network of partnerships
were raising serious concern in Washington. There were allegations of
document-shredding parties. As for those impressive revenue gains, they
were, as it turned out, a preposterous overstatement. Enron had been
booking the gross value of energy and broadband capacity sales as actual
revenue. All that really mattered were the trading profits, which were often not even there. Wall Street, which had cheered the company and its
spectacular revenue growth to the top of the heap, followed it right back
down to the gutter. Even as Enron was collapsing, a number of top Wall
Street analysts continued recommending the stock to investors. Enron fi-

nally filed for bankruptcy protection in December 2001. By then, Enron's shares, which hit an all-time high of $90.56 in August 2000, were trading for just pennies.

Tyco International was also expert at reading Wall Street. Unlike Enron, which had manufactured its revenue growth through trading, Tyco decided to go out and just buy its revenues. Tyco, a big conglomerate, had interests in security and fire-protection services, electronics, medical supplies, valves, pipes, and financial services. That left a lot of territory for exploiting—and that's exactly what Tyco did. The company did literally hundreds of deals. By the time its buying binge ended in 2001, Tyco's revenue stream was pleasantly plumped up. Wall Street cheered. There was just one hitch: Tyco never bothered to disclose its revenue growth methods to investors, so Wall Street was cheering the wrong thing. When Tyco finally did get around to explaining how it had managed to grow revenue so quickly, investors gasped. Tyco, as it turned out, had done more than seven hundred acquisitions totaling $7 *billion* in the 1999–2001 time period that it never disclosed. Tyco's stock price promptly dropped by half.

Enron and Tyco weren't the only ones to read Wall Street brilliantly, only to crash and burn later. Cisco Systems, the hot maker of networking gear, was another poster child for now-you-see-it, now-you-don't revenue growth. Cisco stunned the world by vowing to grow revenue by 30 percent a year, then stunned the world even more by delivering. Wall Street was impressed, driving up Cisco's market cap to around $400 billion. Cisco soon had bragging rights to being one of the fastest-growing companies in the world.

Then the Internet bubble burst, and reality set in. It soon became apparent that Cisco wasn't growing all that much. It was just buying revenues the way Imelda Marcos used to buy shoes—by the truckload. Egged on by Wall Street, Cisco simply used its soaring stock price to buy interests in scores of smaller technology companies. When Cisco's methodology was revealed, its stock price plunged, knocking tens of billions off the company's vaunted market cap. A lot of its technology investments wound up underwater. Suffice it to say Cisco's famous shopping spree skidded to an abrupt halt. So did its growth spurt. As this is being written, John Chambers, Cisco's CEO, is still promising investors that he can deliver impressive growth by focusing on a couple of key areas, including optical and wireless networking.

Trying to please Wall Street has always been a tricky business, of course. The challenge is to meet investors' expectations while not compromising your own long-term strategic objectives. That brings me to another deal motivator: security. And by that I'm referring to the long-term care and protection of a company's strategic goals. For a CEO with a master plan in mind, that's no small thing.

The Disney-ABC merger was classic. Security certainly wasn't the deal's primary driver. But it was a major by-product, and happily so for Michael Eisner, Disney's longtime CEO. The combined company was so formidable that the chances of anybody making a hostile run at Disney were instantly diminished. That's not to say it was impossible to make a run at Disney, particularly if its stock price dipped low enough. But once Michael bought ABC, the challenge of successfully taking out Disney in a hostile manner became a lot more daunting. The transaction even gave birth to a new term: "Disneyfy" (as in doing a deal that makes your company so large and so formidable that your company is "Disneyfied" against hostile suitors).

AOL Time Warner is another example of Disneyfication. The AOL–Time Warner merger made all kinds of strategic sense for both companies, so I'm not even remotely suggesting that security was the primary driver. But one big by-product of the deal, absolutely, was Disneyfication—both for Time Warner and for AOL. During the go-go Internet era, Jerry Levin, Time Warner's CEO, grew concerned that somebody might attempt a hostile takeover of his company. As Internet stock prices gained steam, rumors would start flying that a takeover was in the works. That used to drive Jerry crazy. Once Time Warner merged with AOL, however, Jerry got something he never had before: peace of mind. With AOL by its side, Time Warner was finally big enough—and secure enough—to prosecute its long-term strategy with impunity. Jerry's worries about a hostile takeover pretty much evaporated.

Disneyfication also gave AOL emotional security. Thanks to Time Warner, AOL no longer had to beat the drum about "open access." That was the idea, championed by AOL, that cable operators should be forced to make their cable TV lines available to AOL and others at greatly reduced rates. (Cable operators generally hated the idea and quickly dubbed it "forced access.") Once AOL married Time Warner, it no longer had to worry about gaining access to cable TV systems. Time Warner, after all, was the No. 2 cable operator in America.

For AOL, Disneyfication also brought something else: financial security. No company ever likes to admit that it needs a merger to survive. But in AOL's case I think you can make a strong argument that Time Warner gave it the kind of security that it could never have gotten on its own. In marrying Time Warner, it inherited a big Hollywood movie studio, a publishing business, cable television systems, and lots of other real businesses with real revenue and real profits. Before the merger, AOL was dependent on the whims of its month-to-month subscription customers. AOL figured out that its stock price could fall, quite literally, to zero if market conditions changed dramatically enough, which, of course, they later did. It's virtually certain that AOL, absent Time Warner, would be a far weaker company. It's possible that AOL might even be in financial distress along with all those other former highfliers. Fortunately for AOL, it never had to ride out that storm. And now that it's married to Time Warner, it never will.

The Internet history books are crammed with examples of highfliers that at one time seemed unstoppable. Look at Yahoo!, the big Web portal and onetime archrival of AOL. At the height of the Internet bubble, Yahoo!'s share price topped an astounding $216. The company's founding management team was positively revered on Wall Street. Then the Internet bubble burst . . . and the party was over. Yahoo! got creamed. Before long, it was scrambling to survive just like everybody else. As this is being written in September 2002, most of the Yahoo! management team is long gone. Its vaunted stock price has sunk to about $10. So much for unstoppable.

Those are some of the more clandestine motivators behind big deals. A lot of CEOs rightly enter into transactions for far more obvious, and ultimately sound, reasons. As far as I'm concerned, there are only three reasons to ever consider a big merger. Though their finer points vary, they share a common objective: improving the business "triangle." The triangle, you may recall, is composed of three sides: product, technology, and distribution. The more clever CEOs in this world have figured out that the more you can pack on, the better the odds of trumping the other guy.

A lot of dealmaking these days is built on this simple but important insight.

The first reason to do deals is something I loosely refer to as "improvement." By that I mean that your company's assets need to be amplified or modified, and the only way to do that successfully and expeditiously is to merge with another company. That's what Bernie Ebbers, the CEO of WorldCom, was trying to do when he went after Sprint. Unfortunately for Bernie, regulators killed the deal over competitive concerns. But Bernie's initial instinct to grow WorldCom's presence in the wireless market (representing product, technology, and distribution) by buying Sprint was a good one.

Some improvement efforts go way off track. Amazon, the big Web retailer, is a classic example of good instincts gone bad. The initial idea of Jeff Bezos, Amazon's founder and CEO, was simple but brilliant: to make millions of book and CD titles available via the Web. Books have no urgency to them. Most people don't mind waiting a few days to get a book in the mail if they can get a better price. Books also have an unlimited shelf life—they don't expire or go bad, so to speak. People already know what they feel like, so there's nothing to touch or try on. And they ship really well. Same goes for CDs. Amazon, at its core, was an almost-perfect "triangle" of product, technology, and distribution, a classic example of convergence if ever there was one.

Then Jeff overreached. Addressing a packed e-commerce summit in September 1999, Jeff loudly proclaimed that the Amazon of tomorrow would be a place where online shoppers could find "anything"—from Barbie dolls to lawn mowers to you-name-it. The proclamation gave Amazon a new nickname—the Wal-Mart of the Web. (Jeff, expressing the sort of humility that typified the dot.com era, later said the Wal-Mart comparison was actually too limited. But you get the idea.) For a company that had made a name for itself as an e-retailer of books and CDs, Jeff's announcement was a watershed event.

And no wonder. Wal-Mart isn't Barnes & Noble. It never has been, and if we're lucky it never will be. Wal-Mart sells chain saws, athletic equipment, garden supplies, and a lot of other things that don't sit well or cheaply on the shelf. Barnes & Noble, of course, is books, books, and more books, punctuated by CDs. People who go to Barnes & Noble often have a specific title, or at least a specific category, in mind. At Wal-Mart, it's the Thrill of the Hunt. People tend to wander the aisles picking up items that strike their fancy. A lot of purchases are almost serendipitous. Jeff tried to replicate that "wandering around" experience on Amazon. But not even a talent like Jeff could replicate Wal-Mart's VW-sized shopping carts, or those miles of aisles stuffed with everything from lawn furniture to shower curtains. Jeff's attempts to morph Amazon into the Wal-Mart of the Web fell flat—and Amazon's stock price followed suit.

"Tonnage," or scale, is another big deal driver. As the term suggests, size is the objective. The Daimler-Chrysler merger is a good example of a raw tonnage deal. These two car giants spent a lot of time waxing on about their shared automobile heritage and vision for the future. But don't kid yourself: This deal was about one thing and one thing only—scale. By marrying, each inherited the other's dowry—in the form of improved distribution networks, expanded production capability, design talent, and more. Daimler and Chrysler today cast a long shadow over two continents, putting pressure on the other two big American automakers—GM and Ford—to keep up. The Bell mergers of the 1990s were also raw tonnage deals. By the time their merger dance was over, SBC Communications and Bell Atlantic (now called Verizon) dominated the left and right coasts and a big chunk of the U.S. interior. For all the billions they spent, SBC and Bell Atlantic weren't a lot different from when they started out. But they were a heck of a lot bigger. Instead of just dominating their own local phone markets, SBC and Bell Atlantic dominated their neighbors' markets, and in some cases their neighbors' neighbors' markets. Suffice it to say the business triangles of SBC and Verizon are heavy with distribution capability—and product, and, increasingly, advanced technology—and spinning stronger than ever.

The third and final reason to ever consider a big merger is "Change." And that's Change with a capital C. This is the ultimate poker game, and you need nerves of steel to play it. Why? Because in this game you have to ask for five new cards—then bet the farm. As any poker player knows, asking for five new cards is always a risky move. If you don't play your hand just right or at least catch some lucky breaks, you can get sorry real fast, as you'll see in the next chapter. But going for broke can also pay off brilliantly.

If you want to see brilliance at the (corporate) poker table personified, look no further than Michael Jordan, the former CEO of Westinghouse. Mike's initial hand was a real dog. When he took over in 1993, Westinghouse was so out of step with the times that its triangle was practically a square. The company's assets included a hodge-podge of dated industrial businesses, including one that specialized in the construction of nuclear power plants. Making matters worse, Westinghouse had just taken a $6.5 billion write-off on financial services that had almost pushed the company to the edge of bankruptcy.

It would have been easy, even expected, for Mike to play the weak hand he had and hope for the best. Nobody would have blamed him, least of all his own board. But Mike didn't do that. Instead, he asked for five new cards—then went for broke.

Mike bet the farm on broadcasting and media. It was a bold and risky move, to say the least. Westinghouse was an industrial giant. Its sole media asset was a relatively small broadcasting group called Group W that had sat on the sidelines for years. Group W had only five TV stations and about twenty radio stations. Group W had always been viewed as a wild card that didn't fit in with the rest of the Westinghouse family. In going after media, Mike was basically abandoning Westinghouse's storied history. A lot of people said Mike's plan would never work. Some people thought he was crazy, in fact.

Mike, to his eternal credit, stood his ground. As far as Mike was concerned, Group W was the only ace he had. Against a backdrop of jeers on Wall Street, Mike sold off all the industrial operations, including the nuclear power plant business, then turned around and bought CBS for $5.8 billion and the assumption of another $500 million in debt. The move was incredibly gutsy. At the time, Westinghouse had a market value of only about $4 billion. Mike announced his deal in November 1995, just one day after the Disney-ABC merger had been announced. The Disney deal, as you might expect, got fawning coverage in the press. The Westinghouse-CBS deal didn't fare so well by comparison. Newspapers across the country chided the Westinghouse transaction as nonsensical and ill-fated. Mike, as the deal's driver, personally took a pounding.

Mike ultimately got the last laugh. He subsequently merged CBS into Infinity Broadcasting, creating a media giant with an impressive stable of broadcasting and radio assets. CBS was later sold to Viacom for $34 billion, about six times what Mike paid for it. Not many CEOs have the resolve or backbone to see through a makeover like that. Luckily for West-inghouse and its shareholders, Mike Jordan did.

There is one final deal motivator that I haven't yet mentioned. It doesn't fit very neatly into any of the above categories, but I'd be less than honest if I didn't at least throw it out on the table for discussion: It's a lot of fun. Call it the fun factor, if you must, but make no mistake about it—dealmaking is a real kick.

Dealmaking can be downright addictive. There's even a term for it: deal junkie. I've never liked the term, mostly because I don't like the neg-ative connotation. But there you have it. Some people have accused me of being a deal junkie. And I guess I'd have to admit that to some degree—perhaps even to a large degree—I am. If you told me that I could never run another big company again, I'd manage. If you told me I could never do another deal, however, that would be pretty tough to take. But deal junkie? I prefer to think of myself as somebody who just *really* enjoys his work. I genuinely believe that I always have the best interests of share-holders and employees in mind whenever I contemplate a major transac-tion. My standards are rigorous, and I take pride in delivering value to my investors. But the cold fact of the matter is—I love doing deals.

I'm not alone, of course. I have some friends who have to do at least one deal a month to feel right with the world. Fortunately, some of the biggest deal junkies I know—and a few are discussed in this book—also happen to be some of the finest dealmakers around. As they say, practice makes perfect.

By my count I've been involved in more than 250 business transactions over the course of my thirty-year career. Not all of my efforts were golden. I've certainly had my share of hits. I've also had some misses. But I can honestly say I learned a little something from each and every one about what to do—and what *not* to do—at the negotiating table. Dealmaking truly is an art, not a science. Donald Trump at least got that part right.

All that said, I don't purport to have any "secrets" for successful deal-making. A lot of the art of the deal is in the nuance of the moment, which is totally unpredictable. There's also the deal adversary to consider. If it's John Malone, you are *not* going to clean his clock. Same goes for Rupert

Murdoch, Sumner Redstone, and other world-class dealmakers. But for the other 99.99 percent of deals—and deal adversaries—out there, there is hope. Nobody can guarantee you slam-dunk success, of course. But if you use a little common sense and follow these general guidelines, I promise you'll never embarrass yourself. And you might even come out looking like a hero.

HINDERY'S COMMANDMENTS

RULE 1: DO MORE HOMEWORK THAN THE OTHER GUY.

Really good dealmakers are sort of like the Marines. And remember their motto: "More sweat in peace, less blood in war."

No matter which side of the negotiating table you happen to be on—buy side or sell side—you'll always do better if you're better informed than the other guy. Knowledge, at the deal table, truly is power. Think of it in the context of selling a house. If I'm the seller, I'm going to be real keen to tell you about the new stainless-steel kitchen and lovely garden out back. But I'm probably not going to draw your attention to all those termites I've seen running around lately, or the expanding crack in the corner of the basement floor. I may have to disclose them, but you're going to have to do your own reconnaissance to find out more about those floors.

When I was buying some cable systems from Jack Kent Cooke, the now-deceased billionaire, some years ago, I had some doubts about his subscriber numbers. I thought his figures sounded really inflated. Mr. Cooke (he always insisted on being called Mr. Cooke) said I was crazy, so I decided to investigate for myself. I literally got in a car and drove around to see for myself exactly where his cable lines went, by way of trying to ascertain how many homes were located in the cable franchise area. The cable lines, I discovered, traveled past a couple of hospitals and a prison. Bingo. Mr. Cooke, as it turned out, had been counting each hospital bed and prison cell as a potential customer. His novel methodology had the effect of artificially raising his figures, and therefore my purchase price. (Cable systems are priced according to the actual number of subscribers, as well as the number of homes "passed." For that reason, dense urban markets generally fetch the highest prices.)

Mr. Cooke, who would lie with impunity if he thought he could get away with it, laughed when I confronted him. I laughed, too—right after I told him he'd have to adjust his purchase price accordingly or the deal was off. He did, and we eventually got the deal done to our mutual satisfaction. But if I hadn't done my homework, I would have paid for all those phantom customers—and I would have had only myself to blame.

RULE 2: LOOK BEFORE YOU LEAP TO THE ALTAR—YOU MAY LOVE HIM, BUT YOU CAN'T CHANGE HIM.

Some dealmakers get so jazzed about the idea of doing a deal that they overlook, or badly underestimate, each other's differences. It's a huge mistake because differences in corporate culture can just murder you.

I have no doubt that Daimler and Chrysler, the auto giants, thought their marriage was a match made in heaven. And why not? They shared a heritage. They shared a vision. And they had corporate cultures that . . . weren't even close. It was like Diana Ross trying to sing with an oompah band—it just didn't work. Detroit, the home of Chrysler and Motown, is midwestern to its core. Stuttgart, Daimler's hometown, is an international city with a proud German heritage. Chrysler executives, in keeping with U.S. pay scales, earned a whole lot more money than their German counterparts. Daimler executives understandably resented that a lot. Adding to the tension, most Chrysler executives spoke only English. That forced Daimler execs, who were generally fluent in both languages, to always converse in their nonnative tongue. The Daimler-Chrysler marriage, not surprisingly, continued to be touch and go long after the honeymoon was over.

GE's marriage to Kidder, Peabody in 1986 was also an unhappy union. In this case, the two companies—GE and Kidder—were from the same country. But culturally they might well have been from different planets. In buying Kidder, GE bought into a world of secret handshakes, bizarre compensation, and weird motivation that was so contrary to GE that they simply shouldn't have done it. Not surprisingly, the marriage went downhill almost immediately. GE eventually sold most of the firm to PaineWebber. Jack Welch, GE's CEO at the time, later admitted in his own memoir that the whole episode had been a huge mistake.

So pick your partner carefully—because you'll be living with the son of a gun for a long, long time.

RULE 3: DEALS SHOULD BE DONE AS FAST AS POSSIBLE . . . BUT NO FASTER.

This is a variation on Albert Einstein's famous observation that "things should be made as simple as possible . . . but no simpler." The idea, in both cases, is that it's good to push yourself to the limit. But recognize that there *is* a limit, and don't go beyond that.

Speed is critical to successful dealmaking. So is the element of surprise, especially when you're dealing with big publicly traded companies whose stock prices can get whipsawed by news of a deal. But sometimes you can move so fast that you trip yourself up. Depending on how fast you're moving, you can land flat on your face.

Brian Roberts, the president of Comcast, is a case in point. When Brian made a run at AT&T Broadband in the summer of 2001, he kept his plans a big secret from everybody in the industry until the last possible moment. One reason for Brian's radio silence: He was concerned that John Malone and I were going to make a run at Broadband. At the time rumors were circulating that we were going to take out Broadband in a hostile run.

Brian's tactic worked, all right—a little *too* well, in fact. His announcement stunned the media world. It also stunned AT&T, which turned him down flat. Mike Armstrong, AT&T's CEO, was none too pleased with the timing of Brian's offer, which was delivered just as Mike was laying plans for an initial public offering (IPO) of Broadband. Brian's offer put Broadband in play, thoroughly trashing Mike's IPO plans. Mike promptly got on the phone to drum up competing offers. He called Microsoft, Disney, AOL Time Warner, and others. All Brian could do was sit on the sidelines and pray that Mike got no takers.

Brian would have been a lot smarter—and I told him so later—if he had taken a few extra days and given the cable CEOs, Disney, and some others a heads-up on his plans. If he had done that, Brian could have figured out right away if he was going to find himself in a competitive bidding situation and planned his response accordingly. As it was, Brian wound up sitting on the sidelines for more than five months while Mike tried to gin up a bidding war.

The irony of Brian's predicament was that John and I never had anything more than a passing interest in taking a run at Broadband. Despite some press reports to the contrary, our interest never got beyond the back-of-the-envelope planning stage. Fun to think about? Always. But as I've already indicated, serious deals need serious reasons to exist. So take a tip from Brian and learn to hustle quickly—but not so quickly that you hustle yourself into a corner.

RULE 4: REMEMBER THAT YOU ARE ONLY AS GOOD AS THE WOMEN AND MEN AROUND YOU. (AND SO IS THE OTHER GUY.)

There's an old joke about two guys trying to run away from a charging tiger. One says to the other: "This is useless; a man can't outrun a tiger." To which the other guy says: "I don't have to outrun a tiger. I just have to outrun *you*." This same logic applies to dealmaking.

In the middle of a big deal it's easy to get seduced and think that it's all about you. But it's not. It's about the team. Because no matter how good you are, or how good you *think* you are, you do not know more than the men and women sitting around you know in the aggregate. I guarantee it. So make sure that your team is quicker, harder-working, and more experienced than the one sitting on the other side. Otherwise you're just begging to get creamed.

Look at the TCI-AT&T transaction. I was on the TCI side, and I was surrounded by an incredibly bright, experienced, hard-working group. We made it our business to know every twist, turn, and nuance of that deal—and it showed. Mike Armstrong, AT&T's chairman and CEO, no doubt thought his negotiating team was quite capable. And some members of his team were extremely talented. But Mike himself was a novice dealmaker, so he was ill equipped to distinguish the good ones on his team from the not-so-good ones. Mike was also relatively new to the cable business. So were a lot of Mike's bankers and other advisors.

Talk about a gift-wrapped deal. A lot of AT&T's investment bankers didn't even know the basic terms of the cable business. And forget about the more creative financial constructions of TCI, which, to be honest, could confuse a math Ph.D. AT&T didn't bat an eye when we told them they'd be obliged to pay Liberty Media, TCI's programming arm, exorbitant rates for Starz! and Encore programming for twenty-five years. That was about twenty years longer than normal. After the TCI deal closed,

AT&T got a good look at what it had agreed to and screamed bloody murder. But by then it was too late.

I've gotten sandbagged a few times myself over the years. When I was CEO of GlobalCenter, the Internet arm of Global Crossing, I had a deal in place to buy a controlling stake in Digex, a "Web-hosting" company that managed Internet traffic. I was flying to New York to sign the final deal papers when I got the word that Digex had just accepted a last-minute offer from WorldCom, the big telecommunications carrier headed by Bernie Ebbers. By the time I landed, my deal was dead.

I later discovered that a prominent Wall Street analyst with ties to my bankers had tipped off Bernie. That allowed Bernie to sneak in the back door and cut his own deal while I was still in the air. I was furious. But there also wasn't a whole lot I could do. My deal was dead. In any event, my point holds: You're only as good—or as ineffective—as the men and women around you, so pick your team carefully.

RULE 5: LEARN HOW TO WALK AWAY.

One of the hardest things in business is to walk away from a deal that you really want. But sometimes it's the only way to get what you want or, even more important, what you need.

Rupert Murdoch, chairman of News Corp., showed great courage in pulling the plug on his talks with DirecTV, the big satellite TV operator controlled by General Motors, in fall 2001. Rupert at that point had spent more than a year trying to buy DirecTV. GM's board strung him along for much of that time. Just when Rupert thought he had the deal nailed, the GM board did the equivalent of sticking a sharp stick in Rupert's eye. It entered into talks with Rupert's old rival, Charlie Ergen of EchoStar, a competing satellite TV operator. Rupert finally withdrew his offer and walked when GM's board delayed voting on his offer—once again—so that EchoStar could work up a better financing package. For Rupert, who had solid financial backing from day one, that was the last straw. Charlie eventually secured his $26 billion offer by putting up his own EchoStar stock as collateral.

Even before the GM board accepted EchoStar's offer, many lawmakers predicted the deal would have a lot of difficulty gaining regulatory approval. And no wonder. The deal would combine the No. 1 (DirecTV) and

No. 2 (EchoStar) satellite TV services, leaving Charlie with a virtual monopoly in the market. The combined company would have 19 million customers and a lock on satellite TV customers who live in rural areas. Rupert's bid didn't have that problem. As this is being written in the fall of 2002, regulators have turned down the EchoStar-DirecTV merger on anticompetitive grounds. The action paves the way for Rupert to resurrect his bid for DirecTV. Given the weakness in media valuations, it's now likely that he'll even be able to buy it for far less than what he originally offered. Perseverance, as I said, counts for a lot.

RULE 6: HAVE ADVERSARIES, IF NEED BE. BUT DON'T HAVE ENEMIES.

Part of the art of the deal is anticipating the responses of your adversaries. That's pretty hard to do if your opposition is determined to do everything within their mortal power to see you to the Gates of Hell. Once that happens, predictability sort of flies out the window.

Consider the unfortunate case of MediaOne, the big Denver-based cable TV company (later sold to AT&T; see Chapter 5). When MediaOne bought Continental Cablevision in 1996, it vowed to keep Continental's headquarters in Boston. That might not have sounded like such a big deal to an outsider, but to Continental's founder and chairman, Amos Hostetter, it was a *huge* deal. Amos at that point had spent thirty years of his life in Boston, and most of his executive team also had longtime ties to the area.

Enter Chuck Lillis, MediaOne's CEO. Less than a year after the Continental deal closed, Chuck announced plans to relocate Continental to Denver, which was Chuck's longtime base. Amos hit the ceiling. He was outraged that Chuck would go back on his word like that. Amos immediately protested the decision, going so far as to make a personal plea to the MediaOne board. Chuck still wouldn't budge. Amos eventually resigned, and most of his Boston executives followed him out the door.

Now the fact of the matter is that if a company spends billions to buy a company, it can darn well do what it wants with the assets—and if Chuck wanted to move Continental to Denver that was his call. But it just wasn't smart to treat Amos with such indifference. Even if Amos was being a tad emotional, he was still a respected cable pioneer and had a lot of pull in the industry. Amos was also one of MediaOne's largest stockholders, so that gave him pull of another sort entirely.

Unfortunately for Chuck, Amos turned into a blood enemy. It turned out to be quite a lucky break for me, however. As CEO of AT&T Broadband, I later enlisted Amos's help to kill Chuck's proposed merger between MediaOne and Comcast. We later installed Amos as the nonexecutive chairman of cable—based, of course, in Boston. And Chuck? Once the AT&T-MediaOne merger closed, he resigned, and most of his top executives followed him out the door. Talk about symmetry.

So do yourself a favor and watch your manners out there. The deal you save could be your own.

RULE 7: READ THE FINE PRINT.

People routinely take things for granted that they shouldn't. That's true in life in general, and it's certainly true in dealmaking. The problem, in dealmaking, is that assumptions can really do you in if you're not careful, or at least a little lucky.

Volkswagen AG was neither. In 1998 it spent $790 million to buy the ultra-luxury carmaker Rolls-Royce. The purchase price, unfortunately, didn't entitle VW to the vaunted Rolls-Royce name. Oops. VW's deal, you see, was with Vickers PLC, which controlled Rolls-Royce Motor Cars Ltd. The unit manufactured the Rolls—but didn't own the rights to the world-famous brand name. The name, as it turned out, was actually controlled by Rolls-Royce PLC, the fine English maker of aircraft engines. Negotiators for VW assumed the branding issue would work out. After all, why spend almost a billion dollars for rights to Rolls unless you could also buy the gold-plated name? Why, indeed.

BMW, which had just lost Roll-Royce to VW in a bitter bidding war, got the last laugh. BMW, which had an established relationship with Rolls-Royce PLC (they had been working together to develop aircraft engines), circled back and bought the rights to the Rolls-Royce name for just $66 million. A veritable blue-light special, if ever there was one. And VW? It got stuck with Rolls-Royce's other luxury brand name, Bentley, the stodgy cousin of the Rolls. BMW gamely agreed to license the Rolls-Royce name back to VW free of charge until January 1, 2003. After that, BMW takes control, and VW gets shuttled off to luxury-car Siberia with its Bentley nameplate. Enough said about the importance of fine print.

RULE 8: DON'T KEEP SCORE ON THINGS THAT DON'T MATTER.

In the heat of a deal, people sometimes ask for concessions just because they can. Resist this urge, which will only distract you from the bigger picture and eat up precious time. It can also make you look like a jerk.

Some years ago I helped engineer the sale of Teleport, a telecommunications company that was jointly owned by TCI and several large cable companies, to AT&T for about $11 billion. At the last minute, AT&T's chief negotiator, Dan Somers, presented us with an urgent demand: He said Teleport's top six executives had to agree to stay at the company and work for AT&T, or the deal was off. We were dumbfounded. We just couldn't hand over Teleport's top executives like that. Not only that, the deal was supposed to be announced the very next morning.

A fast-thinking attorney on our side, Len Baxt, took the bait. Len grabbed the list of managers that Dan had just handed us, turned it face down on the table and loudly challenged Dan to name any three out of the six people on the list, along with their titles. If these executives are important enough for you to risk blowing up the deal, he goaded, surely you can cite at least three of their names.

Dan drew a blank. After hastily conferring with his colleagues, Dan managed to come up with exactly one name, and he wasn't even sure about that person's title. Chastened by the exchange, Dan backed off his demand, and the Teleport deal proceeded as planned. So resist the urge to push buttons you really don't have to. The face you save may be your own.

RULE 9: HANG IN THERE.

Albert Einstein once said: "It's not that I'm so smart; it's just that I stay with problems longer." Whether you're trying to come up with the theory of relativity or just trying to do the deal of your life, perseverance counts for a lot.

When I was trying to buy $1.5 billion worth of cable systems from Jack Kent Cooke some years ago, negotiations dragged on through two successive Christmases. There weren't any other bidders for the assets, mind you (see Chapter 7). But that didn't keep Mr. Cooke from trying to wear me down. Both years he set meetings on Christmas Eve in Los Angeles. The timing of the meetings practically guaranteed that I'd have a difficult time getting back home to San Francisco in time for Christmas with my family. (And, in fact, I did.) I suspect that was the point of the whole exercise.

Looking back on it now, I think Mr. Cooke deliberately pushed me to the edge because he wanted to find out how far I was willing to go. How bad did I want to deal, *really*? And my answer then, and now, is that I'll do almost anything to get a deal done. Anything. You want to meet with me on Christmas Eve in Los Angeles? Sure, I'll do that. Want to do it two years in a row? Sure, I'll do that, too. Want to torture me day in and day out over minute details so insignificant they make your eyes glaze over? I'm there. My resiliency (some call it stubbornness), my refusal to ever say die, is one reason I've racked up more than seven million air miles over the course of the past twenty years. And it's the reason I'll still get on a plane to this day, anytime, anywhere, to get a deal done. So don't try to outlast me, and don't let others think they can outlast you, either.

RULE 10: LEARN TO KEEP YOUR MOUTH SHUT.

Sometimes things just fall into your lap. It doesn't happen all that often among experienced dealmakers. But when it does, just thank your lucky stars and keep your mouth shut. There will be plenty of time for war stories after the deal is done.

For the mother of all jackpot stories, consider Cox and Comcast. Their experience is a good reminder to us all that, yes, miracles *do* happen. (I would never be so trite as to declare that good things happen to good people, but you can read on and draw your own conclusions about that.)

In 2000, Dan Somers, the head of AT&T Broadband, called up Brian Roberts, the president of Comcast, and told him AT&T wanted to buy out the @Home shares of Cox and Comcast. At the time, neither company was looking to sell. A similar call went to Cox. Brian, accompanied by Comcast's co-CFO, Larry Smith, subsequently sat down with Dan to talk about terms. Jim Robbins, Cox's CEO, couldn't make the meeting, so Brian agreed to take the lead and see what he could work out.

What Brian came up with was, to put it mildly, a grand slam right out of the park. AT&T ultimately agreed to buy the @Home shares of Cox and Comcast for $48 a share, or about $3 billion. As part of the deal, Cox and Comcast agreed to cede control of @Home to AT&T, which at the time was @Home's biggest shareholder. @Home shares were trading in the 30s at the time. AT&T, confident that the share price would shoot up, didn't bother to ask for a "collar" on the deal. ("Collars" allow for the fluctuations of stock prices—up and down—between the time a deal is announced and the time it actually closes.) Absent a collar, @Home's share price could drop off a cliff and AT&T would still be obliged to pay the full $3 billion. Brian was dismayed that Dan didn't at least *ask* for a collar, or at least some sort of price protection. Brian, being the good poker player that he is, said nothing, of course. If AT&T was happy with the terms, then so was he.

AT&T didn't stay happy for long. @Home's share price subsequently did fall off a cliff along with the rest of the Internet world. Because there was no collar on the Cox-Comcast deal, AT&T was forced to fork over the full $3 billion for @Home stock that was only worth, at the time, about $200 million. For tax reasons, AT&T ultimately paid Cox and Comcast $3.4 billion and told them to just keep their @Home stock, which was basically worthless anyway. @Home later filed for bankruptcy.

3

AT&T: HOOK, (PHONE) LINE,
AND SINKER

In 1997, Tele-Communications, Inc. was the biggest cable television operator in America. And it was in serious trouble.

TCI had 7 million customers; 11 million if you counted "affiliated" cable partners. TCI also had a formidable presence in the "content" world. Liberty Media, TCI's longtime programming arm, had stakes in dozens of media companies, including Time Warner, Discovery, and QVC. TCI's bragging rights to being the No. 1 operator, unfortunately, had come at a very steep cost. After years of heavy spending to acquire dozens of smaller cable operators, TCI's debt load was staggering—$14.5 billion. The nation's big debt-rating agencies weren't so sure TCI even had much of a future. Moody's no longer classified TCI's senior debt as "investment grade." It was—literally and figuratively speaking—junk. At Standard & Poor's, TCI's debt was right on the edge of junk. The ratings made it expensive for TCI to tap into the capital markets. Since cable operators need capital—and lots of it—for virtually everything they do, the problem wasn't insignificant.

TCI's rapid expansion, coupled with years of pinching pennies, had taken a heavy toll on TCI's basic cable-TV business. Some of TCI's cable systems hadn't been upgraded in years. Customer service was practically nonexistent. Overall service quality, at least in some markets, was truly awful. It was also relatively expensive. TCI's fat customer base, for years a source of pride, wasn't growing. If anything, it was beginning to shrink.

The exodus didn't help TCI's dwindling cash flow. Though TCI had enough money to keep up with day-to-day operations, it was unclear how, or even if, the company could get enough money to proceed with upgrades. TCI was tapped out with lenders, who had made it clear they wouldn't be giving TCI any more money, not until it cleaned up its balance sheet, anyway. To all appearances, TCI was losing its grip on cable—one customer at a time.

TCI was also on shaky ground politically speaking. As it was America's biggest cable operator, regulators and politicians looked to TCI to set an example for the rest of the cable industry. And they were none too pleased with TCI's arrogant ways, expensive fees, and lousy service. Even the White House weighed in. Al Gore, the former vice president, in one speech famously referred to TCI as the Darth Vader of the cable industry. The label, unfortunately, stuck. All this pain showed up in TCI's stock price, which was struggling to stay in the double digits. Since all boats tend to rise and fall together in the cable industry, other cable operators wound up getting shellacked. Every time TCI's stock price got whacked, so did the stock prices and valuations of everybody else. Needless to say, other cable operators weren't too happy about this. TCI's name was mud in some cable circles.

TCI's pain wasn't just financial. Bob Magness, TCI's much-beloved founder and chairman, had just passed away. John Malone, TCI's longtime president, was immediately elevated to chairman. Bob had been out of day-to-day management of TCI for some time. Still, his passing rocked John's world. John was despondent over Bob's passing. He was also lonesome. The two of them had been friends and business associates for almost a quarter of a century. For the first time ever, John was alone at the top of TCI. For most of his twenty-five years there, John had spent most of his time doing what he does best—cutting deals. Now that Bob was gone, John would have to refocus on day-to-day management.

John was fully aware that TCI had some serious problems. The biggest, by far, was TCI's executive team. Over the years the top ranks had become populated with a lot of highly paid outsiders—from the airline industry, consumer products, and such—who knew next to nothing about the cable business. Field offices, the heart and soul of any cable operation, were treated like foreign outposts. RIFs (Reductions in Force—a euphemism for firing people without replacing them), which had been initiated to save cash, had employee morale in the sinker. By the beginning of 1997, the effects of mismanagement were painfully apparent. When TCI's subscriber numbers for the fourth quarter—traditionally the strongest—came in, they showed that TCI had actually lost customers. The drop-off was alarming. John felt that TCI had lost its way. Something had to give.

John considered a couple of quick-fix solutions. He briefly considered merging TCI with Comcast, the big Philadelphia-based cable TV operator, and letting Comcast run the whole thing. He also thought about bringing in a big gun from outside the cable industry as TCI's new CEO. One person on his short list of contenders was his old pal Craig McCaw, the cellular billionaire. John ultimately decided to stay put and fix TCI himself. Anything less would have been a repudiation of all that he and Bob had worked for. There was also a financial consideration. If John sold TCI right then, as badly broken as it was, he would have had to accept a fire-sale price. John might have been distressed, but he would never be *that* distressed.

That's when John called me. I'd known John since the mid-1980s. We first crossed paths when I was working in San Francisco as Chronicle Publishing's chief financial officer. John tutored me about the cable industry and later encouraged me to start my own company. When I finally struck out on my own in 1988 and founded InterMedia, John was one of my biggest investors. Over the years we'd grown quite fond of each other. We also trusted each other without reservation. To be sure, we had our differences. I've always been far more willing to compromise to get a deal done than John will ever be. John, by comparison, is a long-term thinker who doesn't mind riding things out—for years—to get his way. But our thinking was similar enough that we figured it would be a good partnership. Most important of all, we both loved the cable business, especially TCI. And we were both dealmakers to the bone.

John was a legendary dealmaker. Since his arrival at TCI in 1973, John had overseen more than five hundred deals. He was expert in every type of deal, including mergers, reverse mergers, divestitures, joint ventures, you name it. One of his specialties was "tracking" stocks, which are issues that "track," if you will, the performance of specific company assets. (Tracking stocks allow investors to see how distinct businesses within a single company are performing. Liberty Media, for example, was a tracking stock of TCI. The two issues traded alongside each other on NASDAQ, even though Liberty was controlled by TCI.) John's deals were notoriously complex. Some were so complicated they could make your nose bleed. But for John, that was just business as usual. I don't claim to have John's smarts—few do. But I could certainly hold my own with him at the negotiating table. By then I'd done a couple of hundred deals, including a ton of cable television transactions. So I guess you could say we spoke the same language.

Trying to get TCI back on track, John had stepped back into day-to-day operations a few months earlier. Though things had begun to perk up a bit, John said he no longer had it in him to run the cable business. After twenty-five years, he was basically worn out. Bob's passing was the last straw. John also had Liberty, which was his real passion, to attend to. John asked me to join him at TCI as president and help turn things around. I was deeply honored. John was somebody I looked up to and admired. I didn't hesitate. I told John I would do anything I could to help him.

We agreed that my No. 1 job as TCI's new president was to fix the company's broken balance sheet. I would also have to make fast tracks to mend relationships—with shareholders, employees, customers, and regulators. TCI's senior management team would also have to be overhauled. Though John would continue to oversee TCI's long-term strategy, he gave me full authority to make decisions affecting day-to-day operations.

John's real passion, as I said, was Liberty Media. He loved Liberty so much he used to say that he didn't know where Liberty ended and he began. He'd even named his yacht—*Liberty*—after it. If you knew anything about John, his devotion to Liberty wasn't all that surprising. John was an engineer by training. But he was a futurist in his heart and soul. John used to spend hours talking about the evolving nature of technology and its impact on the world. Under John's leadership, Liberty had begun investing in all sorts of emerging-technology companies. Given his druthers, John probably would have dumped TCI's cable systems many years earlier and just focused on Liberty Media. But the time had never been right, especially when Bob Magness was around.

But now Bob was gone, and things were different. John loved TCI. He also believed deeply in the company. Though John owned millions of shares of TCI stock, he had never sold even a single share. The fact that John Malone, the most feared cable operator in the universe, was stepping back spoke volumes about the shifting nature of the cable business. John was the face of the U.S. cable industry—and he was growing tired of the burden. He was tired of having to defend TCI to regulators, to consumer groups, and even to other cable operators. It really pained him to have TCI derided as the Darth Vader of the industry. It pained him even more that some cable operators privately agreed. All that said, John would never abandon TCI in its hour of need. That's why he had called me in. Though we didn't talk about it right then, I could sense that a far bigger change might be in the works. If we could whip TCI into shape and get the stock price up, I felt John might finally be ready, after twenty-five years in the business, to sell TCI outright.

By then, the Telecommunications Act of 1996 was firmly in place. The new law, ten years in the making, was Congress's attempt to jump-start competition in the phone and cable TV industries. Cable operators for years had argued that they were under intense pressure from competitors. That was a bit of a stretch. Until the passage of the 1996 act, the cable industry enjoyed a virtual monopoly in their local franchise areas. But now, thanks to the bold legislative action, the threat of competition was finally real. Cable companies owned one of just two direct connections to the home. It would be only a matter of time before competitors started nipping at the industry's heels looking for a free ride into the home. The Bells, likewise, had been sniffing around our borders for years. It was possible that the regional phone companies, egged on by Congress, would finally get their acts together and storm our cable markets. Cable companies, with their thirty-year-old cable networks, were hardly ready for the coming war. For the first time ever, I was really worried about the future of the cable television industry.

My main concern was the basic cable-TV plant—all those millions of miles of "coaxial" lines that collectively form America's cable infrastructure. "Coax," as it is called, is basically a solid piece of metal wire covered with insulation and surrounded by a metal sheath. On the plus side, coax is a high-performance conduit that can carry a ton of voice, data, and video signals quickly. On the downside, coax has to be maintained regularly to retain its integrity. It also has to be periodically upgraded with new technology to keep pace with the marketplace. And there's the rub. A lot of cable operators, including TCI, hadn't yet made those investments. As a result, their cable systems were woefully behind the technology curve, and thus ill-prepared for anything even resembling real competition. To catch up, America's cable operators would have to retrofit their aging cable lines with new "fiber-optic" electronics and related gear. To do that, however, they'd have to dispatch crews to install the new equipment by hand. That meant digging up streets and ripping out old lines. Such a huge task would take billions of dollars and millions of man-hours to complete.

My appointment as TCI's president was announced on February 7, 1997, which was a Friday. I showed up for work on Monday. One of my first orders of business was to assess TCI's management ranks. I knew from my own dealings with TCI that most of its senior managers in Denver were out of touch with the industry. What I didn't realize was how out of touch they were with their own employees. I was about to find out.

Not long after I arrived at TCI, President Clinton came to Denver for an economic conference. Hoping to inspire a little company pride, I chartered buses to take all our workers in the Denver area to TCI's satellite transmission center, where President Clinton was scheduled to give a speech on the importance of technology to the future of America. I thought the experience might inspire some company pride. I also hoped the outing might serve as a good bonding experience for managers and employees.

I was standing outside with everybody else waiting to board a bus when something caught my eye: a purring black limousine. I tapped a few employees on the shoulder and asked they knew anything about it. Nobody did. When we had all boarded the bus and were ready to depart, I asked the bus driver to wait a few minutes. I just had to see for myself who the car was waiting for. A few minutes later, a senior TCI manager came bounding out of the building. She waved a big "hello" in our direction, then climbed into the back of the waiting car. She was immediately whisked away to the same speech the rest of us were attending. We all followed along in the bus.

I was dumbstruck. I was also furious. Here I was trying to promote employee appreciation and company pride, and this manager has the unmitigated gall to order up a chauffeur-driven limousine? And she does this knowing that all the other employees and managers are following behind in a bus? The sheer arrogance of it was overwhelming. I used my cell phone to leave her a voice mail, telling her I wanted to talk as soon as we got back. When she showed up that afternoon, I fired her on the spot.

That was just one story. Within six weeks of my arrival I fired twenty-five top TCI executives. That was more than half the senior management team. John was taken aback at the extent of the firings. But, true to his word, he didn't interfere. I soon replaced all of those executives with ones I knew I could count on. Fortunately for me, TCI's middle-level managers were wonderfully capable. I replaced twenty-one of the twenty-five terminated managers with people from inside TCI. The other four were people I knew from around the cable industry.

Once the new team was assembled, we rolled up our sleeves and got to work. We immediately decentralized TCI's decision-making authority in favor of the field offices. The previous management team in Denver had insisted on making all major decisions, which was exactly the wrong approach. Managers in Denver had no idea how to deal with a marketing issue in, say, Portland. It was ludicrous to even try. Under the new edict, TCI's local cable offices once again had broad discretionary authority over their marketing, budgeting, programming, engineering, and regulatory plans.

To help boost employee morale, we offered financial incentives—to just about everybody. We made a tenfold increase in the number of managers with stock options. We also offered cash rewards and other financial incentives to cable installers and our other frontline people. In deference to our employees, we took the strongest possible stand on diversity. Martin Luther King Day, which had never been recognized by TCI, became a paid company holiday. We also liberalized company policies on rolling over sick days and vacation days, and for the first time we provided family leave and benefits for gay and lesbian couples.

We also got busy reorganizing TCI's cable systems, which at the time were incredibly spread out. TCI controlled only a few whole markets. In many cases, we shared markets with two or even three other cable operators. This approach had always struck me as nonsensical. It was inefficient for cable operators and confusing for customers. I strongly believed that the entire industry, including TCI, would benefit enormously by "clustering" cable systems into specific markets, with one cable operator per market. To make this plan work, however, we'd have to convince other cable operators to voluntarily swap systems across the country. This was no small challenge. To pull it off, we'd have to get everybody to agree to basic valuations and stick to them. But I knew it was quite doable, provided we could get everybody rowing in the same direction.

Next we turned our attention to TCI's use of advanced technology. Under John, TCI had begun deploying "digital" set-top boxes, permitting TCI to expand channel capacity in some markets. The beauty of digital set-tops, for John, was that TCI didn't have to spend money upgrading the underlying cable plant. With a little technical rejiggering, the boxes could ride on TCI's existing plant, as old and as worn as it was. But that was just a quick fix. To roll out data and phone services, TCI's networks would have to be upgraded. And that meant we'd have to spend money—money that we didn't have.

Even by the rather liberal standards of the cable TV industry, TCI's cable systems were antiquated. In some of TCI's smaller rural systems, the basic plant hadn't been touched in years. The lines were old and cracked, making them vulnerable to disruptions from snow, rain, and other weather conditions. Cable outages and service irregularities were far too common. Despite the aggressive deployment of digital set-top boxes, TCI's channel lineups in many markets were downright puny, just thirty-five channels or so.

No matter. We decided to give TCI a new label, anyway—Technology Leader. Like Madison Avenue image-makers, we started churning out press release after press release crowing about our plans. Our message was clear: We would turn TCI into America's showcase for technology. TCI would lead, not follow, the rest of the industry into the Digital Age. (For more on this, see Chapter 6.)

In a series of carefully planned announcements, we said TCI would speed up rollout of digital cable-TV services, an advanced version of cable that offers better pictures and clearer sound. We followed that up by saying that TCI would use advanced "compression" technology to expand TCI's channel lineup—a constant source of customer complaints—in most markets. (Compression technology shrink-wraps "content"—voice, data, and video—so you can squeeze more channels into existing cable lines.) We also set plans to greatly expand the availability of TCI@Home, our high-speed Internet-access service, throughout our territory. Mind you, we hadn't actually done anything. All of our announcements were basically statements of our intentions. But apparently that was enough. Wall

Street cheered the news, sending our stock price a little higher with each successive announcement.

By the summer of 1997, things were humming. Customers were not complaining quite as loudly. Employee morale was perking up. Managers were working hard and rowing in the same direction. (And, I might add, there were no more purring limos waiting in the parking lot.) Regulators weren't beating us up nearly as often. The Darth Vader label was still out there, but you didn't see it nearly as often. Thanks to aggressive system swapping, TCI's cable empire was well on its way to being radically re-configured so that we owned a number of large markets, not just pieces of them. Wall Street noticed the changes. Analysts who had once excoriated TCI suddenly had favorable things to say. A few were even quite bullish. All of this was reflected in TCI's steadily improving stock price. TCI, to all appearances, was on a certified roll.

That same summer, John and I got invited to the prestigious Allen & Co. conference in Sun Valley, Idaho. John, as the CEO of TCI, had been attending the conference for years, but it was my first trip. John and I were asked to make a short presentation. John assured me that extemporaneous comments would be fine. All we had to do, he said, was sit on a stage and talk about the changes we were making at TCI. So don't sweat it, he told me.

I sweated it. The conference, hosted by financier Herb Allen, is the most coveted invitation in the media world. Only the most prominent and influential chairmen and CEOs are even invited. Bill Gates of Microsoft is a regular. So is Warren Buffett and, until her death, so was Katharine Graham of Washington Post Co. (Mrs. Graham tripped and fell at one Allen & Co. conference, and tragically died as a result of her injuries.) Given the influential audience, I felt it was important that our message be crisp and to the point. To help John and me stay on track in our comments, I decided to work up some slides detailing our recent progress. I carefully culled through a recent presentation and pulled out a few bullet points, then had those points converted into a slide format. Once the slides were catalogued and arranged just so, I gave them to John for safekeeping.

I never saw those slides again. Somewhere between Denver and Sun Valley, John managed to lose the slides. They just vanished, and he had no idea where or how. Since it was too late to do anything about it, we did the only thing we could do—we headed over to the conference hall with nothing but chutzpah and our not-so-good looks. John assured me that the attire for the occasion was casual, and so we both wore open-collared shirts.

Oh man. As soon as we walked into the conference hall, our jaws just about dropped to the floor. Jill Barad, the CEO of Mattel, was standing on the stage in front of a packed house. Jill, as usual, was dressed to the nines. As soon as she started talking, her carefully choreographed production unfolded to wild applause. In seconds the stage was consumed with a spectacular display of lights, sound, and images. Everything was timed—perfectly—to Jill's talking points onstage. Jill didn't miss a trick. As she was flying through her tour de force onstage, impeccably dressed aides stationed strategically throughout the hall were handing out Barbie dolls by the handful. It was obvious that Jill and her team had been working on the presentation for weeks.

John and I looked at each other—dumbfounded. Not only were we seriously underdressed, now we had the additional indignity of having to follow this incredible, Broadway-worthy presentation. My heart was pounding. What to do? With my adrenaline pumping, I literally ran to a nearby audiovisual room. I collared the first kid I saw and offered him $500 cash—which was all I had on me—if he would work up a few slides for me right then and there. I must have looked half-crazed—and I was—standing there with a wad of cash in my hand. But I was absolutely desperate.

By the time Jill left the stage to uproarious applause forty-five minutes later, John and I had exactly three makeshift slides. It wasn't much, given the extravaganza that had just preceded us. But it was all we had. When our names were called we walked out on the stage, which was now dark and silent, and took our seats on two stools that had been set out for us. When the spotlight hit us, we just started talking—and talking. I'll never know how much that trio of slides helped. But I do know that by the time we stopped talking an hour later, TCI's stock had moved up by a whole dollar, finishing up $4 for the day. It was, to say the least, a memorable end to a most memorable day.

TCI's stock price continued to steadily improve. By the following spring, TCI's stock price had skyrocketed by an astronomical 300 percent. Wall Street was ecstatic. So were John and I. In just fifteen short months, we had managed to pull TCI back from the precipice of doom and fashion it into a proud—and valuable—market leader. The steep rise in TCI's stock price prompted speculation that John, ever the dealmaker, was thinking about selling TCI. John and I downplayed that idea immediately. After all the big changes at TCI, the last thing we needed was for our employees to worry about another shakeup. But in truth, that's exactly what I was thinking. Given the steep rise in the stock price, I was beginning to think it might be time to start reeling in a buyer. But not just any buyer, mind you—I wanted to sell, specifically, to AT&T.

Why AT&T? For starters, it had a great brand name. The vaunted AT&T name, at least at the time, was right up there with Coke, Sony, and IBM. AT&T also had a ton of cash, which is always nice for a rainy day. Best of all, it had a new CEO who was just itching to put his imprint on the company. Not only that, AT&T needed to do *something*. AT&T's long-distance business was drying up. It still threw off a ton of cash. But price wars had cut profit margins to the bone, and the outlook for the whole sector was getting worse by the quarter. AT&T was nowhere on local phone service. The company had hoped to resell the Bells' services under its own brand name, then bundle up local with long-distance and other services and sell it for a discounted price. Things didn't exactly work out. The Bells, not surprisingly, set their rates so high that there was no way AT&T could turn a profit. The Bells' sucker punch left AT&T reeling—for years.

The Bells' posture was especially tough considering that AT&T and the Bells used to be part of the same family. Back then, life was relatively simple. AT&T only sold long distance, and the Bells only sold local phone service. Technically, AT&T had to "pay" the Bells to handle its long-distance calls on the originating and terminating points. But that was just window dressing, since the money was just going from one pocket of AT&T to another.

Everything changed in 1984. That year, the AT&T phone monopoly was broken up by court decree. The Bells—there were originally seven of them—were carved out and spun off as independent local phone companies. AT&T got the long distance business, their manufacturing subsidiary, Western Electric, and Bell Labs. All of a sudden, the Bell "handling" fees that had seemed almost irrelevant before became a make-or-break issue for both sides. AT&T started pushing the Bells to lower their fees, which had always been high. The Bells refused. Soon, AT&T began accusing the Bells of price gouging. The Bells returned fire. This went on for years. The tension got ratcheted up even more after the Telecom Act of 1996 passed. As soon as it passed, the Bells started pushing really hard to enter the long distance market. That, of course, was AT&T's bread-and-butter market. AT&T returned the favor by announcing that it planned to invade the Bells' local phone markets.

But AT&T had a big problem: It had no way to actually reach local phone customers. AT&T had one of the best long-distance networks on the planet. It had every bell and whistle imaginable. But it had zero direct connections to the home. For that, it still had to go through the Bells, just as it did back in the good old monopoly days. And the Bells? They could get along just fine without AT&T, thank you very much. The Bells, owing to their network heritage, controlled everything they needed to offer local and long-distance services, including the all-important "last mile" of phone line that connects directly to homes and businesses (sometimes called the "local loop"). The Bells were required by law to lease out these local loops to AT&T and other rivals. But the Bells, being no dummies, made sure those fees were sufficiently expensive so that nobody, especially AT&T, could beat them at their own game.

AT&T, as you might expect, tried every trick in the book to get around the Bells. It tried the courts; it tried appealing to regulators. It even tried using "fixed" wireless, a lame version of wireless aimed at the home market. Nothing worked. But the one silver bullet that AT&T didn't try, at least not all that seriously, was cable TV. America's cable TV operators controlled the only other "last mile" into the home—the cable TV connection. Even better, cable TV lines use coaxial technology, which, as I've mentioned, is a real workhorse. True, the Bells' local lines are far more ubiquitous—local phone lines go virtually everywhere, while cable TV lines only serve about 85 percent of the United States. But even 85 percent access was a lot better than what AT&T had, which was no access.

John and I figured AT&T could use cable TV lines as a launching pad to get into the $100 billion a year local phone business. To be sure, America's cable lines would have to be seriously upgraded with new gear and electronics to accommodate Bell-quality phone service. But once the lines were fitted with new gear, they could be used to offer local, long distance, cable TV, Internet services—you name it. Best of all, AT&T could sidestep the Bells and all their billions of dollars in annual handling fees. On paper, at least, the plan had a lot of merit.

There was just one little hitch. AT&T had already nixed the idea. In the summer of 1997, I secretly met with Bob Allen, AT&T's longtime chairman and CEO, to pitch him on the idea of using TCI's cable TV lines in the manner I just described. Bob laughed out loud at the notion, then turned me down flat. Bob was emphatic. He didn't believe that cable TV plant—those decrepit coaxial cables—could ever be engineered to support AT&T-quality phone service, local or otherwise. No way, no how, he said. There was nothing I could say to convince him otherwise, so I said okay and that was it. I was disappointed, but it was clear Bob wasn't going to budge.

But now Bob was out, and it was a whole new ballgame. As luck would have it (for me, at least), Bob subsequently got caught up in his own political web at AT&T, leading to his earlier-than-planned retirement. Bob's successor was named in October 1997—Mike Armstrong, the CEO of Hughes Electronics, the aerospace arm of General Motors. Mike was the consummate corporate salesman—tall, good-looking, charismatic. He'd spent thirty-one years working his way up the sales and marketing ladder at IBM. By the time he left, he was chairman of world trade for IBM, with responsibility for all operations outside the United States. Mike had been at Hughes for six years by the time AT&T came calling.

As far as John and I were concerned, Mike was perfect. He had the full support of the AT&T board. And he was looking to make some big changes at AT&T. (AT&T always described Mike as a "turnaround artist," though it was never clear what, exactly, Mike had ever turned around.) He was also a relative novice at dealmaking. Best of all, at least for our purposes, Mike considered himself a "cable guy." Mike's experience with cable was limited to his association with DirecTV, a satellite-TV service operated by Hughes. Mike, to his credit, championed DirecTV once he became CEO of Hughes. He helped develop a business plan for DirecTV, and made sure it got adequate funding from the GM board. But he'd had little to do with its actual creation. But no matter. If Mike wanted to think of himself as one of the cable guys, that was more than fine by us.

John and I were anxious to take Mike's measure and to find out how serious he was about shaking up AT&T. We needed a hook. How about the Internet? We knew that AT&T was badly in need of an Internet strategy. AT&T had never managed to leverage its powerful brand name in the Internet space. TCI, by comparison, had an aggressive Internet strategy. It was a founding member and major shareholder in @Home, a fast-growing high-speed Internet-access service that was akin to AOL and Earthlink.

Unlike AOL and Earthlink, @Home had exclusive carriage agreements with TCI, Cox, Comcast, and other big cable operators. As a result of those agreements, @Home had exclusive cable access to markets with 72 million households. Though @Home wasn't set up to offer traditional phone service, with a little retooling it could be used to offer Internet Protocol (IP) phone service. IP, considered the wave of the future, allows PC users to make phone calls over the Internet. (PC users also have to install special software and equipment.) Best of all for AT&T, IP could be used to transmit all sorts of digital information—voice, data, and video.

We called up Mike and invited him to Denver. Mike immediately agreed, and flew out a short time later. During that first meeting, we asked Mike, almost casually, if he might be interested in using @Home's lines across the country to offer AT&T-branded (IP) phone service. (In addition to helping out AT&T, John thought such a partnership might also enhance the value of TCI.) Mike was game. He was a longtime believer in the power of cable TV lines, a belief that had only been strengthened by his experience with DirecTV. There was just one snag: John and I couldn't let Mike into @Home on our own. While TCI had a lot of pull at @Home, we were by no means the final word. TCI had a 23 percent stake in @Home, plus "soft" control. That meant nothing got done at @Home without TCI's approval. But we also couldn't jam things down our partners' throats, either. If Mike wanted to lease out @Home's lines, he'd have to sell the deal to Cox and Comcast, which had veto rights over big deals affecting @Home.

Practically speaking, I knew Cox and Comcast might object. Cable and phone companies basically don't trust each other. The mistrust owes in part to the infamous "last mile." Cable and phone companies, as I said, control the only two direct connections to the home. So they're constantly on red alert for turf intrusions by the other side. (And, indeed, cable and phone companies have occasionally made half-baked attempts to go after each other's markets over the years.) The cable community is also a fairly tight-knit group (some say insular) and doesn't easily take to outsiders, much less a telecom bigfoot like AT&T. Still, John and I were hopeful that Mike, a super salesman, might be able to charm his way into the group.

After all, Mike was a telecom outsider himself. We figured that could only help.

It didn't. The @Home talks, right out of the gate, were incredibly strained. Cox, in particular, was concerned about AT&T's larger agenda. Cox had its own phone plans and didn't want to diminish its prospects by giving AT&T too much leeway. Mike pushed back. He didn't want cable operators controlling how or on what terms AT&T phone services got introduced. Even the @Home name was a bone of contention. AT&T obviously favored using its gold-plated brand name. But @Home, by mutual agreement, had always been sold under its brand name, and the cable operators weren't too keen on giving that up. We spent weeks going round and round on these and other issues, to no good effect. In the end, neither side was willing to yield. The talks finally broke down for good in January 1998.

Mike, however, was far from done. All the weeks of arguing the merits of a deal with @Home had only convinced him of the appeal of the idea of using cable TV lines for AT&T-branded phone service. Mike was hot on the idea, in fact, and I mean really hot. If he could gain access to enough cable TV lines, Mike was convinced he could turn AT&T into a major player in the Bells' local phone markets. Hmmm. Sounded like an opportunity to John and me. That's when John and I decided to take a calculated risk: We'd help arrange for Mike to meet the CEOs of all the major cable television companies. That way, Mike could personally pitch them on the idea of doing a big, industrywide phone deal with AT&T. It was a somewhat risky gambit on our part. If Mike succeeded, it would blow our chances of enticing him to do a big joint venture with just TCI. But if he failed, it could set the stage perfectly for John and me to circle back in as White Knights and bail Mike out. In reality, of course, Mike would be helping us out. But that was just semantics.

All the big cable operators agreed to meet with Mike at the national cable show in Atlanta that May. Details of the meeting were kept top secret. We all agreed to assemble in a private room at the convention center. At the appointed hour, all the major cable heads showed up—Joe Collins of Time Warner, Chuck Lillis of MediaOne, Brian Roberts of Comcast, Jim Robbins of Cox, and, of course, me. Together, the five cable companies represented more than 80 percent of the cable households in America. That was more than enough to give AT&T a good jump-start into the

Bells' local phone business. There was some nervousness in the air. For most of these CEOs, it was the first time they would be meeting the new AT&T CEO face to face.

After everybody said their greetings and sat down, Mike launched right into his pitch. He described a future in which AT&T and the cable industry could, quite literally, change America. If cable operators joined with him, consumers would, for the first time ever, have a real choice in local phone providers. AT&T would benefit from the cable industry's direct links to its customers; the cable industry would benefit from its close association with one of the most respected companies on the planet—AT&T. Mike made it clear that the union could be a financial win-win for both sides. On top of that, regulators would love it. That could only help the cable industry over the long term. Mike's passion was clear. His words were eloquent.

The cable CEOs listened patiently to Mike's pitch—then shot him down like a tin can on a fence. Chuck Lillis, the CEO of MediaOne, acted as the group's spokesman. Chuck just couldn't say enough about what the cable heads wanted from AT&T—which was the sun, the moon, and the stars. Even if the cable heads ultimately agreed to some sort of arrangement with AT&T—and that was far from clear—Chuck said the cable heads wanted AT&T to shoulder most of the financial costs of upgrading their respective cable systems for phone. And that was just the beginning.

Chuck said MediaOne and the others wanted $6 billion in cash—up front—for upgrade work. For that, AT&T would get access to 25 million cable homes, upgraded for phone service, within a year. The cable operators would still charge AT&T an "access" fee, he explained, but these fees would at least be less than what the Bells were charging. Cable companies also wanted a healthy cut of AT&T's phone revenues. (Never mind, apparently, that AT&T was going to finance the entire upgrade and lend its vaunted brand name.) To make sure AT&T didn't get in the way of the cable industry's long-term broadband plans, AT&T would also have to limit itself to narrow-band (traditional) phone service only.

Chuck's preposterous demands were made even worse by his arrogant, high-handed delivery. To hear Chuck talk, you'd have thought he was dressing down a junior executive, not the CEO of AT&T. It was really awful. Chuck, a longtime telecom executive, was a newcomer to cable himself. Given his background, you'd have thought he would have given Mike a break. Or at least been gracious about it.

The CEOs from Cox, Comcast, and Time Warner basically let Chuck do all the talking. That was no accident. The CEOs had decided ahead of time to let Chuck act as the lead dog . . . and take the heat. Comcast and the others were just as wary of AT&T's motives, to be honest. But they were also smart enough to know that they probably shouldn't burn their bridges with Mike just yet. Chuck, who had a reputation for being long-winded, never seemed to notice. He just kept on talking.

When the meeting was over, nobody said much. At that point, there really wasn't much more to say, so we all just shook hands and went our separate ways out the door. I walked out with Mike. Neither one of us said a word. But then again, we didn't have to. Mike was livid. All you had to do was take one look at him to know that. I was sorry for Mike. After all, he had just gotten his head handed to him in a particularly ugly fashion. But I was also privately ecstatic. In my heart I knew that John and I had just won. Thanks to Chuck's graceless display, and the complicit support of the other CEOs in the room, John and I finally had a good shot at cutting our own phone deal with AT&T. And the beauty of it was—I didn't have to say a word.

I was still floating on air when my perfect day suddenly turned into a this-can't-be-happening nightmare.

To understand the gravity of the events that followed, I have to backtrack a few weeks. Just before our Atlanta meeting, I testified before Congress about TCI's intentions with respect to high-definition television signals, also known as HDTV. This technology is a real crowd-pleaser because it offers high-resolution images, CD-quality sound, and vibrant colors. The downside is that cable operators have to install special equipment capable of handling HDTV signals. Depending on which HDTV format is used, HDTV signals can chew up a lot of "bandwidth"—or channel space—on a cable TV system. At the time NBC and CBS were advocating an HDTV standard that John and some other cable operators regarded as a real bandwidth hog. John was concerned that cable operators might have to bump regular programming to accommodate these new HDTV signals. He felt broadcasters, for competitive reasons, were deliberately advocating inefficient standards.

I certainly understood John's concern. But I was also mindful that HDTV was becoming a political hot potato. Broadcasters were beating the tom-toms in Washington. The last thing I needed was to have politicians dictating TCI's technology policy. Hoping to cool things down a bit, I publicly pledged TCI's unwavering support to carry HDTV signals in whatever format broadcasters chose to transmit them. John, as expected, wasn't too happy about this. He felt I had given up too much political ground to make peace with broadcasters. I respected John's opinion a lot. But I was also convinced that we needed to make it clear—to politicians, broadcasters, and consumers—that TCI would work with, not against, our friends in broadcasting. Besides that, I already had handshake deals in place on HDTV with some big broadcasters. So I knew we weren't going to get jammed on technical standards as John feared.

John's misgivings aside, TCI's public pledge to embrace all HDTV standards was widely applauded—by legislators, broadcasters, consumer groups, and regulators. Over time, I assumed and hoped that John would come around, as well.

Anyway, that's the backdrop. Now back to Atlanta.

Not long after the secret meeting with Mike and the cable CEOs broke up, John Malone, as he often does, wandered down to the convention floor. At some point in his wanderings, a reporter asked John something along the lines of: "What do you think about TCI's plans to carry HDTV signals?" The proper answer, of course, was that we would transmit any and all HDTV formats. That was the correct answer. More important, that was what I had just told Congress. But John, for crying out loud, fired back with something like: "Leo can do whatever he wants on his systems. But I have no intention of supporting HDTV on mine." The clear suggestion, of course, was that TCI had just lied to Congress, and planned to renege on its promise to broadcasters.

Everybody went nuts.

Within minutes, the national news wires were crammed with headlines lambasting TCI and accusing us—me in particular—of lying to Congress. The National Association of Broadcasters, which represented NBC, CBS, and other major broadcasters, tore into us. So did the White House, the Federal Communications Commission, and just about every other local, state, and federal official who had ever dealt with TCI. Two FCC commissioners who were headed to the Atlanta airport to go back home happened to hear the news on the radio. They literally turned their car around and came back to the show to hunt down John and me to find out what the heck was going on.

I was mortified. TCI fully intended to carry any and all HDTV signals, and John knew it. Though John didn't intellectually agree with TCI's formal stance on the issue, that was our formal stance on the issue. But John, I guess, was still miffed. By then he had been stewing over my public testimony for weeks. So when the reporter snagged him on the convention floor, John let loose with the answer that he did. Trying to contain the damage, John and I immediately issued a joint statement to "clarify" our position. The statement affirmed TCI's promise to Congress and to broadcasters. We also made it clear that, despite John's off-the-cuff remarks, there had been no change in TCI's official position on HDTV.

But by then a lot of damage had already been done. I felt that my credibility—with Congress, regulators, and my fellow cable operators—had been damaged. I felt that my authority as TCI's president had been severely undercut. I was also concerned about rumors that John and I were at odds. John's remark had only fanned that flame, not put it out. That could only hurt TCI, and all that we had worked for. I also wasn't sure how AT&T would view the controversy. John and I were hoping to approach Mike about doing a big deal with TCI. No company likes to step into the middle of a fight with Congress. My mind was racing with a thousand thoughts. Mostly, though, I was just disappointed.

I spent that weekend agonizing over what to do. I loved John—he was my friend and personal hero. I also loved TCI. It was a great company with great employees. But I also couldn't shake the gnawing feeling of doom in the pit of my stomach. John's offhand comments in Atlanta hurt the company and hurt me. By Sunday night, I had largely concluded that I should probably just resign from TCI. I flew back to Denver to deliver the news in person.

John was already there. He'd returned to Denver right after the dustup in Atlanta. Our last exchange—in Atlanta—had been cross, to say the least. I could tell he was still smarting from our last encounter. We didn't speak right away; we just sort of glowered at each other from across the room. John knew he'd messed up. But he wasn't used to being chewed out, either, much less by a TCI president. He was just as agitated at me as I was at him. He was agitated at me *because* I was agitated at him. The chill between us was palpable. Just as I was collecting myself to speak, John did something I'd never seen him do before or since. He got up from behind his desk, walked right up to me—and gave me a great big bear hug. Then he apologized for the confusion in Atlanta and said we needed to remain partners. I was so stunned and appreciative of the gesture that I didn't know what to do or say. In retrospect, that was probably the only thing John could have done to get me to calm down and stay put. I responded by saying something along the lines of, Yeah, I agree, and that was that. The tension in the room evaporated immediately.

With that drama behind us, John and I got right back to where we had left off—in pursuit of AT&T. It was clear to both of us that Mike was highly annoyed with the cable industry. He was also anxious to do a big deal. We decided the time was right to finally give him one.

John invited Mike to come out to TCI's headquarters in Denver to meet with us. He agreed and flew out. Mike, who was on his way to a ski resort for the weekend, walked in wearing a pair of cowboy boots with big buckles on them. It couldn't have been more perfect. Here was Mike Armstrong, the new cowboy of AT&T, sitting down to talk with the biggest Cable Cowboy of them all, John Malone. That's when John, a master at talking up the future of technology, starting spinning his lariat.

John, who keeps a white board in the TCI boardroom, started sketching out—as only he can—how a combined AT&T-TCI might look. At this point, we weren't even talking about a merger. We were just talking about a joint venture. John told Mike we could put AT&T's consumer long-distance division together with TCI's cable business to offer voice, data, and video services across the country—and over one wire, no less. Using TCI's digital set-tops, which function like mini-computers, Mike could finally turn AT&T into a certified broadband giant. Mike leaned in to hear more. John took that as a good sign, and kept on talking.

The numbers John was throwing up on the board suggested TCI could deliver nearly half of all cable TV households—about 35 million—in one fell swoop. To reach 50 percent, however, Mike would need more than just TCI. He'd also need the support of TCI's affiliate partners, who controlled 4 million customers. To ratchet up to 80 percent coverage, representing a true national footprint, Mike would also need the support of Comcast, Cox, and other big cable operators. It wasn't a slam-dunk, of course. But with continued encouragement from TCI, we thought there was a very good chance that other big cable operators would eventually embrace the plan. Once Mike had the backing of the cable TV industry, everything could work out for AT&T—just as Mike had talked about it in Atlanta. Mike, who was well versed in technology thanks to his runs at IBM and Hughes, fully grasped the implications of what John was saying. And he was more than just a little enthusiastic.

In partnering up with TCI, AT&T would be pumping up the speed and volume of its spinning triangle, infusing it with the might and reach of the biggest cable company in America. It would also mark the biggest gamble of AT&T's life. And it was clear that Mike needed to do something. AT&T's business triangle, heavily weighted with distribution, was terribly out of kilter. AT&T's sleek long distance network, for all its technological muscle, was woefully inadequate to carry AT&T to the next competitive level. For that, AT&T would need direct access to local phone customers—fast. The Bells were already nipping at AT&T's heels, so there was no time to build. He'd have to buy, then leapfrog like crazy. With TCI's backing and a few lucky breaks, Mike might actually succeed in transforming AT&T into a New Media leader, just as he said he would. From where Mike was sitting right then, a deal with TCI must have seemed too good to be true.

And, in fact, it was too good to be true. Like any good seller, we didn't tell Mike everything. We didn't tell him that cable TV plant was never intended to accommodate Bell-quality phone service. Nor did we tell him that, in order to use cable lines for phone service, they'd have to be upgraded at great cost, which would probably take a long time. We also didn't tell him that he'd have to become a trusted member of the cable club—the very same cable club that had beat him up so badly in Atlanta. TCI only had 7 million cable customers; 11 million if you included "affiliate" partners. TCI always emphasized the 11 million because it was a lot more impressive. But in truth, it was an exaggeration. TCI had no formal control over any of those affiliates. We only controlled the 7 million, which isn't a whole lot if you're an AT&T with designs on every one of the 100 million telephone households in America. So it was imperative for Mike to gain the trust and support of other cable operators. Otherwise, the plan would never work.

After we made our pitch to Mike, we shook hands and parted ways. John and I sort of held our breath back in Denver and waited for the phone to ring. It didn't take long. Within twenty-four hours Mike called to say he wanted to do a deal. He was sold—hook, line, and sinker. Mike was sold on the idea of using TCI's cable systems to offer AT&T-branded phone service across the country. He also hoped to forge phone pacts with other cable operators, just as we had suggested. AT&T's days of being beholden to the Bells, to all appearances, were finally coming to an end. Mike was jubilant. So were we. We had just convinced one of the biggest and most respected telecommunications companies on the planet to partner up with the former Darth Vader of the cable television industry. Talk about changing your stripes.

The two sides went to work right away to finalize terms of our joint venture. Talks bogged down almost immediately. The biggest problem, for us, was trying to figure out how to value AT&T's consumer long-distance business. Years of price wars had cut profit margins to the bone, and the margins were still melting away. To be sure, AT&T's long distance business threw off a ton of cash. But it was also a runaway train that would eventually jump over a cliff along with the rest of the long distance sector. TCI, by comparison, was extremely stable. Subscribers were up, cash flow was growing, and the company's future looked brighter than ever. After going round and round with AT&T's bankers for several weeks, we finally concluded it might make more sense for AT&T to just buy TCI outright. By then, John was comfortable with the notion of selling TCI, especially if we could get a healthy premium for it. Mike, who didn't want to run the risk of losing access to TCI's pipes, quickly agreed. As for me, I couldn't have been happier. By then, I'd been thinking about selling TCI to AT&T for more than a year.

We got to work right away on hammering out terms. I was adamant that we have a signed term sheet in hand before the deal was formally announced. The last thing I wanted was a repeat of TCI's fiasco with Bell Atlantic in 1993. That year, John announced plans to sell TCI to Bell Atlantic (now called Verizon). John, unfortunately, had only a memorandum of understanding, not a definitive agreement, so neither side was bound. The deal later died amid a lot of finger pointing. The public explanation for the blowup was that the two sides couldn't agree on financial terms. To be sure, price was an issue. After the deal was announced, the Federal Communications Commission slashed cable rates by a whopping 20 percent. That created a lot of uncertainty about TCI's future cash flow. Bell Atlantic was understandably concerned and tried to renegotiate terms. John wasn't willing to slice 20 percent off his price and dug in his heels.

But the rate rollback was only part of the story. After the Bell Atlantic–TCI deal was announced, Ray Smith, Bell Atlantic's CEO, traipsed around the country and personally visited some TCI sites. He also assigned more than two hundred people to look at various aspects of TCI's business, with instructions to file reports on what they found. As the reports started landing on Ray's desk, the conclusions were all the same: TCI was a wreck. Ray, to his credit, figured out that TCI didn't actually control any of its affiliate partners. He correctly deduced that TCI's affiliates were free agents and could do as they pleased. By the time the FCC whacked cable rates, Ray had already decided to pull the plug on the TCI deal. The rate rollback just gave him an easy out.

We couldn't afford to have AT&T back out at the last minute as Ray had done. We didn't have a backup plan—AT&T was our first, second, and third choice. Hoping to curtail the chances of a Bell Atlantic redux, we told Mike that we felt it was important to get the deal done as quickly as possible, and as quietly as possible. John, to be honest, was less concerned about this than I was. But no matter—I was worried enough for both of us.

Luckily for us, Mike insisted on his own that we sign our definitive agreement quickly and in utter secrecy. Given the size of the deal, Mike said he was afraid word of it might leak out if we waited too long. John and I were happy to oblige. The last thing we wanted was for the press to get wind of the deal. By the time they got done raking TCI over the coals, the press would wind up doing Mike's due diligence for him. We figured we'd fare a lot better if Mike did his own research, especially given who was heading his deal team—Dan Somers, AT&T's chief financial officer.

We considered it a definite plus for us that Dan was heading up the AT&T team. Prior to joining AT&T in 1997, Dan was chairman and CEO of Bell Cablemedia PLC in London for about two years. Though Bell Cablemedia was always described as one of the largest cable companies in the United Kingdom—and it certainly was in terms of its expansive franchise area—it had only about 100,000 customers. Early in his career, Dan was the chief financial officer of Hardee's, the fast-food chain. He later became chief financial officer for Bell Canada International. Dan was the guy who put together the deal that is still considered one of the sorriest cable transactions ever—the partnership between Jones Intercable and BCI Telecom Holdings. (BCI was controlled by BCE, Canada's version of Ma Bell.) Jones Intercable was controlled by its namesake and founder, Glenn Jones. Glenn, one of the cable industry's original pioneers, was a master at crafting complex partnership structures. By the time Glenn sat down at the negotiating table with Dan, Glenn had twenty years in the business and hundreds of cable deals under his belt. Glenn ran circles around Dan. Glenn got Dan to pay a "control" premium for Jones Intercable—but didn't give him any control. BCI spent $290 million for a 30 percent stake in Jones—and agreed to kick in another $55 million for options to buy out Glenn's controlling stake a few years later. Glenn and BCI later wound up in court squabbling about—what else—control-related issues. It was a real mess.

Dan didn't disappoint us, either. In May 1998, both negotiating teams moved into conference rooms in New York to work out final details for what was now a full-blown merger. Dan showed up for the TCI negotiations with a group of highly respected telecom bankers who didn't know jack about the cable business. A lot of them didn't even know the basic terminology of the business, so they got lost pretty easily in conversations and presentations. To be fair to these bankers, the cable industry, like many industries, has its own jargon and style of speaking. It can get really confusing really fast if you're not from that world. In conversations, for example, cable guys rarely use last names. "John," for example, is John Malone. You don't have to say his last name—and nobody ever does—people just know. Depending on the context of the conversation, "Jerry" could be Gerald Levin (formerly of Time Warner), Jerry Kent (formerly of Charter Communications), Gerry Lenfest (formerly of Lenfest Communications), or Geraldine Laybourne, known as "Gerry," of Oxygen Media. Likewise, cable guys automatically know that "5000" is a reference to the DCT-5000, a digital set-top box sold by General Instrument, which everybody still refers to as "GI" even though it's been owned by Motorola for years. There are about a hundred other inside-baseball terms like that.

After briefings with the bankers who were brought in to assist AT&T, our people would literally high-five each other because it was just so apparent that they didn't have a clue what we were talking about. They were too embarrassed (or proud, which is even worse) to ask us to slow down and explain. So, of course, we didn't. The tip-off was their silence. The AT&T bankers rarely asked questions. They kept notes like mad, mind you. But they rarely asked questions. We kept thinking that Dan and Mike would catch on and bring in some cable bankers to fortify their ranks. They never did.

AT&T's lack of understanding of the cable business became painfully apparent when we got a good look at some of their business projections. They were extraordinarily, and unrealistically, optimistic. AT&T's projections for our cash flows, in particular, were factors beyond what we believed to be true. Our cash flows were improving, to be sure. But there was no way that we would ever meet the rosy expectations of Dan and his bankers. It was also clear that these bankers had little understanding of tracking stocks—one of John's specialties. The lack of expertise wasn't insignificant. A major part of the deal, at least early on, called for AT&T to put all of TCI's cable assets into a separately traded tracking stock.

AT&T's bankers had lots of ideas for the tracker—most of them bad. The AT&T team at one point advocated selling just 5 percent of the tracker to the public and letting AT&T keep the rest of the equity. It was a ridiculous idea on its face. Why? At the time, about half of TCI's shares were held by large institutional investors that had owned the stock for years. That meant, on a public float of just 5 percent, only about 2 to 3 percent of the shares would actually wind up being actively traded by the public. In practice, then, you'd be basing the entire worth of the company on the trading whims of just a handful of individual investors. John about hit the ceiling when he heard about that one. He was so upset he called some of the AT&T bankers into his office to basically give them a tutorial on tracking stocks and explain why their plan wouldn't work. I guess they got the message because AT&T quietly dropped the idea for a 5 percent tracker right after that, and it was never brought up again.

One of the last issues we wrestled with was the all-important ratio, which would determine how many shares of AT&T stock our shareholders received in exchange for each TCI share they owned. For obvious reasons, deal ratios are hugely important. It's not the sort of thing you ever want to short-change in terms of time. AT&T, however, was in a lather to get the deal done quickly. We were happy to oblige.

Dan led the ratio talks for AT&T. I represented TCI, though I conferred almost nonstop with John on the phone. By then, Dan and I had been dis-cussing the ratio for a few hours. The offer on the table was good but not great—and I wanted great. That's when I decided to play a little liar's poker, if you will, with John Malone as my wild card. John has always been known for his willingness to walk away from a deal if things don't suit him. (And, indeed, he is one of the best walkers I've ever seen in my life.) So I decided to use that. I told Dan he'd have to substantially improve his offer for TCI, otherwise I was afraid that John might walk. I tried to look really concerned when I relayed this bit of information, even though I knew the chances of John walking were exactly slim to none.

Dan was in a tough spot. John, after all, was eccentric and somewhat unpredictable. It didn't help that Mike was breathing down Dan's neck. Dan's career was riding on his ability to get this deal done to Mike's satis-faction, and he and I both knew it. I have no doubt that John would have walked if he hadn't been happy with the final terms. But Dan, of course, wasn't about to let that happen, not with Mike Armstrong and the future of his career on the line.

In the end, Dan and I agreed on a ratio that was well within the range that John and I had deemed acceptable. That's putting it mildly. Since so many years have passed I guess I can admit it now: John and I thought we would be lucky to get a 20 to 25 percent premium—tops—for TCI share-holders. We wound up getting 37 percent, exceeding our wildest expecta-tions. That translated into an extra $10 billion for TCI shareholders. (As John always says: You win some, you lose some.) By the time I folded my cards that day, suffice it to say, I was one happy poker player.

LOOKING BACK

Dissecting a major deal you were involved in is never easy. Recollections always get colored by which side you happened to be sitting on, and by the twists and turns of history that followed. But I think it's fair to say that AT&T made a number of missteps, some of which were exacerbated by the inexperience of the two dealmakers at the top, Mike Armstrong and Dan Somers. A few of these oversights were rather small, though still instructive. Others were more significant.

One of the biggest goofs, in hindsight, was Mike's insistence on pushing through the deal so quickly. In twelve days you can't possibly do proper due diligence—and AT&T didn't. (Remember Rule 3: Deals should be done as fast as possible, but no faster.) What Mike should have done is what Ray Smith of Bell Atlantic did—he should have gotten out there and kicked the tires himself. To be sure, AT&T's bankers and other advisors got a good feel for TCI's business during our laborious joint venture talks. Those talks, as I mentioned, went on for weeks. But nothing takes the place of hitting the road and taking a look for yourself. As Ray Smith discovered, anything less is just an educated guess.

Since John and I were on the sell side, we were happy to accommodate AT&T's request to seal the deal quickly. Faster is always better when it comes to selling—less time for second thoughts, cold feet, and due diligence. But it was a huge tactical error on AT&T's part. The deal stood to fundamentally change AT&T forever. It was also a huge selling price. AT&T should have taken the time to do proper due diligence, because once it signed on the dotted line there was no looking back. (Rule 1: Do more homework than the other guy.) It's possible, even probable, that Mike would have proceeded with the deal for strategic reasons, no matter what due diligence revealed. But if Mike had done his homework, at least he could have used his findings to try to negotiate more favorable terms for his shareholders.

As for Dan Somers, AT&T's CFO and lead negotiator, common sense alone should have told him not to stack his team with bankers who didn't have much experience in cable. I also fault AT&T's bankers. Even though they had millions of dollars in fees riding on the successful completion of the TCI deal, it was their job to look out for Mike and Dan. (Rule 4: You're only as good as the women and men around you.) By not insisting on thorough due diligence, Mike's negotiating team let him down. Even worse, they let down AT&T and its shareholders. To be fair, there were a few notable exceptions. Larry Grafstein and Gordon "Gordo" Rich, then co-heads of the telecom and media practice at C.S. First Boston, were real standouts on the AT&T team. Both were incredibly insightful. AT&T could have used a few more people like Larry and Gordo. (So could Wall Street in general, I might add.) In addition to being a gifted banker, Gordo was also a decent and caring human being. He tragically died in late 2000. Larry later became head of the telecom practice at Lazard Frères.

SPUR IN THE SIDE

In about the eleventh hour of the merger discussions, we found ourselves in the middle of a slight emergency. A cattle ranch, as it turned out, was buried in the collection of assets that TCI was selling to AT&T. The place, called the Silver Spur, was a sprawling ranch in Wyoming that was stocked with prize beef cattle. The Spur was an emotional reminder of TCI's decidedly western roots. It was also a reminder of Bob Magness, TCI's much-beloved founder, who had recently passed away. Bob had always loved the ranch. John (Malone) used it occasionally for investor and manager meetings, and it had a lot of emotional importance to him because of its history. John had always planned to buy the ranch and add it to his growing portfolio of western properties, but had never quite gotten around to it. When John saw that the ranch was about to go to AT&T, he got really upset. He told me I had to get the ranch back for Liberty or the merger was off. While I didn't believe John would actually kill the deal over the Spur, I also didn't want to test him, either.

I dropped in on Dan Somers to explain the situation. Dan was very nice about it. He listened patiently, then asked me the following question: "What's the ranch worth?" I said I didn't have a clue—which was absolutely true. I had never even visited the ranch and barely recalled that TCI owned it. When I didn't answer right away, Dan followed up with another question: "What's it on the books for?" I paused momentarily. I knew that the Spur was quite valuable. The entire ranch, including its cattle, was probably worth $20 million. But Dan hadn't asked me what it was worth. All he asked me was how much we had it on the books for. So I told him—$1.5 million. The answer was absolutely truthful. The Spur was on the books for $1.5 million. If Dan wanted to know the market value, however, he'd have to probe a bit. Dan didn't do that. So in the end that's what AT&T agreed to take for the ranch—$1.5 million.

BLINDED BY STARZ!

John started Starz! and Encore, two pay TV services controlled by Liberty Media, from scratch. Over the years, they had turned into substantial competitors to HBO—and big moneymakers for Liberty. Once the AT&T-TCI merger closed, Liberty, of course, would be on its own. John understandably wanted to preserve long-term carriage for the two channels on TCI's systems. With that in mind, we sent deal papers over to AT&T that spelled out, in detail, TCI's obligations to the two channels once the merger closed.

In plain black and white, we told AT&T it would have to pay $300 million a year to carry Starz! and its suite of thirteen movie channels. But there was a catch: $300 million was just the *floor*; the fees would ratchet up over time. At $300 million, AT&T would be paying about $3 per subscriber a month. That was twice the going rate of similar movie services. And the term of the contract—twenty-five years—was about twenty years longer than normal. Most companies won't agree to contracts beyond five years.

In the cable world, movie services are typically based on the number of subscribers. Not in this case, however. Under the Starz! contract, AT&T would be obliged to treat TCI's entire customer base—7 million, plus another 1 million or so customers controlled by TCI affiliates—as Starz! subscribers, even though it would be lucky if 15 percent actually signed up. (That was assuming, of course, that AT&T decided to offer Starz! on an à la carte basis.) Even worse, AT&T would have to apply these same terms and conditions to any new customers it obtained over time through acquisitions, swaps, and such.

As if all that wasn't enough, AT&T would also have to pay for two-thirds of any cost overruns that Starz! incurred to obtain movie rights. So if Starz! projected spending $1 million to buy the rights to a movie but actually wound up spending $2 million, AT&T would be on the hook for two-thirds of the overrun, or about $670,000. There would be no cap on AT&T's overrun obligations. The sky, quite literally, was the limit.

We sent the Starz! and Encore documents over to AT&T—and held our breath. AT&T didn't bat an eye. The company immediately agreed to everything we requested. Given the generous terms, I had expected some discussion, or at least a few questions. All I could figure was that AT&T hadn't bothered to read the documents, or it read them but didn't understand the implications. In any event, AT&T said nothing, so we considered the matter closed.

I guess AT&T finally did get around to reading, or least understanding, the Starz! agreement. About two years after the TCI deal closed, AT&T started complaining about the contracts and tried to redo the terms. John, who was on the AT&T board at the time, said no dice. After

John resigned from the AT&T board in 2001, Starz! sued AT&T to enforce the contracts. AT&T pushed back, claiming they were unenforceable. As this is being written the two sides are still slugging it out in court.

The irony, of course, is that AT&T could have avoided the whole messy situation if it had only heeded Rule 7: Read the fine print. Consider yourselves warned.

A TAXING SITUATION

John Malone is a master at dreaming up clever ways to defer taxes, or at least minimize them greatly. He truly outdid himself on the AT&T deal.

AT&T has always been one of the biggest taxpayers in Corporate America. In the AT&T-TCI merger, we decided to seize on that fact and turn it to the advantage of Liberty Media. John's plan was simple but elegant: We would ask AT&T to pay—in cash—every calendar quarter for Liberty Media's tax losses. By going this route, AT&T would be able to use Liberty's losses to lower its net income line, thereby lessening its own tax hit. (Think of your own personal tax filings: the more write-offs you can claim, the lighter your tax load.) The arrangement would be no skin off AT&T's nose. It was going to have to pay taxes regardless. The only questions were how much, and to whom.

The plan offered legitimate, albeit modest, tax benefits to AT&T. But it was a huge windfall for Liberty. Rather than just racking up "paper" (carryforward) losses as it had done for years, Liberty would get somebody (AT&T) to hand over a fat wad of cash to cover those losses—every single quarter. After the AT&T-TCI merger was announced, a lot of people singled out the tax-sharing arrangement as a good example of how TCI had outfoxed AT&T at the negotiating table. John always blanched at that a bit. He just considered it good tax planning. So did AT&T.

AT&T, for its part, always tried to treat the tax arrangement as a nonevent. To some extent it was. But it was also a make-or-break issue for John. If AT&T had grasped this early on, it's possible that Dan or Mike could have used it to push for givebacks in other areas. As it was, AT&T treated the tax arrangement as a throwaway, allowing a good opportunity for deal leverage to slip away unused.

ROLLING THE DICE

As I've said time and again, there is no substitute for doing your home-work (Rule 1). Nothing drives that point home more than AT&T's ill-fated attempt to use TCI's cable systems to offer local phone service nationally.

Mike was betting AT&T's future, and the future of the men and women of that company, on his belief that TCI's cable TV lines could do certain things within certain time frames, and do them well enough to carry the company to the next level. Mike, in short, was betting on spe-cific outcomes by specific dates. For all his hopes and dreams, Mike knew relatively little about what it would take to turn TCI's cable systems into ones that could support a Bell-quality phone product. Bob Allen, the for-mer CEO of AT&T, knew instinctively what an army of AT&T bankers ei-ther didn't know or didn't want to tell Mike—his phone-over-cable plan wasn't going to work, at least not in the short time frames he was talking about.

We on the TCI side were fully aware of the challenge of trying to turn cable networks into phone conduits. We knew it would be incredibly ex-pensive and take an extraordinarily long time to accomplish. Therefore, I was very careful to keep our names off all the business models and pro-jections that Dan (Somers) and his advisors put together over the course of our merger discussions. Hewing to Rule 10 (Learn to keep your mouth shut), we made a blood pact among ourselves on the TCI side to simply stay out of it. We offered no opinions to AT&T about its projections for the cable business. If asked, we would offer facts about TCI's past perfor-mance, but that was about it. As far as we were concerned, the onus was on the AT&T advisors—not us—to make sure their models were good and that they would hold up to scrutiny on Wall Street.

We were amazed at what the AT&T bankers came up with. At one point, Dan and his team predicted that TCI's cash flows would improve by two to three times once it was merged into AT&T. How was that possible? As far as I was concerned, there was nothing to support that, financially, operationally, or otherwise. AT&T was also unduly optimistic about when, and in what volume, it would be able to offer cable telephony (phone over cable TV lines). Incredibly, AT&T at one point predicted it would be able to have a substantial number of cable telephony customers in hand by the end of 1999. That was preposterous. The merger wasn't even expected to close until March 1999.

Dan and other members of his team would occasionally ask us what we thought about AT&T's projections. We always found a way to take a pass. (Gee, Dan, I'm not sure. Can I get back to you on that?) We'd offer facts—about current cash flows, operating profit margins, that sort of thing—by the buckets. We were also happy to talk about TCI's past performance. But we offered no opinions whatsoever about the future performance of the systems. Nor would we say anything that even smacked of being a forward-looking statement. You'd have thought our silence would have raised suspicions on the AT&T side. Nobody seemed to notice.

Once the deal was done, we assumed AT&T's projections would wind up buried in the bottom of a filing drawer somewhere. Once radio silence was lifted, we also assumed that AT&T would crunch out more realistic numbers to present to Wall Street. We were wrong on both counts. On the day the AT&T-TCI merger was announced, Mike Armstrong got up in front of a packed conference room and repeated many of those same, rosy projections. Some of our bankers standing in the back room just looked at one another in disbelief.

When I got up to the podium, I deliberately focused on AT&T's broader strategic objectives. Since I knew I would be joining AT&T, at least for a while, to run its new cable business, I was already thinking about ways to help Mike deliver on his optimistic promises. I believed in AT&T's cable plan as much as Mike did, and I was determined to do everything within my power to make sure he succeeded. But I wasn't AT&T's hired gun just yet. On the day the TCI deal was announced, I was still very much a representative of TCI shareholders, and I would continue to look out for their interests until the day—the *minute*—the AT&T-TCI merger closed.

I've been asked if, in retrospect, I wish I'd given Mike and AT&T an easier ride. Maybe offered a little more guidance, that sort of thing. And the answer, quite frankly, is no. As I've said before, buyers and sellers have different jobs to do at the negotiating table. My job, as the seller, was to protect the interests of TCI's shareholders and get them the best deal possible. All I can say is, I did my job.

ALL THE NEWS THAT'S (NOT) FIT TO PRINT

Despite the big stakes on the table, relations between TCI and AT&T remained fairly cordial for the entire twelve days. But there was one rather curious episode that I've been asked about repeatedly. In an effort to put this matter to rest, or at least lend my own perspective, I'd like to talk about it now.

The weekend before we announced the deal, *The New York Times* published a lengthy story in its Sunday business section about TCI. On balance, the story was positive. The reporter, Geraldine Fabrikant, acknowledged TCI's rather dramatic turnaround and singled out my efforts as a major contributing factor.

But the story also contained a brief and, for me, extremely painful discussion of my family. I've been estranged from some of my family members for years. So the subject, on its face, was a difficult one for me personally. Ms. Fabrikant basically accused me of embellishing my personal history to make my childhood seem more impoverished and anguished than it actually was. My mother was quoted as saying that she didn't recall that I had ever served in the merchant marine. Other family recollections about my formative years were also presented as fact.

I have no problems with anybody checking into my background, mind you. But the operative word is "check." If Ms. Fabrikant had bothered to contact the Coast Guard or the seamen's union, for example, she would have discovered that I did, indeed, serve in the merchant marine in 1966, when I was eighteen, on the SS *Avila,* a Union Oil tanker. With additional research, Ms. Fabrikant would have discovered that other citations in her story were similarly inaccurate, incomplete, or misleading.

I was deeply distressed about the article. But I also had no interest—then or now—in publicly debating the events of my childhood. Since I couldn't exactly put out a press release refuting my own family, I did the only thing I felt I could do—I said nothing publicly and just hoped the whole thing would blow over.

When I walked into the conference room that very Sunday to continue working on the TCI deal, there was a surprise waiting for me: There in the middle of the table was a big stack of *Times* business sections, with the TCI story prominently displayed on the front. I have to assume that whoever placed the papers there was trying to send a message, though exactly what that message was I'll never know. In any event, Gordo Rich and one of my associates promptly (and, for me, graciously) removed the stack of papers in a rather decisive manner, and we proceeded with the negotiations.

I wish I could say that I learned some valuable lesson as a result of this unfortunate episode. But I really didn't. It was just hurtful. I don't think there are too many people who would like to see their family problems and dysfunctions splayed across the pages of *The New York Times,* and I'm no different. But as I said, I just wanted to offer my perspective. And now I have.

A FOOTNOTE

On balance I'd have to say I was pretty darned pleased with how things turned out on the TCI deal, with one rather embarrassing exception.

A few months after the $48 billion deal was announced I got a rather nasty surprise: I learned that all of my equity holdings in AT&T were restricted for up to five years. That meant, in effect, that I couldn't resign from AT&T for five years or I would lose my unvested options. The only way to get out of it was to get fired.

I went nuts. I had always planned to leave AT&T fairly soon after the deal closed. John knew that; everybody around me knew that. But unbeknownst to me, Mike had insisted that I stick around—and John had agreed! Worst of all, I'd actually approved the change myself. There were so many papers flying across my desk that, somewhere along the line, I managed to sign two unattached signature pages. Those pages later got attached to a document saying that a very large part of my stock options were exercisable only after five years, locking me into AT&T's employment for that period of time.

After I found out, I actually looked into suing AT&T, or suing somebody. I got over that real fast. How could I go to a judge and explain that, in the middle of one of the biggest mergers in history, which I was overseeing, I didn't bother to read documents before I signed them? The fact was, I had nobody to blame but myself. Because of that, I never even bothered to bring up the matter with Mike directly. (I had a whole lot to say to John, however.)

I finally did manage to get around that stock provision. I wish I could say that I came up with some clever exit for myself. The fact of the matter is, I got fired. But even that has a rather interesting story behind it (see Chapter 5). Because I was fired, I was able to get out of my employment contract a lot earlier than the allotted five years. Even so, I figure the delay cost me more than $65 million, given the dramatic decline in AT&T's share price during that period.

But that's just the way it is in fast-moving deals. When you make mistakes, you take your lumps. That is both the beauty and burden of high-stakes dealmaking. The rewards can be great, but so are the consequences of failing.

4

YES I CAN

NOTHING is ever easy in New York. To paraphrase E. B. White, the great American essayist, it's a city that can fulfill you or destroy you, depending a good deal on luck.

I knew it would take some doing to start a new regional sports network dedicated to one of the reigning symbols of the city—the New York Yankees. The Yankees are hometown heroes in New York (unless you happen to be a Mets fan, of course) and the most storied ballclub in America. The team is presided over by the one and only George Steinbrenner. He's a national sports icon, and in New York he's as big a celebrity as the mayor.

This new regional network would also include broadcast rights for other high-octane teams around the region, including the New Jersey Nets of the National Basketball Association. I knew it would be challenging to balance the interests of all these marquee names and their equally effusive—some say obsessive—fans. As it turned out, that would be the easy part.

The idea of forming a new regional sports network featuring the Yankees dated back to 1999. That's when the three team owners—George Steinbrenner (Yankees), Ray Chambers (Nets), and Lew Katz (Devils)—got together and decided to form their own business triangle, if you will. By pooling their content (sports rights) and acting as their own distributors, George and the other team owners figured they could, in effect, become a version of the Madison Square Garden Network (MSG). So named because of its affiliation with Madison Square Garden, MSG and its predecessor at that point had been broadcasting Yankees games for nearly fifteen years. MSG was (and as of 2002, still is) controlled by Cablevision, a cable operator that has about 3 million customers in greater New York. MSG, a big sports and entertainment network, had about 7.5 million subscribers in the Northeast. In addition to the Yankees, MSG broadcasts the Knicks, Rangers, New York Mets, and other sporting events.

Why, you might ask, would George and the other team owners want to go to all the trouble and expense of reinventing the wheel? Pure economics. By cutting out the middleman—MSG—the Yankees could collect revenues both from cable operators and from advertisers. The numbers were compelling. MSG by 2000 was paying $52 million a year to the Yankees for broadcasting rights. To be sure, the $52 million was astronomical in comparison to what other top teams were getting—the Cincinnati Reds got $6 million for their local TV rights; the Minnesota Twins got $5 million. The Montreal Expos, one of the weaker teams in the league, had no local broadcast revenue. But the $52 million was a pittance in comparison to what Cablevision was making off subscriptions and advertising. Some industry estimates suggested MSG was raking in operating cash flow of $80 million to $100 million a year, and a big chunk of that was from the Yankees alone.

Sports rights have been an issue, in one form or another, for the better part of a century. The Chicago Cubs signed a local broadcast deal with WMAQ radio in 1926, marking one of the first deals of its type. For years, fans had to rely on the national broadcast networks—ABC, NBC, or CBS—which could always be counted on to carry a handful of nationally televised games. If you were lucky, your hometown team wound up on the *Game of the Week* on Saturday afternoons. If you weren't so lucky, you had to tune in by radio or read about games in the paper. Local TV stations were good for a handful of games a season. That wasn't a lot considering there were 162 games in the regular season.

The explosion of capacity on cable TV systems beginning in the early 1990s changed everything. Local cable operators suddenly saw their channel capacity almost triple. Cable operators, scrambling to fill air time, quickly bid up prices for sports rights across the board. In response, broadcasting rights for NFL football doubled to $2.2 billion; NBA basketball rights increased to $600 million from $275 million. By 2000, NASCAR stock car racing quadrupled to $400 million. There was even a heated bidding war for PGA golf. The elevated prices got a lot of razzing in the press.

Cable operators quickly latched on to baseball. With its long playing season (six months, plus another month for the playoffs), 162 regular season games, and legions of devoted local fans, it was ideal for local cable operators looking for a way to fill air time. Even better, baseball offered the opportunity for all sorts of related programming—pre- and postgame shows, sports talk shows, and running analysis by current, former, and armchair baseball celebrities—all of which could be used to fill hundreds upon hundreds of hours of air time. Best of all, it was programming with a guaranteed return audience. Even the most popular TV shows—think *Seinfeld* or *E.R.*—could only hold on to a television audience for six or seven years, tops. Baseball has been drawing legions of devoted fans for *decades*. For advertisers, baseball was a veritable grand slam.

The ones left out, so it seemed, were the actual team owners. Though the sports rights fees continued to escalate throughout the 1990s, the fees being paid to owners were still modest next to the subscription and advertising revenues that the actual distributors were raking in. Baseball's revenue-sharing rules, which require stronger teams to subsidize the weaker teams, didn't help. George, as head of one of the strongest teams in the league, already had to contribute about 20 percent of revenues—local TV revenues, concession sales, you name it—to the baseball kitty. Adding to George's financial pain, the baseball league was talking about doubling the percentage to a full 40 percent. There was also the matter of players' salaries: They were going through the roof. Team owners tried increasing ticket prices to help defray costs. But not even substantial increases could keep pace with the ever-rising salaries of some players. The Yankees, of course, had some of the most expensive talent in the league. George's reality was this: His net revenues from baseball operations were going to continue to get whittled away, while Cablevision's profits from the Yankees were going to continue to rise.

A few teams over the years had tried starting their own regional sports networks à la MSG. Nobody really made much headway. In the late 1990s Tom Hicks, owner of the Texas Rangers and Dallas Stars, got his rights back from Fox Sports and tried to launch his own networks. Things didn't work out, and Tom eventually signed a long-term deal with Fox. Even Disney, which owns ESPN, has had its problems on the regional level. Disney tried to bundle up its two sports franchises in California—the California Angels baseball team (now called the Anaheim Angels) and the

Mighty Ducks, a hockey team—into a regional sports network. Even Disney, with all its resources and pull, couldn't secure adequate distribution from local cable operators to get it off the ground. Disney finally threw in the towel and sold the broadcasting rights for both teams to Fox. One notable success was the New England Sports Network, which was formed out of the sports rights of the Boston Red Sox and Boston Bruins.

For the Yankees, things started coming to a head in the summer of 1999. That July, a thirty-day window opened up for Cablevision to negotiate an extension of the Yankees broadcasting rights for the 2001 season and thereafter. The talks ran into a brick wall over price. By then, it was clear that relations between the two camps were fraying. Just a year earlier, Cablevision had tried to buy the Yankees for about $450 million. George felt the team was worth $650 million, at least, but Cablevision wouldn't budge. Talks finally broke down over management. Cablevision offered to give George a twenty-five-year "consulting" agreement but insisted on retaining final authority over talent hires. George, who has the best eye on the planet when it comes to spotting baseball superstars, told Cablevision to take a hike, and that was it.

By the fall of 1999, George was ready to take it to the next level. (Talking about leadership, George once offered this rather succinct piece of advice: "Lead, follow, or get the hell out of the way.") He and the other team owners were convinced that a new cable network, anchored by the Yankees and buttressed by the sports rights of the Nets and other area teams, could be a huge financial winner. To be sure, parting ways with MSG represented a huge gamble. But if things worked out, they could also hit the ball right out of the park. With the financial future of his beloved Yankees on the line, George planted his feet in the batter's box for the clutch hit of all time.

And thus the YankeeNets was born. Since the team owners had no experience in running a sports holding company, much less a sports network, they went outside for help. Harvey Schiller, a prominent Turner Broadcasting executive, was hired in 1999 as CEO of YankeeNets. Harvey got an annual salary of $2 million. In two years' time, Harvey spent another $6 million hiring staff and getting offices set up at Rockefeller Center in Manhattan. He also struck a partnership with IMG, a sports management group. The Yankees and IMG cut a new, ten-year deal whereby the Yankees would own 95 percent of a new regional sports network. Though the

Yankees sports rights were still tied up with Cablevision and MSG, George and the other team owners figured Harvey could at least get started. That way, once the Yankees sports rights freed up, the new venture would be ready to go.

Taking all this in on the sidelines was Cablevision, which was none too happy at the prospect of losing the Yankees. The team, as I mentioned, was a huge cash cow for MSG. By the following year, Cablevision had seen enough. It sued the Yankees to stop the team from forming its own regional sports network. Cablevision argued that the Yankees were trying to use the IMG deal to get around their contractual obligations to MSG, which had the right to "match" any competing offers. The two sides went round and round for months. So much dirt got hurled you could have built a new ballfield with it.

The court ultimately sided with Cablevision. But then, in a monumental stroke of good luck, the court threw George a big meatball straight down the middle: It laid out a road map telling George exactly how to recapture his sports rights. In the end, that's exactly what George did. The Yankees wound up paying Cablevision a onetime fee of $30 million to secure his sports rights beginning with the 2002 season. Since final terms were worked out with a legal mediator, technically nobody won. But in truth it was a grand slam for George, who for the first time since 1985, finally had his sports right exactly where he wanted them—in his own back pocket.

That's about the time I came into the picture.

Joe Ravitch, head of media and investment banking at Goldman Sachs, contacted me in May 2001 to discuss the possibilty of teaming up with George to launch a new sports network. By then, Joe had been sounding out a number of possible investors, including Vivendi, MGM, AOL Time Warner, and Comcast. Though everybody was interested, Joe said the terms had never been right. AOL Time Warner and Comcast, for example, wanted to create a sports network featuring the Yankees that they would jointly own fifty-fifty. The problem was that they wanted to charge themselves just $1 per subscriber to carry the service, about half the going rate.

I didn't know a lot about the inner workings of YankeeNets, to be honest, but I could spot an opportunity when I saw one. I was certainly aware of the Yankees' fight with Cablevision. I didn't consider that a big problem, at least not right then. More important, for my purposes, I had a lot of confidence in Joe. We'd worked together on a couple of deals over the years, and I really liked his style. He was a sophisticated investor and really knew the media ropes. He also knew the Yankees' organization inside and out, so I said sure, let's talk.

In early June, Joe and I met with Randy Levine, president of the Yankees, and Lonn Trost, chief operating officer, at the Four Seasons Hotel in New York. Over coffee, Randy and Lonn talked about their interest in starting up a new sports network. The challenges would be huge. YankeeNets broadcasting wouldn't be a start-up in any conventional sense. It would be a company with specific dates by which it had to be fully functional—no ifs, ands, or buts. YankeeNets would be obliged to launch in March 2002 in time for baseball's Opening Day, so there was zero flexibility on timing. Most start-ups, by comparison, have the luxury of evolving their businesses and product offerings over a period of *years*. Likewise, the new network would owe the Yankees $54 million in broadcasting fees, which was slightly more than what MSG had been paying, starting on the first day of the 2002 baseball season. So there'd be no time to ramp up on revenues, either. The New Jersey Nets' $7 million fee for the 2002–03 season would be due when the fall basketball season began in October 2002.

Then there was the product itself: Yankees and Nets games. The new network would have to televise all 150 Yankees games that weren't televised nationally by Fox or ESPN, Major League Baseball's TV partners. There would also be seventy-five Nets basketball games to contend with in the fall. To be credible, the new network would have to launch as a twenty-four-hour-a-day, seven-day-a-week product. There would be no time to ramp up on anything. We'd have to scramble to backfill the rest of the schedule that wasn't occupied with baseball games with other programming. That meant coming up with creative concepts, hiring production crews, and so on. None of this would be easy or cheap. Since we'd also be making our television debut in the fishbowl of New York, we'd have to be perfect right out of the chute. We couldn't afford second-rate productions, uninformed commentary, or lousy camera work.

Nothing we did would even matter, however, unless we could convince cable TV operators to distribute the network. As I said, a number of teams over the years had tried to launch their own networks but had to fold when they couldn't secure adequate distribution from local cable-TV operators. MSG had the luxury of guaranteed distribution thanks to its ownership by Cablevision, which, as I said, had three million cable sub-scribers in the New York area. Cablevision could also leverage its distribu-tion power to get other cable companies to carry MSG—the industry's version of "You scratch my back, and I'll scratch yours." The new Yankees network would have no such distribution affiliation. We couldn't offer the lure of carriage to other networks as a carrot. Absent that sort of incen-tive, we'd have to convince cable operators to carry the network solely on the strength of the programming.

Cablevision was still smarting over losing the Yankees. Given the ragged way things had ended, I knew Cablevision might not be so anxious to do the right thing and carry Yankees ballgames. That could be a prob-lem. Securing distribution on Cablevision's cable systems would be cru-cial. After all, Cablevision was a hometown cable operator in New York. It provided cable service across Long Island and in the neighborhoods surrounding Manhattan, including Brooklyn and the Bronx, which, of course, was the official home of the Bronx Bombers. If Cablevision balked at carrying the network, satellite TV operators could step in and pick up some of the slack. But satellite TV operators could only do so much for us. A lot of people in and around New York City live in apartments, many of which aren't set up to accommodate satellite TV dishes.

But Cablevision, while important, certainly wouldn't make or break the new network. Time Warner Cable, America's No. 2 cable operator, had nearly 2.7 million New York–area subscribers in various markets, includ-ing Manhattan, Queens, and parts of Brooklyn. If we could get distribu-tion on Time Warner, that would go a long way to influence other cable operators. Comcast, another big national player, had about 900,000 cus-tomers in New Jersey and Connecticut. To make the new network a suc-cess, we'd have to convince everybody to pay about $2 a month per subscriber for the service. That wasn't exactly a slam dunk. Cable opera-tors were already getting clobbered with rising programming costs. ESPN, MSG, and Fox Sports New York (also part-owned by Cablevision), all of them cable sports networks, were already costing cable operators $1.50 to $2 a month per service. Now the YankeeNets would be asking them to cough up even more. That could lead to a revolt among consumer groups, or, even worse, cable operators, not exactly the kind of attention a new network needs.

But just getting carriage wouldn't be enough. It would have to be the right kind of carriage. We'd have to have carriage on the "basic" tier where CNN, ESPN, Lifetime, and other popular channels are carried. This tier, which is the equivalent of beachfront property for programmers, was already quite crowded on most cable TV systems. In some markets, cable operators had run out of room on basic. To squeeze in new channels they actually had to kick off other channels or move them to another tier. Basic has always been the most attractive tier to programmers because it reaches the largest number of eyeballs, and therefore commands the highest advertising rates. (In the cable industry, ad rates are based on the number of subscribers a cable network can deliver.) We couldn't afford to be relegated to a special "pay" tier that customers had to subscribe to, and pay for, separately. That would be instant death.

Though the challenges were significant, the upside potential was huge. Here was an opportunity to create a premier New York–based regional sports network from the ground up using one of the icons of the baseball world—the New York Yankees. And I'd get to do it in one of the most high-profile media markets on the planet—New York City. Throw in the Nets and other area teams, and the venture had all the makings of a World Series grand slam. The opportunity was just too good to pass up. I called up Joe Ravitch and told him that I was definitely interested.

The next step was to meet George Steinbrenner, the Yankees' principal owner. Like most people, I was well aware of George and his many accomplishments. But we had never actually met. We agreed to meet at the Regency Hotel in New York. During our first meeting, we didn't talk about business. We talked about our families, our upbringing, our responsibilities toward people, and how we managed things. The more we talked, the more it became apparent that we had similar philosophies about business, and about life in general. It was also obvious that we both like to win. George was once quoted as saying that second place is really just the first loser. I can't say I disagree.

Like me, George can be rather direct with people. But he can also be incredibly polite. Not long after we met George pulled me aside to let me know that he was prone to swear, and he hoped I wouldn't be offended. I told him not to worry. I'd worked in a shipyard and served in the merchant marine earlier in my life. I was the last guy who was going to be offended by harsh language, and I told him so.

George is one of the best judges of baseball talent around. In the thirty years that George has owned the team, the Yankees have won nine pennants and six World Series. (For a guy who claims to check all the restrooms of Yankee Stadium to make sure they're clean before every World Series game, that's a lot of walking.) George is rightly proud of hiring Joe Torre, the Yankees' incredible manager. Joe had been fired by a couple of clubs, including the New York Mets, before George hired him in 1996. George took a lot of heat for the hire. A local newspaper ran a headline calling him "Clueless Joe." George said he never forgot that—and never let Joe forget it, either.

Like many of us, George is respectful of, and humbled by, the Yankees' winning tradition. In the previous seventy-two years before George owned the team, the Yankees won twenty-nine pennants and twenty world championships. The Yanks' astounding record has turned it into the most famous ballclub in history. Under George, it's also become one of the most valuable sports franchises on the planet. George and some other investors bought the team in January 1973 for $8.8 million. As of 2002, the club was worth more than $850 million.

After a few phone conversations with George, I was in. Things moved along pretty quickly after that. The more I saw of the deal, the more I liked. It was also financially attractive, to say the least. Goldman Sachs and I figured the new Yankees network would be worth about $835 million. Our assessments were predicated on the assumption that we could deliver a fully functional network, including full distribution, reasonable subscriber fees, and advertisers. And that $835 million valuation would kick in on *day one* of the 2002 baseball season.

The actual structure of the venture would be fairly straightforward. George and the other team owners would contribute their broadcast rights to YankeeNets, then sell 40 percent of the company to private investors for $335 million. The team owners would own the remaining 60 percent of the venture, which would become a unit of YankeeNets, a limited partnership composed of George and the other team owners. George would receive more than half of the owners' 60 percent stake in recognition of the high value of his Yankees asset. Goldman Sachs agreed to invest $300 million, which would be used to pay down some junk bond debt. The remaining $35 million would come from me and a couple of other private investors.

Then, just as we thought the YankeeNets deal was about to be a done deal, a curious, three-way horse race began to develop on the sidelines. Unbeknownst to anybody, Ray Chambers, the principal owner of the New Jersey Nets, was trying to bring another investor into the group. But this wasn't just any investor, it was Quadrangle Group, a new firm headed by Steve Rattner. Steve, who was Ray's longtime investment banker, had struck out on his own about a year earlier to set up Quadrangle. Over time, Steve hoped to turn Quadrangle into a major player in the media world.

Quadrangle, at that point, hadn't made much of a splash. By then Quadrangle had done only a couple of deals that were only worth about $10 million to $15 million. Quadrangle needed a big score to put it on the map. Steve immediately offered to split the $300 million investment with Goldman, effectively making Quadrangle an equal partner with one of the most prestigious firms on Wall Street. The mere fact that Steve offered up $150 million on the spot like that said a lot about his enthusiasm for the project. I couldn't say I blamed him.

I was quite familiar with Steve's track record. I first crossed paths with Steve in the mid-1980s when he was a young investment banker and I was chief financial officer at Chronicle Publishing Co. in San Francisco. I'd retained Steve's firm to help me assess some television assets we owned, and Steve was part of the team that worked with me on that project. I ran into Steve a few years later when I was buying the cable TV assets of the late Jack Kent Cooke, the former owner of the Washington Redskins football team. You'll recall that among this rather irascible character's quirks was his insistence that everybody, including his longtime senior managers, call him "Mr. Cooke." Steve, who was brash even then, always insisted on calling him "Jack." That used to amuse everybody—except Mr. Cooke, that is.

Steve's most famous media deal, however, may be the one he was never able to pull off. In late 1996, Bob Magness, TCI's beloved founder and chairman, passed away. Bob, unfortunately, didn't make arrangements for the disposition of a big block of his TCI stock that had "super voting" rights. After Bob passed on, the block went to his estate, which was controlled by his two sons. The problem, for TCI, was that whoever owned the block would be able to wield a lot of control over TCI. Enter Steve Rattner. Steve secretly tried to buy the shares on behalf of Brian Roberts (the president of Comcast) and Bill Gates (the chairman of Microsoft), who had recently become business partners. (Microsoft had just announced plans to invest $1 billion in Comcast.) Adding to the intrigue, Steve refused to identify his client, leaving the impression that something shady was up. Brian never let on that Steve was working for him. Even so, John and I figured out real fast what was going on and put a stop to it. Needless to say, there was never any love lost between Steve and me after that. Steve later claimed that the Magness estate, trolling around for multiple bids, had actually contacted him, not the other way around. As for Brian, he later apologized for the whole sorry stunt.

As the summer of 2001 wore on, so did the drama. A third investment house, Blackstone, soon registered its interest in getting a piece of the action. Blackstone said that it was willing to step forward with full funding for the new venture. The vote of confidence was not insignificant. Blackstone, founded by Pete Peterson and Steve Schwarzman, had a lot of respect in financial circles. It was also a certified media heavyweight with a long track record for picking winners. Founded in 1985 with just $400,000 in assets, the firm by 2001 had raised more than $8 billion for private investment purposes. I read Blackstone's aggressive interest as yet another sign that YankeeNets was, indeed, a very hot ticket.

That's when the trouble began. As Ray's talks with Quadrangle heated up, I started getting signals through back channels. Word soon got back to me that Ray had decided to check on my personal "references," presumably to gauge my fitness to serve as the network's CEO. I have no problem with anybody checking my references. They include people like Rupert Murdoch, John Malone, Chuck Dolan (chairman of Cablevision), and Dick Parsons, then co–chief operating officer of AOL Time Warner. (Dick later succeeded Jerry Levin as chairman.)

But Ray wasn't interested in talking to these references. He wanted to talk, instead, to my two previous bosses—Mike Armstrong, the chairman of AT&T, and Gary Winnick, the chairman of Global Crossing. I'd had ragged partings with both firms and had never made any bones about that. (I was fired by AT&T and left Global by mutual agreement.) I spent a grand total of seven months at AT&T and a year at GlobalCenter, the Web arm of Global Crossing. So Ray's picks were hardly representative of my thirty-year career, which I'm very proud of, warts and all. Even though I thought Ray's selection of references was somewhat curious, I said nothing and continued finalizing our deal package with Goldman.

In the end, just two groups were invited to draw up proposals—Goldman Sachs/Hindery and Quadrangle. Blackstone, which had softer support coming in, would have to sit this one out. In July, the YankeeNets board convened to hear presentations. Goldman Sachs went in first. Joe Ravitch was our lead presenter. In pitching the board to select our group, Joe pointed out that my many, longstanding relationships with cable operators could be a huge asset to the new venture. Given the importance of Cablevision to the long-term success of the venture, he noted that it probably didn't hurt that I had good relations with Charles Dolan, Cablevision's chairman, as well as his son, Jim, Cablevision's CEO. My friendships with Chuck and Jim certainly didn't guarantee carriage (as we will see). But Joe said they probably wouldn't hurt, either (as we will see).

Joe also highlighted my fourteen-plus years as a cable operator, during which time I had served as, among other things, chairman of the industry's leading trade organization, the National Cable Television Association. He touched on my experience at InterMedia Partners and TCI and my involvement in some landmark transactions, including the AT&T-TCI and AT&T-MediaOne mergers. At the end of Joe's presentation, we fielded questions from the board. The last question came from George Steinbrenner. He asked me how long I thought it might take for us to complete deal papers. So I told him: ten days. If everybody worked really hard and cooperated, I honestly thought we could have everything done in just ten days.

After we cleared out, Steve Rattner came in and made his pitch for Quadrangle. Steve had never run a cable business, or any kind of business, for that matter, on his own. But he did have a solid connection to the cable world in the form of Quadrangle's chairman, Amos Hostetter. Amos was a highly respected cable pioneer. He was also on the board of AT&T, which at the time—thanks in no small part to the TCI deal—was the largest cable TV operator in the country. After making his case for Quadrangle, Steve segued off into a little negative campaigning. Among other things, Steve suggested that I might get bored with YankeeNets over time and pointed to my rather short tenure at AT&T Broadband as evidence of that. He also implied that, given my strong personality and hands-on

management style, I might not get along all that well with the team owners. Steve also argued that the new network, as a start-up, didn't need the
kind of horsepower that somebody of my stature would bring to the table.
(So, according to Steve, I was either a prima donna or an overqualified
success story, I could never figure out which.)

Once the presentations were over, the YankeeNets directors thanked
everybody for their time, then hunkered down to consider their options.
When they emerged from their deliberations, George and the other team
owners threw us a real knuckleball: They wanted Quadrangle and us
(Goldman/Hindery) to kiss and make up, because they wanted the two
groups to become coinvestment partners. They also wanted me to become
the venture's new CEO, just as we had discussed.

This was not our ideal outcome, to say the least. From day one we—
meaning Goldman Sachs and myself—had wanted to fund and manage the
YankeeNets network by ourselves. We didn't need and, to be honest,
didn't want a partner, much less one that had been so willing to take pot
shots at me. But the deal was the deal—and we wanted in. So we said
okay, and that was it. Despite the change, I was still confident that we
could have final deal papers in hand within ten days, just as I had told
George. By then we had already submitted a very detailed letter of intent,
also known as an LOI, to the YankeeNets board. The LOI spelled out my
role as CEO and other management details, including the compensation
of my executive team. To be sure, the LOI wasn't the final word. Unlike
definitive agreements, an LOI isn't binding. But given the fact that the
YankeeNets board had just approved our plan, we assumed Quadrangle
would at least be hospitable. While we assumed there would be some tin-
kering with final terms, we also assumed that the two camps, now joined
as partners, would be able to make fast work of the final agreement. Ten
days, in fact, seemed more than reasonable.

Boy, did I get that wrong.

Within days it became readily apparent that it was going to be a tough
slog to the finish line. As for getting final deal papers done in just ten
days—not a chance. All you had to do was take one look at the staggering
number of lawyers who were involved to know that.

Shortly after we'd shaken hands to seal the deal, George and I walked
into a conference room at the Regency Hotel to review deal papers. When

My longtime mentor, tutor, and great friend Ed Little-field, the retired chairman of Utah International. This photo was taken in May 1986 at a reunion of former Littlefield assistants in San Francisco. Ed passed away in September 2001 at the age of eighty-seven.

Bill Daniels, chairman of Daniels & Associates. Bill, a great friend and mentor, was instrumental in encouraging me to strike out on my own and start my own company, Inter-Media Partners, in January 1988. Bill passed away in March 2000 at the age of eighty.

Golfing with (*left to right*) Brian Roberts, president, Comcast; Jim Robbins, CEO, Cox Communications; Bill Gates, chairman, Microsoft; Greg Maffei, chief financial officer, Microsoft. This photo was taken in May 1998 in Atlanta during the national cable show—just one day after the secret meeting with Mike Armstrong that had turned so ugly. The TCI-AT&T merger was announced about a month later.

Here I am at the 24-hour road race in Le Mans, July 2002, flanked by my racing partners, Tony Kester (*left*) and Peter Baron (*right*). (Though the team had a good showing, we were forced to pull out of the race in the sixteenth hour due to a broken axle.)

This photo was taken at the Allen & Co. conference in July 1997, just a few months after I'd been appointed president of TCI. That's me (*second from left*) with (*left to right*) Mike Jordan, CEO, CBS; Dick Parsons, then the vice-chairman, Time Warner (and later Jerry Levin's successor); and Howard Stringer, CEO, Sony U.S.A.

This photo, from the same Allen & Co. conference, was snapped just after John Malone (*left*) and I had finished our presentation. Over the course of our 45-minute address, TCI's share price rose more than $1, which is one reason we look so happy.

Rupert Murdoch, chairman, News Corp. Rupert is one of the most feared (and revered) programmers on the planet. He's also one of the most visionary deal guys you'll ever meet in your life.

Courtesy of News Corporation

Courtesy of Alan Levenson

Mike Armstrong, chairman and CEO, AT&T. Though Mike had good intentions in buying $100 billion worth of cable TV assets, he was never able to transform AT&T into a global broadband leader. He ultimately sold AT&T's cable assets to Comcast for a fraction of what he paid.

Ted Turner, founder, Turner Broadcasting. Ted's vision of a 24-hour network—CNN— changed our perceptions about news, and in the process changed the world.

Sumner Redstone, chairman, Viacom. Sumner had the courage and vision to combine Viacom with CBS to create one of the most vibrant media empires around.

Mel Karmazin, chief operating officer, Viacom. Mel parlayed CBS, a traditional broadcaster known for such TV classics as *60 Minutes*, into a dominant media power by merging with Viacom.

Barry Diller, chairman and CEO, USA Interactive, and chairman and CEO, Vivendi Universal Entertainment. Barry turned a rather dowdy shopping channel, HSN, into a major media player by rolling it up into Seagram. To make sure he'd never be fired, Barry demanded—and got—a watertight employment contract.

Edgar Bronfman, Jr., former CEO, Seagram. Edgar transformed his family's Canadian liquor business into one of the biggest and most influential media organizations in the world, only to become part of the troubled Vivendi conglomerate.

George Steinbrenner, principal owner, New York Yankees. In recapturing his broadcast rights from Cablevision, George set the foundation of what would become a powerful regional sports network, YES.

Courtesy of Associated Press

Jerry Levin, former chairman and CEO, AOL Time Warner. The $165 billion merger of AOL and Time Warner radically redefined the competitive landscape. Though Jerry was later criticized for the deal, the strategic logic of combining the two companies made eminent sense.

Courtesy of Darryl Estrine

Courtesy of Sam Bolton for PMC

Thanks to the support of George Steinbrenner and the other team owners, YES is well on its way to becoming the biggest and best regional sports network in the country. This picture was taken at the Chrysler Building, another New York icon, where our main office is located.

we walked into the room, we couldn't believe our eyes: No fewer than forty people, mostly lawyers, were crammed into the room waiting for us. Everybody was waiting to pore over a document that was so long and complicated you'd have thought it as was a nuclear disarmament pact. (In retrospect, I guess it sort of was.) Not being one to mince words, George expressed his displeasure immediately: "Shakespeare was right," he yelled out to nobody in particular. "Kill all the lawyers!" Then he literally started walking around the room and started pointing at people and directing them to stand by the wall and shut up or take a seat at the conference table. George didn't know most of these people, so he just randomly pointed and barked orders. Senior law partners were just gasping because they were getting stuck at the wall while first-year associates were being instructed to sit at the conference table. Not wanting to confront George, most people did as they were told. One brave soul who was banished to the wall tried to protest, saying something like: "But *I'm* the partner." George, without missing a beat, boomed right back: "No, *I'm* the partner." We saw a lot fewer lawyers at meetings after that.

Too many lawyers, as it turned out, would be the least of our problems. A far bigger issue was Quadrangle's seeming ambivalence about whether it really wanted to invest in the new venture. Quadrangle by then had shaken hands on the deal. But as far as we could tell, that was just window dressing. In practice, Quadrangle tried to use the postagreement period up to the financial closing (when money actually changes hands) for the sort of diligence, review, and examination that should have been done *before*—not *after*—the firm agreed to participate. As a result, the process of working up final papers for the deal, known simply as the "documentation process," became the deal itself.

It was clear that Quadrangle wanted to put its imprint on the new venture. But lacking any real experience in running a cable business, they simply didn't know how. As a result, we wasted an incredible amount of time on some of the most mindless, insignificant details you could imagine. My discussion with Quadrangle about cameras was representative of the problem. In going over our deal papers and business model, a Quadrangle associate told me he had concluded that we had budgeted far too many cameras to broadcast Yankees games. I knew how many cameras we needed not because I knew anything about that—I've never actually produced a baseball game in my life—but because I had extremely capable people who had made their living doing precisely that. They told me how many cameras I needed, and that's what we budgeted.

I was perplexed by the question, so I asked the associate to explain the basis of his criticism. He demurred, then finally told me that Quadrangle had actually hired a consultant to review the camera "issue." I pressed further and discovered that this so-called camera expert was a young man who used to sell advertisements for me in the Bay Area when I was head of InterMedia. This young man, who later moved to New York, somewhere along the line had obviously fashioned himself into a media "consultant." But he had absolutely no experience in producing baseball games, and therefore no basis for his recommendation. I pointed all this out to Quadrangle, and they eventually relented.

The biggest issue we tangled over, by far, was corporate governance. Even though I was the CEO, Quadrangle wanted an active role in management. In order to do that, however, they needed to find a way to get around me. Nothing was said explicitly, of course. But you didn't have to be a rocket scientist to figure out what was going on. Quadrangle soon began pushing for changes in the corporate governance that would limit my decision-making powers and give Quadrangle a more active voice in day-to-day operations. Though our original plan hadn't called for a "chairman," Quadrangle said it wanted to name Quadrangle's chairman, Amos Hostetter, as the new nonexecutive chairman of the venture.

Amos was a longtime friend of mine from the cable industry. And I liked and admired him a lot. Amos was perhaps best known as the founder and former chairman of Continental Cablevision, a Boston cable operator. Under Amos, Continental grew to be one of the biggest and most respected cable operators in the country. He finally sold Continental to U S West, the Denver-based regional Bell, marking the beginning of what would turn into a lengthy merger dance between cable and telecom companies. As mentioned in Chapter 5, Amos later resigned when the company decided to uproot Continental, which by then had been renamed MediaOne, from its longtime Boston base and move it to Denver. Most of Amos's top executives followed him out the door. As the CEO of AT&T Broadband, I had worked with Amos to buy MediaOne. Once the deal closed, Amos became the nonexecutive chairman of cable, restoring him to a position of power.

Given our history together, I wasn't resistant at all to the idea of Quadrangle bringing in Amos to the YankeeNets network. But I was *very* resistant to the idea of any management structure that limited my ability to make decisions and manage the network. The clock was ticking. We would have less than eight months to take the YankeeNets network from the drawing board to the living room. That was like tomorrow. To do my job properly, hundreds of decisions affecting every part of the operation, from personnel to equipment purchases, would need to be made. To stay on schedule and move things along, I would need broad discretionary authority to make decisions quickly, and with impunity. If we resorted to decision-making by committee, we would never be ready in time. Even George Steinbrenner, who potentially had the most on the table, had agreed to limit his authority to approval over Yankees announcers.

Quadrangle, insistent on gaining some management control, refused to budge. With each successive draft of my employment contract, Quadrangle would insert language to limit my control and broaden Quadrangle's authority. We'd get a look at that, then insert language to neutralize the language that Quadrangle had just proposed. Then Quadrangle would propose changes to undo our changes, and so on. If we hadn't been so under the gun for time, the whole thing would almost have been comical.

By then we were well into August, and I had plenty of concerns. I was having my doubts about how good a partner Quadrangle would be going forward. Good partners trust each other: They have to, otherwise nothing works. My concern wasn't just for myself. I was on the verge of bringing in a group of very talented, very committed, and very successful executives to start this new company. They included people like Matt Bond, a seasoned programming executive from Denver; Mark Coleman, a media lawyer from San Francisco; and John Filipelli, one of America's top baseball producers. About a dozen executives in all had indicated a willingness to move to New York. That meant uprooting families, putting children in new schools, and selling homes. I'd known most of these people a long time. I needed to make sure they couldn't be terminated capriciously, and that their talents couldn't be ignored, overridden, or unduly second-guessed. At a minimum, I figured I owed them that.

Quadrangle's main beef seemed to be that I would have too much management control. I needed to figure out a way to satisfy Quadrangle's concerns about me without compromising my need to be able to make decisions quickly. That's when we hit on an idea: How about appointing a special "independent" director to act as referee? Providing the board had this person's approval, or at least concurrence, it could fire me or any member of my senior management team. The authority of the independent director would be absolute. Even if all twelve members of the board, including myself, wanted to make a senior management change, the express approval of the independent director would still be needed. That meant I couldn't hire and fire in a willy-nilly fashion—and neither could Quadrangle.

I discussed the idea with George (Steinbrenner). George said he liked my solution, and even agreed with me on who the independent director should be: Bill Bresnan. Bill had long ties to both the Yankees and the cable TV world. Bill was the father-in-law of Brian Cashman, the general manager of the Yankees. George and Bill had met each other through Brian and liked each other a lot. Bill was also a retired cable operator. We'd worked alongside each other for years in the cable business. I'd known Bill sixteen years and absolutely adored him. So if Bill was compromised in my eyes by being Brian Cashman's father-in-law, he was equally compromised in George's eye by virtue of being my longtime, cherished friend.

Our decision to bring in Bill as the independent director was communicated to our various partners, including Quadrangle. We didn't get any complaints from Quadrangle. And we didn't expect any, to be frank. Bill, you see, was also an investor in Quadrangle. Given Bill's ties to Quadrangle, we figured Steve would be pleased, if anything, that one of his own investors was going to be playing such a critical role.

With that behind us, we moved on to another big issue: compensation. Though compensation of my senior management team had been laid out in great detail in our LOI, Quadrangle had some concerns. The firm basically considered YankeeNets to be a start-up, and thought the salaries of top executives, including my own, should be commensurate. At the height of the dot-com bubble, for example, starting salaries for senior executives were typically in the $100,000–$200,000 range. These salary packages were usually buttressed by loads of stock options. That way, if the company performed well once it went public—and a lot of them performed spectacularly, at least for a while—then executives could make a fortune on the back end.

I flatly disagreed with this approach for YankeeNets. Our new network wasn't a start-up in the traditional sense. As I said, the network would have to be fully functional from day one. It would also have enormous financial obligations from the first day of broadcasting. By the time the first pitch of the 2002 baseball season was thrown, we'd have to be the equivalent of ESPN or MSG. From my perspective, in fact, there was nothing "start-up" about this start-up. I expected starting salaries to be commensurate with the task ahead. At that point I had budgeted $500,000 in annual salary for myself, plus another $250,000 to cover my expenses, including expenses associated with a private airplane I sometimes used. Given that my predecessor had earned $2 million annually, I didn't consider this at all excessive. There was a lot of sniping about my plane expenses, in particular. But that was also bogus. I travel frequently between the two coasts on business and had made it clear to everybody that my travel habits would continue.

Quadrangle also had a lot to say about my practice of treating all my senior managers equally from a compensation perspective. For years, I have given equal salaries, options packages, and even titles to my top executives. Quadrangle didn't like or understand the uniformity of compensation. They also said I couldn't have eight executive vice presidents. One Quadrangle associate even asked me: "What is this, a Communist country? Why is everybody the same?" He looked so perplexed when he posed the question I almost had to laugh.

I understood why Quadrangle was confused. In highly competitive investment banking environments, it would be unthinkable for all partners to be compensated equally. One partner might receive a bonus five times larger than another depending on the number and size of the deals that he or she landed that year. From an investment banking perspective, the very thought that there could be flat compensation was just unfathomable. But that was beside the point. That was the way I did things, and that's the way I intended to do things at the new network. Moreover, I had made it clear in the LOI that this was my plan.

Quadrangle had lots of other objections. Among other things, the firm was unhappy with my decision to permit two of my senior managers to commute for the first year from their respective homes in other parts of the country. I explained that both of these employees were tops in their field, and I considered them very important. Unfortunately, both had personal situations that limited their ability to move their families to New

York immediately. Quadrangle finally relented. But the fact that Quadrangle would even think to dicker over something like that was surprising to me. It also chewed up a lot of valuable time.

Our biggest street rumble, by far, was over stock options. Quadrangle felt I was being far too generous with my own staff. They wanted me to trim the number of stock options far below what I felt they deserved. I could certainly understand the firm's concern. The practice of liberally padding compensation packages with stock option awards, as I've said, is probably one of the worst business trends to develop over the past ten years or so. But I didn't have the time or interest to debate the trend, or come up with a new one, right then. The clock was ticking.

In structuring the compensation packages of my senior executives, I deliberately weighted them in favor of stock options (they each got exactly the same type and number, of course) as an incentive to work hard and participate in the future success of YankeeNets. If the network bombed, these options would be worthless. But if the network was a hit, then the options had the potential to become quite valuable—and everybody won. Quadrangle was unhappy, but I refused to budge. I was prepared to ask a dozen highly seasoned executives across the country to help me launch the network. But I was only going to do that if I was certain that my team would be compensated properly for their efforts. I haggled with Quadrangle for weeks over this particular issue. By late August, I'd had enough.

I certainly wasn't anxious to drop out of the project. Quadrangle aside, I had a really good feeling about the YankeeNets network. People just unabashedly loved the Yankees and the other teams, and that affection showed through in some of the most surprising and delightful ways. The experience of Mark Coleman was typical. Mark, an attorney who had worked for me for years in San Francisco, happened to attend a wedding in New York and wound up chatting with the officiating priest at the reception. During the conversation, Mark mentioned that he was involved in the YankeeNets. Upon hearing that, the priest lit up and immediately ripped open his cassock to reveal—I kid you not—a Yankees jersey. The priest told Mark that he had worn the jersey in honor of the Yanks' last regular-season game that weekend. At Mark's request, I later gave that priest box seats to the divisional playoffs in New York. I happened to attend the same game. He showed up wearing a cassock, and stayed glued to his seat rooting for the Yankees all night. I'll never know if he was wearing a Yankees jersey underneath, but I would have bet money on it.

But raw enthusiasm from fans alone wouldn't do it. To make this network fly, I needed a dedicated team I could count on. I'd also need broad authority to make decisions quickly and with impunity. There could be no second-guessing of my decisions, no debating the alternatives. This was not a democracy, and I had no intention of treating it like one. Somebody had to be in charge, otherwise the network didn't stand a chance of launching on time. I also knew I couldn't build the kind of network I envisioned if I had my hands tied.

Reluctantly, I called up Joe Ravitch at Goldman Sachs and told him that I was out. I told Joe that I really believed in this project, and had fully intended and wanted to see it through. But I was tired of the haggling, and tired of having to explain my business practices and procedures to a bunch of investment bankers who had no clue how to launch and run a media business. All the weeks of arguing about titles, cameras, and stock options had chewed up valuable time, time that we could never get back. At this pace, I told him, the network would never launch on time. I told Joe I'd be happy to help him find a replacement for me.

Joe, to his credit, heard me out, then asked me to come down to Goldman's offices to talk about it. Randy Levine, the Yankees president, was there when I showed up. Randy and Joe both urged me to stay. Randy also told me not to worry about Quadrangle—he'd take care of that. As a good-faith gesture, Randy offered to set up an emergency meeting with the YankeeNets board to talk about my concerns.

Randy, true to his word, hastily arranged a meeting of the YankeeNets executive committee the very next week. During the meeting, I walked the directors through my entire executive structure. I discussed, in detail, my proposed compensation structure, including the controversial stock options packages. I also talked about my longstanding habit of treating all my top executives equally. In my concluding comments, I acknowledged that my way of doing things wasn't necessarily the right way—but it was *my* way. If the board members weren't comfortable with that—and that was certainly their call, I told them—then I'd be happy to help find a replacement.

Gratefully, Randy Levine, acting as George's representative, and the others made it clear that they supported my plans. For me, that made all the difference. So long as I knew that the team owners supported me, I was on board 100 percent. With that assurance in hand, I wiped my slate clean and went to work. As a conciliatory gesture to Quadrangle, I soon offered to take 20 percent of my own stock options and disperse them— equally, of course—among my top managers. By doing so, I was able to satisfy Quadrangle's concerns that I was being too generous, while also bringing my team up to a compensation level that I considered appropriate. Once that hurdle was cleared, Quadrangle and I were done. Or so I thought.

On September 10, 2001, we formally announced the formation of the YES Network, short for Yankees Entertainment and Sports. (YES was a lot easier to say than "YankeeNets," plus we needed a three-letter acronym that would fit easily into the TV guide listings.) Goldman Sachs and Quadrangle each agreed to invest $152.5 million. I agreed to personally invest $15 million. Amos Hostetter, Quadrangle's chairman and the new nonexecutive chairman of YES, agreed to invest $10 million. Bill Bresnan, the independent director, would put in $5 million. The grand total: $335 million.

YES seemed to strike a chord. Even before we had formally announced the network, I'd gotten 350 unsolicited résumés from people wanting to work at the fledgling network. I happened to mention this fact during an interview on CNBC the day the network was announced. As I was walking to my car afterward, my cell phone rang. It was a producer thanking me for my appearance on the show—and asking if I'd be interested in résumé No. 351 (from him). I told him sure, send it along.

The timing of our announcement would prove fateful. The very next day, September 11, terrorists launched horrific attacks on the World Trade Center in New York and on the Pentagon in Washington, D.C. Thousands of people died. Fearful that other attacks might follow, the New York Stock Exchange was closed for the remainder of the week. As a result, the closing of our deal, which had originally been scheduled for Friday, September 14, was pushed back to the following Tuesday.

Quadrangle, I would soon learn, was getting a serious case of cold feet. On Friday, just four days before the deal was set to close, Steve Rattner of Quadrangle put in an unexpected call to Bill Bresnan. The message Steve delivered was a blockbuster: Given Bill's connections to the Yankees and me, Steve said he didn't think Bill should be the independent director. Bill immediately pointed out the obvious—Bill already *was* the independent director, and the documents Steve had previously signed guaranteed as much.

Steve didn't call me directly to discuss his concerns. But one of his associates did call my attorney, David Klott, in San Francisco that weekend. David caught up with me on the phone Sunday night. I was walking home from dinner when David called me on my cell phone and explained the situation. I listened. Then I told David to tell Steve to go jump in a lake. The whole situation was absurd. The deal was done, announced, over. We were set to "fund" the deal (actually transfer money) in less than two days. The U.S. financial markets were bound to be in a mess when they opened up on Monday because of the terrorist attacks. I wouldn't even consider reworking key pieces of this deal under normal circumstances, much less under those unfortunate circumstances. David delivered the message, prompting one of Steve's partners, Peter Ezersky, to hunt me down at home later that night. I told Peter the same thing: no way.

Steve wasn't giving up. On Monday, with the financial markets in a nosedive, Steve put in an emergency call to Randy Levine, the Yankees president. Steve made an impassioned pitch for dumping Bill as the independent director. Steve said he thought it was bad enough that Bill was my friend. But Steve said he had just found out that Bill was also the father-in-law of Brian Cashman, the Yankees' general manager. Steve said he was deeply troubled by the discovery, and suggested Bill might be too compromised to do his job objectively. The problem with this tactic, of course, was that everybody—except Steve, apparently—already knew about Bill's longstanding relationship to Brian. In any event, Randy relayed all this to George Steinbrenner and the other team owners. They all told Randy to tell Steve to go jump in a lake, and that's exactly what Randy did.

Quadrangle pulled out of the YES deal that day. Quadrangle's pullout had zero impact on the venture. Goldman Sachs, which had always wanted to act as sole investor, immediately stepped in and picked up Quadrangle's piece of the investment. Steve spent a good part of the week explaining why he backed out of the deal at the last minute. As for us, we had a job to do, so we put our heads down and got to work. The clock, after all, was still ticking.

LOOKING BACK

E. B. White pretty much hit it right on the head: "No one should come to New York to live unless he is willing to be lucky." We were willing to be lucky, and in the end our gamble paid off. To be sure, it took a lot longer than I thought—sixty-seven days in all. I initially told George I expected us to have deal papers in hand in ten days. So I guess I missed the mark on that. But no matter. As soon as we shook hands and agreed to participate in the YankeeNets project, we were in. For us, all the deal details were just that—details. We were 100 percent committed, and happily so.

Quadrangle's handshake agreement indicated something quite different—an opportunity to *begin* negotiations. By the end it was clear that Steve Rattner of Quadrangle couldn't get comfortable with the corporate governance. Though I never discussed this with him directly, I suspect Steve felt he had no other option but to walk. On one hand, I do give him credit for being willing to pull the plug on a deal that didn't feel right to him. (Rule 5: Learn how to walk away.) On the other hand, it's unclear if Steve's decision served his investors well. Only time can be the judge of that.

It never feels good to have a deal—or, in this case, part of a deal—go south. It's also never a point of pride to have trust with a potential deal partner break down altogether. But it does happen, and in this case it happened to us. Amos Hostetter, Quadrangle's chairman, called me up later and apologized on behalf of the firm. Amos, who lives in Boston, said he'd been watching the whole soap opera from afar. And it was clear to him that Quadrangle didn't view YES as a passive investment. Amos said it was clear to him that Steve and his associates wanted to be actual managers of the business. As a result, Amos said, he realized the potential existed for contentiousness to develop between the two of us. Amos said he didn't want that to happen under any circumstances, which was one reason for his call. I told Amos I was on the same page with him on that, and we ended the conversation just as we have all of our conversations over the past fifteen years—as friends.

BASIC STYLE

It all went back to the cameras. The fact that Quadrangle would even think to ask how many cameras I planned to use to broadcast Yankees games said it all. Quadrangle wanted to dominate YES, not just be an investor.

That's not to say people shouldn't be careful when making investment decisions. As I've said before (Rule 1), you should always try to do more homework than the other guy. I could understand, up to a point, why Quadrangle was so cautious. Quadrangle was looking at the biggest investment of its short life. YES, after all, represented an investment of more than $150 million. But there's a big difference between being prudent and being excessively cautious or, worse yet, meddling in things you know nothing about.

Contrast Quadrangle's behavior to that of Goldman Sachs. Goldman had just as much financial exposure. But its investor profile was much different. Goldman, like many experienced investors on the private side (outside the venture capital community, that is), viewed its role as far more "passive"—meaning it planned to leave management of YES up to the people who actually had experience in this area. So whereas Goldman wanted a strong, experienced CEO (me) to counter the strong personalities of the team owners, Quadrangle wanted a less forceful CEO (not me), or at least somebody who would be beholden to it (again, not me), so that Quadrangle could have more influence.

Quadrangle's hands-on style, unfortunately, isn't all that uncommon among some investment houses these days. I personally blame this on the dot-com era. The private investment side used to be characterized by an arduous decision and diligence process. But once the decision to invest was made, the investor stepped back and let the professional managers run things. Then came the dot-com boom. All of a sudden, not only did due diligence go flying out the window, but investors who had zero experience running companies started showing up on boards—and everybody had an opinion about everything. It was a disaster, of course, and a lot of investors got burned. But rather than realizing that maybe the original approach—aggressive diligence, passive investment—was the right way to invest, some investors actually redoubled their efforts to get involved. After the dot-com crash, traditional financing dried up and almost any investor willing to step up with funding was routinely invited to join the board. Never mind that a lot of these investors had no actual business expertise or insight to offer.

Part of the push to a more hands-on style of management also owes to the changing nature of business start-ups. More and more, they're about whole business models—think eBay or Amazon—not just individual products. A lot of these start-ups, however, are no more than concepts that have been dreamed up by creative, clever people, many of whom have little if any experience in business. It probably didn't occur to a lot of these people that it might be wise to populate their boards with people who actually had some business experience. After all, in many cases the founders themselves had no firsthand business experience.

It didn't used to be that way. When Dave Packard and Bill Hewlett started Hewlett-Packard, they weren't trying to change the world. Dave and Bill, both of them engineers by training, were just trying to get an invention—a device that that measured electronic waves—manufactured. There was no master plan, no revolutionary "killer app" in mind. The HP company mushroomed from there, but the seed, if you will, was that one invention, a cleverly designed instrumentation device. In today's evolved business start-up environment, it's questionable if Dave and Bill would have been taken seriously by investors. With no grand plan and no larger business model in mind, I suspect they would have been sent packing.

They say history repeats itself. In the case of historical investment styles, at least, one can only hope so.

OVERPLAYING YOUR HAND

A classic mistake some people make at the negotiating table is to overplay their hand. And as that old saying goes, pigs get slaughtered.

To be sure, dealmaking can be frustrating, especially if things aren't going your way. But as any poker player can tell you, overplaying your hand is ultimately a losing proposition. Consider the rather unfortunate examples of Quadrangle and Cablevision.

Against rather long odds, Quadrangle succeeded in landing a plum spot as coinvestor on a very attractive media deal. It not only managed to beat out Blackstone, a respected investment firm with a long track record of picking media winners, it had equal billing with one of the top firms on

Wall Street—Goldman Sachs. The deal terms, for the most part, were set. So was the management structure. All Quadrangle had to do was row in the same direction with the other partners. That was pretty much it.

But instead of just taking the deal, Quadrangle reverted to form. Showing its true investment banking colors, Quadrangle decided to use the postagreement period to rework the terms of the deal. It was ultimately Steve's decision to pull the plug. But the events that led up to that decision were largely of Steve's own making. I suspect he thought Goldman, myself, and the other partners would back down once it became apparent that he was going to walk. After all, we had just announced the deal. The financial markets, due to 9/11, were in a meltdown. We wouldn't dare let him walk, right? Wrong. Steve classically overplayed his hand, and in the end managed to bounce Quadrangle right out of the deal.

Cablevision also overreached. Cablevision, as I said, tried to buy the Yankees from George in 1998. George wasn't too happy with the price that Cablevision was offering—around $450 million. George thought the team's worth was closer to $650 million. But price wasn't the dealbreaker. The thing that really annoyed George was Cablevision's insistence on having final approval over player hires. George, of course, is legendary for his ability to spot baseball talent. And he wanted to continue doing that even after Cablevision owned the team. I would have jumped at the offer. Having George on hand to scout baseball talent would have been like Tiger Woods offering to help me improve my golf swing. It doesn't get much better than that. But Cablevision didn't see it that way, and the deal eventually died.

Too bad for Cablevision. Today the Yankees are the most valuable sports franchise in the world—thanks in no small part to George's keen eye for baseball talent. And they continue to gain value with each passing season. As of 2002, the team was worth more than $850 million. The Yankees sports rights are the anchor of the new YES Network, which, as of 2002, was worth more than $850 million. So not only did Cablevision lose an opportunity to own the most valuable team in baseball history, its heavy-handedness also gave rise to an aggressive new competitor.

THE YES LAWSUIT

Chuck and Jim Dolan, who control Cablevision, are some of the toughest negotiators you'll ever meet in your life. When I was at TCI, John Malone actually bet me $20 I couldn't convince Chuck and Jim to sell a third of Cablevision to TCI in exchange for some New York–area cable systems. After a lot of heartache (mine, not Chuck's and Jim's), I finally did get that deal done. I also collected my $20.

But there's a big difference between being tough and engaging in discriminatory business practices. Chuck and Jim, I'm sorry to say, stepped over that line after they lost the Yankees sports rights. Despite repeated attempts by YES to get carriage on basic, the Dolans turned us down—time after time after time. True, they did offer to carry YES on a "premium" tier like HBO. The offer, on its face, was preposterous. As sports programmers like Chuck and Jim know, carriage on basic is crucial to the long-term success of any sports network. Business models in that world are predicated on access to basic, which offers the most "eyeballs" and thus the best ad rates. For these reasons, MSG and Fox Sports Net New York, also owned by Cablevision, are both carried on basic. So are ESPN and almost every other sports programmer out there.

After months of trying to work out terms, YES finally did the only thing we felt we could do—we sued Cablevision on antitrust grounds. The suit, which was filed on April 29, 2002, accused Cablevision of blocking distribution of YES for purely anticompetitive reasons. By then, all the other big cable operators, including AOL Time Warner and Comcast, had signed up. Though we had more than thirty distribution contracts in place, getting Cablevision was critical. The company controlled 3 million subscribers in the New York area, including the Bronx, the longtime home of the Yankees. Since we had no interest in turning the suit into an indictment of the U.S. cable industry at large, we tried to keep our language targeted specifically at Cablevision. That said, we recognized that any legal remedy that might arise from this action had the potential to affect other cable operators. That was—and is—most regrettable. But in the face of intractable opposition from Cablevision, I felt, as a fiduciary matter, that I simply had no other choice.

Admittedly, sports programming is extremely expensive, and becoming more so thanks to spiraling sports salaries. Cable operators for years have complained about it. I complained about it myself when I was an operator. Still, I never shut out anybody just because I didn't like the pricing. And I certainly didn't try to railroad anybody to programming Siberia—the "premium" tier. Instead, I did what any good operator should do—I worked out mutually agreeable terms.

To be sure, I knew going in that Chuck and Jim wouldn't be happy about paying monthly fees for something that, up until then, had been a real money-maker for Cablevision. Before I even agreed to join YES, I had a private dinner with Chuck to sound him out. I told Chuck that I considered his support essential. To my pleasant surprise, Chuck didn't hesitate—he offered hearty congratulations and wished me well. Chuck said he'd rather have somebody he knew running YES as opposed to somebody he didn't know. Likewise, Jim and I agreed up front that we wouldn't allow our YES fight to turn personal. Not long after that, Jim invited me to his wedding in Palm Beach. As a wedding present I gave him a toaster. Jim seemed to get a kick out of that.

Those warm feelings, unfortunately, evaporated rather quickly after YES sued. Not long after the suit was filed I got a package in the mail from Jim—it was the toaster. In a handwritten note, Jim said he didn't need the toaster or "this sorry excuse of a friendship." That hurt.

As this is being written in October 2002, the YES lawsuit is still working its way through the courts, and we are nowhere close to reaching a carriage agreement with Cablevision. But we are nowhere close to a shutout, either, as evidenced by our thirty-plus carriage deals with AOL Time Warner, Comcast, DirecTV, and others. George Steinbrenner and the other team owners continue to be wonderfully supportive of YES, and we look forward to a long and prosperous run as America's biggest and best regional sports network.

BILL BRESNAN

Quadrangle's handling of the issue of the independent director was exceptional on a couple of levels.

Bill, just to remind you, was the person George Steinbrenner and I agreed early on should be the sole independent director for the new network. Bill's vote or concurrence was needed to terminate me or any member of my senior executive team. Quadrangle initially agreed to Bill's appointment, and on that basis we announced the formation of YES. A few days later, Steve Rattner of Quadrangle cried foul. Steve said he'd just found out about Bill's connection to the Yankees. He said it was bad enough that Bill was my friend, but the fact that he was also the father-in-law of Brian Cashman, the Yankees' manager, was just too much. Steve wanted to dump Bill as the independent director and appoint somebody else.

Steve's about-face was curious, to say the least. Bill had been Brian's father-in-law for years, so it wasn't exactly a secret. Bill's relationship with Brian was common knowledge among the YankeeNets partners. It was also common knowledge in New York sports and media circles. Since Bill was also an investor in Quadrangle, you'd have thought Steve would have been more clued in. It's possible, of course, that Steve was out of the loop.

I think a more plausible explanation, however, is that Steve simply got a bad case of cold feet. The terrorist attacks of 9/11 had the financial markets in a tailspin. Investors across the board were shaky. Quadrangle was about to make the biggest investment of its young life—$152.5 million. That was no chump change, even for a sophisticated group of investors like the ones in Quadrangle. It was never clear to us if Quadrangle had the money handy, or whether it would have to go outside for funding. If the latter was true, the prospect of having to raise money in such a shaky financial environment probably wasn't too appealing.

Personally, I was glad the firm pulled out. But as a matter of principle, Steve should have hung in there. By pulling out at the last minute like that, Steve not only robbed his investors of an attractive investment opportunity, he left his own firm looking timid and unsure of itself. I'm not saying I've never had butterflies in my stomach on deals—do enough of them and eventually you do. But that is the nature of dealmaking. Once you agree to take a deal—you take the deal. No waffling. No whining. No "can we change one more thing" after everybody has signed on the dotted line. You take the deal. Anything less is a waste of your time and my time, not to mention your investors' resources.

YOU WANT WHAT?

After Quadrangle pulled out, we had to quickly redo hundreds of pages of paperwork to reflect the change. Rather than redrafting everything, we asked Quadrangle to simply sign a one-page amendment stating that it had dropped out (a standard procedure in such situations). Quadrangle resisted, saying it would sign the document for us only if we agreed to pay the $2.5 million in lawyers' fees that it had racked up over the course of the YankeeNets discussions. We refused, noting that Quadrangle had pulled out of its own volition. Quadrangle dropped its demand only after Randy Levine, the president of the Yankees, gave Steve a call and showed him the light.

To be fair, Quadrangle was perfectly within its rights to ask for lawyers' fees. But as I've said before (Rule 8), it's not a good idea to ask for things just because you can. The mere fact that Quadrangle would even raise the issue suggested sour grapes. The simple moral of this story: Try to keep the bigger picture in mind. And if all else fails remember Rule 10: Keep your mouth shut!

DEAL ETIQUETTE

Some people have asked me if I'd ever do another deal with Steve Rattner of Quadrangle. I have a lot of respect for Steve's investment banking talents, and I wish him good luck with Quadrangle. But the answer to that question, quite truthfully, is no, not if I can help it.

My problem with Quadrangle and with Steve, specifically, boiled down to this: trust. You can and should fight right up until the time the decision to proceed with the deal is made. But once you make the decision to proceed, you do just that—you take the deal. Of course, you always retain the option of walking away from any deal that doesn't suit you. But that, by definition, is a losing strategy. As dealmaking pros know, it doesn't matter how many transactions you can gin up; it's how many deals you can successfully close that counts.

My dear friend John Malone is notorious for his habit of negotiating deal terms long after everybody has shaken hands. But even John has discovered that there are consequences to this particular style of dealmaking. It ticks people off. It makes then unnecessarily wary of you, even fearful. A lot of people to this day hate doing deals with John because they always worry he's going to fiddle around with the terms after the deal is agreed upon. I suspect John doesn't get a crack at some opportunities that might be attractive for his shareholders simply because people are afraid to sit down at the negotiating table with him. That's not good for anybody—especially John.

In retrospect, I probably shouldn't have been surprised at Quadrangle's reaction. Quadrangle is top-heavy with former investment bankers, who tend, by nature, to be transaction-oriented people. There's a big difference between raising money and investing money; between doing a deal and running a company. They're yin and yang. That you can do a deal doesn't necessarily make you a good investor. Bruce Wasserstein, the head of Lazard Frères, is one of the best deal guys you will ever meet in your life. He's utterly masterful at landing big deals. As far as Bruce is concerned, the bigger and tougher the better. (His specialty is hostile takeovers, which in itself should tell you something about Bruce.) But Bruce—and this is not a criticism—knows absolutely nothing about running a business, and he doesn't pretend to. Quadrangle, it seems to me, could learn a lesson or two from Bruce on that.

5

MEDIAONE GROUP—
ROLLING THE DICE

MEDIAONE GROUP was the ultimate trade bait.

The big Denver-based cable TV operator had 5 million subscribers in some of the best markets in America, including Boston, Atlanta, and Los Angeles. Like prime waterfront property, these were the types of markets that cable operators tended to hold on to for life—and the kind that other cable operators would do almost anything to get.

It was August 1998. Just two months earlier, AT&T had announced plans to buy Tele-Communications, Inc. (TCI), for $48 billion. AT&T planned to upgrade TCI's cable TV systems to handle AT&T-branded local and long distance phone service. Over time, AT&T planned to sell consumers a bundle of phone, cable TV, Internet access, and, eventually, interactive TV services. Regulators and politicians were ecstatic at the prospect that consumers would finally have a choice of local phone companies. AT&T was just as ecstatic at the prospect of finally getting a piece of the Bells' $100-billion local phone market. AT&T had plenty of "distribution," to be sure. But, unfortunately for AT&T, it was the wrong kind. For all its long-distance might, AT&T had no direct connections to the home. Therefore, it had no way to challenge the Bells' stranglehold over local phone service. Cable companies, like the Bells, also had direct connections to the home. Once cable lines were upgraded and outfitted with new technology, they could be used to deliver all sorts of new digital services, including high-speed

Internet access, interactive video, and, of course, local phone service. By then, AT&T had been trying to bust into the Bells' markets for years with no success. Cable was its last hope.

Mike Armstrong, AT&T's chairman, was on a mission to remake AT&T's ailing business triangle. In buying TCI, Mike was loading it up with better distribution, new technology, and an array of new products. A triangle like that could easily carry AT&T into the next century. You had to give Mike credit for going for broke like that—*somebody* needed to. AT&T's core long-distance business was dying. The market was eroding as if piranhas were eating it. Years of long distance price wars had driven profit margins to the bone, and the financial picture was growing bleaker by the quarter. To make its huge investment in cable pay off, AT&T would have to launch phone-over-cable services as quickly as possible.

I was still CEO of TCI, and fairly consumed with gaining regulatory approval for the pending TCI-AT&T merger. It was the biggest deal of my life, and I wanted to make sure things went smoothly. I'd already agreed to become AT&T's cable chief once the merger closed, at least for a while. As usual, I was trying to think ahead. To be successful in the local phone business, AT&T would need broad access to America's cable TV systems. But AT&T had a problem, and it was a big one. AT&T couldn't, by law or by economics, buy enough cable to secure a national platform. Regulators wouldn't allow it, and even if they did, AT&T didn't have enough money. TCI had only 7 million customers, 11 million if you counted "affiliate" cable partners. Those were huge numbers for a cable operator—but not if you were AT&T and wanted direct access to America's 100 million–plus telephone households.

How to get around that conundrum? By teaming up with every big cable operator in America. It wasn't a sure thing that cable operators would go for it. But if we could convince them to let AT&T lease out their lines to offer AT&T-branded local phone service, AT&T could reach every major market in America in no time. That was really the only way. Without the industry's help, the chances for success were dismal. How to entice cable operators to cooperate? That was easy: MediaOne. It owned a treasure trove of cable systems in markets that other cable operators had lusted after for years. AT&T could buy MediaOne, then carve up the company like a Christmas turkey and distribute its parts to various cable operators. That would truly be an offer that nobody could refuse. If we got everybody rowing in the same direction, AT&T could easily gain access to 80 to 85 percent of the United States. That was more than enough to give AT&T a big jump start in the local phone business.

Mike, as I've said, was quite bullish on the power of cable TV lines. He just fundamentally believed in the power of upgraded cable TV systems to triumph in the emerging world of New Media. He was also on board with the idea of using MediaOne as trade bait to land big phone deals. We talked it over, and Mike agreed that we should buy MediaOne as soon as possible. We couldn't move on our plan right then, of course. Regulators were still mulling our $48 billion merger proposal for TCI and AT&T. The Bells were already complaining that the AT&T-TCI merger gave AT&T too much power in the market. If we'd tipped our hand on MediaOne, it would have been regulatory suicide. That being the case, we did the only thing we could do—we said nothing publicly and worked on the TCI deal.

In anticipation of going after MediaOne, I turned my attention to Lenfest Communications, a cable TV operator in Pennsylvania. Lenfest had about 1.25 million customers in New Jersey, Delaware, Maryland, and Pennsylvania. TCI owned a 50 percent stake in Lenfest; the other 50 percent was controlled by Lenfest's founder and chairman, Gerry Lenfest. TCI and Gerry shared control of Lenfest Communications fifty-fifty. That meant Gerry couldn't make any big decisions without TCI's approval, and we couldn't make any big moves without Gerry's okay. I wasn't a big fan of Gerry, and vice versa. Some of Gerry's overseas businesses, which TCI had no control over, had cost TCI a ton of money. Gerry and I made a number of attempts to dissolve the partnership, but we could never agree on terms. We eventually tabled the talks.

After Mike and I decided to go after MediaOne, however, I figured it was time to restart my buyout talks with Gerry. Lenfest had an East Coast concentration of cable systems that included the lucrative Philadelphia market. Given AT&T's larger phone aspirations, it occurred to me that Lenfest could also come in handy as trade bait. I didn't know for sure, of course. But I had a good hunch. I resurrected buyout talks with Gerry in the fall of 1998. I deliberately didn't let on that AT&T was interested in buying MediaOne. Gerry and I didn't have the best working relationship to begin with. If he found out what I was up to, I was afraid his buyout price would go through the roof or, worse yet, he might dig in his heels and not sell to us at all.

Even though Mike was enthusiastic about buying MediaOne, I had my concerns, the biggest of which was whether Mike would have the stomach to stick with it. His strategy of using cable TV to remake AT&T was somewhat risky. Mike was banking on particular outcomes—using TCI's cable TV lines for phone service—in a rather short time frame. TCI's cable lines weren't even close to being ready. Before TCI's systems could support Bell-quality phone service, AT&T would have to spend heavy and move fast. If problems cropped up—and no doubt they would, given the size of the task ahead—Mike would feel the heat on Wall Street. Other cable operators had already rejected his phone-over-cable plan as far too ambitious. To make his plan work, Mike would have to be willing to turn a blind eye to critics. Like any good leader, he'd have to believe in himself, stay focused, and, most important of all, stay the course. If he could do that, however, I was convinced that Mike could turn AT&T into a New Media giant, just as he had promised investors.

By then we were deep into talks with Time Warner, America's No. 2 cable operator, about a big phone pact. AT&T wanted to use Time Warner's cable TV systems across the country to offer AT&T-branded local phone service. Once Time Warner was on board, we figured other cable operators would follow more easily. Time Warner, after all, was one of the most closely watched, admired, and emulated cable companies on the planet.

On February 1, 1999, we hit the jackpot. AT&T and Time Warner announced they were forging a twenty-year strategic relationship on phone service. The deal called for Time Warner and AT&T to set up a jointly owned phone venture to offer AT&T-branded local phone service. The venture would use cable TV lines (Time Warner's and AT&T's) to offer local phone service to 20 million households and small businesses in thirty-three states. The venture, which would be 77.5 percent owned by AT&T and 22.5 percent owned by Time Warner, planned to pilot phone service in one or two cities by the end of 1999 and begin broader deployment in 2000.

Market reaction to the deal was swift and overwhelmingly positive. And no wonder. The landmark agreement was proof positive that AT&T could, indeed, get the U.S. cable industry to embrace its big phone plan. And its first cable partner out of the gate was no less than Time Warner, one of the world's leading media and entertainment companies. After months of agonizing over whether AT&T's gamble on cable would pay off, there finally was light at the end of the tunnel. Or so we thought.

The AT&T-TCI merger closed about a month later on March 9, 1999, marking AT&T's official entry into the world of cable TV. AT&T promptly went into a "quiet" period because of a large debt financing that was under way. During quiet periods, companies aren't permitted to make any public statements about plans and such that haven't been included in formal filings to regulators. So even though we had just completed a $55 billion merger and had plenty to talk about, AT&T went radio silent.

On March 22, 1999, Comcast Corp. dropped a bombshell. The big Philadelphia-based cable TV operator announced that it was buying MediaOne for $60 billion. The deal would combine Comcast, America's fourth-largest cable operator, with MediaOne, the No. 3 cable operator, to create a broadband giant with 11 million cable TV customers and systems that passed more than 18 million homes. The combined company would leapfrog AT&T to become the biggest cable TV operator in the country. Brian Roberts, Comcast's president, could hardly contain his enthusiasm: "This is a breathtaking moment in the history of Comcast," he said in a press release. Indeed, the deal marked a pinnacle in Brian's career, a capstone that would decisively move him and Comcast to a leadership position in the U.S. cable industry.

My reaction to Brian's deal? Over my dead body.

Brian longed to turn Comcast into a media powerhouse. Under Brian and his father, Ralph, the company's founder and chairman, Comcast had grown into a sizable cable player. Comcast had about 5.7 million cable TV subscribers; its systems served markets with about 9.4 million homes. Comcast, which had been expanding its business triangle for years, also had a growing stable of programming. In addition to QVC, the big home-shopping cable network, Comcast owned a controlling interest in E!, a general entertainment cable network, and Comcast SportsNet, a regional sports channel. For all its ambitions, however, Comcast was still a middle-rung player. The MediaOne deal stood to change all that.

AT&T could hardly show its upset publicly. That would have tipped our hand too much. Plus, we were still in our quiet period and couldn't talk about our plans. Following proper decorum, Mike Armstrong put in a call to Brian on the day he announced his deal and offered his hearty congratulations. Brian seemed relieved. He shouldn't have been. Mike was like the hit man who shows up at the funeral of a guy he has just knocked off. As Brian was about to find out, things weren't exactly what they appeared to be.

Brian had tried for years to push Comcast into the cable big leagues. In 1997, as you may recall, Brian and Bill Gates tried to secretly buy a big block of TCI shares with super-voting power that had been owned by Bob Magness, TCI's founder. Bob had just passed away. Bob hadn't made plans for disposition of the block, which wound up in his family trust. The problem, for TCI, was that whoever controlled the block could also exert a lot of control over TCI. An investment banker in New York tried to secretly buy the shares for Comcast and Microsoft. Brian never bothered to tell John (Malone) what he was up to. John and I found out anyway and put a stop to it. That Brian would even consider raiding TCI like that said a lot about how far he was willing to go. By then, Brian had been chasing MediaOne for more than two years.

Right then, however, Brian's career ambitions were the last thing on my mind. While Brian might have wanted MediaOne, I *needed* it. Without MediaOne, AT&T wouldn't have sufficient trade bait to win cable operators' support for its big phone-over-cable plans. The way I saw it, without unflagging support from the industry, AT&T was doomed. For Brian, MediaOne was a rocket-ship ride to the top of the cable industry. For us, MediaOne was the difference between success and utter failure. We had to get MediaOne—no ifs, ands, or buts.

Because AT&T was still in a quiet period, I couldn't just pick up the phone and call Brian to hash things out (translation: yell at him). But I also knew there was no way I was going to let Brian waltz off with the MediaOne prize without a big fight. The way I figured it, there were three ways for me to blow up Brian's deal. The first way was perhaps the easiest: AT&T could simply outbid him. That approach, however, was also the dumbest. AT&T was already stretching itself financially to get the TCI deal done. To voluntarily get into a bidding war on MediaOne would have been suicide.

The second way to topple Brian's deal was to pick it apart. Ross Perot used to describe dealing with General Motors as herding a lumbering elephant—to move things along, you get a sharp stick, then start poking around until you find the soft spots. Most deals have their vulnerable points. And Brian's deal, fortunately for me, had a big one: voting control. Under Comcast's proposal, Brian and his father, Ralph, would have 82 percent of the votes in the combined company, even though they'd own less than 2 percent of the equity. That translated into hard control for Brian and Ralph—and almost no influence for anybody else. The "anybody else," in this case, included some pretty big shareholders. I figured some of them might not be too happy about that.

Our third and final option to break up Brian's deal was to resort to the tried and true carrot-and-stick approach. To make this gambit work, I'd have to find a big stick. I'd also need a carrot to offer in exchange for good behavior. The stick? How about a big shareholder who's unhappy at being frozen out of voting control? And the carrot? That was a no-brainer: Lenfest. Comcast for years had been trying to buy Gerry's cable TV systems in the Philadelphia suburbs. I could use Lenfest's Philadelphia systems as bait to entice Brian to walk away from MediaOne. There was just one snag with that approach: Lenfest still wasn't mine to give away. I was still haggling with Gerry Lenfest about his buyout price, and we were nowhere close to a final agreement.

After mulling our options we decided on No. 3—the carrot-and-stick approach. Deciding on which shareholder to recruit for our proxy fight was also a no-brainer: Amos Hostetter, the founder and former chairman of Continental Cablevision, a big Boston-based cable operator. Amos, you might recall, sold Continental to MediaOne (then called U S West) in 1996 for $10.8 billion on the firm understanding that Continental would not be moved out of Boston. MediaOne's CEO, Chuck Lillis, agreed—then uprooted the company and moved it to Denver shortly after the merger closed. Amos was outraged. He made an impassioned plea to the U S West board in a last-gasp effort to derail Chuck's plan, to no avail. Amos's pleas fell on deaf ears, and he resigned shortly thereafter. The whole thing was a big embarrassment for MediaOne and for Chuck, in particular. Chuck, a longtime telecom executive, was still trying to ingratiate himself with the cable industry when the whole Amos blowup happened. A lot of cable executives despised Chuck after that. But nobody despised him more than Amos.

Right after his run-in with Chuck, Amos called me at TCI to talk through his situation. I was really upset for Amos, and distressed over Chuck's heavy-handedness. But I had some concerns of my own. Amos, on behalf of MediaOne, had just cut a deal with me to consolidate TCI's cable systems in the Chicago area with those of MediaOne. In return, TCI agreed to give MediaOne some TCI systems in Florida. Once Amos left, I was worried that MediaOne wouldn't honor our handshake agreement. Amos assured me that everything would be fine.

It wasn't fine. After Amos resigned from MediaOne, I didn't hear a peep from MediaOne. The days turned into weeks, and still no word. I was more than just a little perturbed. One day Bill Fitzgerald, TCI's M&A head, introduced me to Doug Holmes, a MediaOne executive who was in Denver for a meeting with us. Doug's business card said he was head of acquisitions for MediaOne in Boston, which, of course, was Amos's stomping grounds. I naturally assumed that Doug was one of Amos's guys and promptly tore into Chuck Lillis. Using every choice word I could think of, I blasted Chuck for his poor treatment of Amos and for trying to rework the terms of our handshake agreement. I was in a real mood that day, so I didn't hold back at all.

Instead of chiming in, as I had expected, Doug got red as a beet and stormed out of the room. As it turned out, Doug was not one of Amos's guys. He was *Chuck's* guy. Not only that, but Doug adored Chuck, and considered him a personal hero. I'd ripped into Chuck so fast that Bill didn't have time to explain that Doug, at Chuck's request, had temporarily relocated from Denver to Boston to help out on cable. Even worse, Doug was a devout Mormon who rarely cursed or even raised his voice. Oh boy. The next morning I called Doug to apologize. By the tone of Doug's voice, I knew I was toast. Our cable deal, as I'd feared, went nowhere.

Okay, so I didn't have such a great relationship with the MediaOne guys. But I had a *great* relationship with Amos. In addition to being a longtime friend and industry colleague, Amos was hugely influential in the cable TV industry generally and within MediaOne in particular. Even though he'd just gotten booted from MediaOne, Amos and his family still owned 9.3 percent of the company. (Amos converted most of his ownership stake in Continental into MediaOne stock.) That made Amos, at least for the moment, a truly powerful force in the world of MediaOne. Best of all for me, he despised Chuck Lillis, the MediaOne CEO, for reneging on his promise to not move Continental out of Boston.

I called up Amos right away and told him, in so many words, that I intended to blow up Chuck's deal with Brian, and that I needed his help.

Amos was game. As I'd expected, Amos was upset about the voting control issue. Under Comcast's proposal, he'd get left with low-voting shares and no voice in the combined company. Brian and Ralph, who would only own less than 2 percent of the combined company, would wind up with hard control. Amos was peeved that Brian and Ralph would even consider cutting him out of the power structure like that. Amos, perhaps energized by the prospect of turning the tables on Chuck, immediately hit the phone trying to drum up support from other big shareholders.

I was still working to get my carrot lined up: Lenfest Communications. Gerry Lenfest and I were still going round and round on price in our buyout talks. Gerry was pushing for a rich price for his 50 percent ownership stake, which, as I mentioned, carried veto control over the company. Gerry still didn't have a clue what I was up to on MediaOne. If I had any luck at all, he wouldn't find out until it was all over. My secretiveness, while regrettable, was necessary. I was convinced that Gerry would never sell to me if he knew I was going to flip Lenfest over to Comcast. The two companies were crosstown rivals in Philadelphia. They spent a lot of time trying to outdo each other on just *everything*. Take the annual Mummers Parade in Philadelphia. The New Year's Day event features marching bands and a bunch of guys dressed up like ultra-glamourous women. Comcast and Lenfest used to compete like crazy to sponsor it. You'd have thought they were going after Macy's Thanksgiving Day Parade.

Comcast and Lenfest didn't compete head-on, mind you, but they did have to share the same market. Comcast provided cable service in downtown Philadelphia; Lenfest served the sprawling outer suburbs. Comcast had only 300,000 area subscribers. Gerry had more than 1 million. Brian had tried to buy out Gerry over the years, but he would never budge. Gerry considered Philadelphia a major anchor. And he had a lot more customers, to boot. Gerry had tried at various times to convince Brian to set up a local cable partnership, but Brian was never interested. Part of it was pride. Philadelphia, after all, was Comcast's headquarters city. The face-off had been going on for years.

My talks with Gerry, as I said, had been going on for a while. That was a huge stroke of luck for me. If I had called up Gerry *after* the Comcast-MediaOne deal was announced, Gerry probably would have been suspicious. Though Gerry could be a pain in the neck, he was an old cable hand and could sniff out opportunity like a bloodhound. I crossed my fingers and hoped my luck would hold up. If things went my way, Gerry wouldn't find out what I was up to until it was too late for him to do anything about it. At the same time, I secretly pushed ahead with plans to also take out Brian.

On April 22, AT&T finally announced plans to buy MediaOne for $62.5 billion in cash, stock, and assumed debt. AT&T's offer represented a rich premium of 17 percent, or $8.6 billion, over the value of Comcast's all-stock offer, which had continued to lose steam thanks to gyrations in the marketplace. (By then, Comcast's original offer of $60 billion was worth only about $54 billion.) In our press release, we pointedly noted that AT&T's offer would leave MediaOne shareholders with full voting rights and a cash dividend. That was a straight shot to the jaws of Brian and Ralph Roberts of Comcast, who were only offering low-voting shares and no dividend. Amos Hostetter also got a measure of vindication. Upon completion of the merger, Amos would become nonexecutive chairman of cable in the combined company. (You didn't have to be a rocket scientist to figure it out: Amos was in; Chuck was out.) The deal also offered a small measure of vindication for me, personally. Once the deal closed, AT&T would finally get the Chicago cable systems that MediaOne had promised to TCI—and then reneged on—two years earlier. (As you might recall, that was the handshake deal that went south after Amos got forced out.)

That night, I called up Brian and laid my cards out on the table. I told him I knew he was probably disappointed at the turn of events, but made it clear that AT&T needed MediaOne. More important, for his purposes, AT&T was prepared to do whatever was necessary to get it. If you get into a bidding war with us, I warned him, we'll win. (Mike Armstrong, AT&T's chairman, relayed the same message to Brian's father, Ralph.) The threat was plausible. AT&T, after all, was a monster compared to Comcast. What Brian and Ralph didn't know, however, was that we were bluffing. AT&T was in no position to get into a bidding war with Comcast, or anybody else, for that matter. AT&T had just spent $55 billion to buy TCI. (Thanks to the run-up in AT&T's stock price, the AT&T-TCI deal, originally announced as a $48 billion transaction, was actually worth $55 billion on the day it closed.) It would be all we could do just to make good on our offer for MediaOne. We had no plans—or ability—to improve our bid. As far as Brian knew, however, I was dead serious. And that's all that mattered to me right then.

Brian was in a tough spot. He'd just announced to the world that he planned to buy MediaOne. Not only that, but Brian had positioned the deal as a transforming transaction that was vital to Comcast's future success. Now we were threatening to take it all away from him. I could tell that Brian was uneasy at the prospect of taking us on, which I read as a good sign. But I also knew I had to be careful. It would do AT&T no good to blow up Brian's deal in a manner that left him looking beaten or foolish. Nor did I want Comcast, a respected, well-run company, to be hurt by the turn of events I was trying to force through. Brian was fast on his way to becoming one of the industry's more thoughtful leaders. I respected Brian, and I respected his resolve to turn Comcast into a leading cable company. But all that said, I couldn't let him have MediaOne.

For days Brian and I traded threats and counter-threats. That was just part of the game. But the game, at least for AT&T, had a time limit. We had a phone strategy to execute, and the clock was ticking. So we made Brian an offer we thought he couldn't refuse. I told Brian we'd give him a couple of million cable customers once our MediaOne deal was done. We planned to parcel out systems to other cable operators, so why not Comcast? Though we didn't discuss the Lenfest systems specifically, I'm sure Brian got my message: If he played ball with us now, he'd get Lenfest later. Lenfest, of course, was Brian's Holy Grail. My gambit was a calculated risk. AT&T still didn't own Lenfest, so it technically wasn't ours to barter. But I figured that was a detail I could wrap up soon enough if I had to.

Brian pushed back with a couple of counter-offers, including one that called for AT&T to hand over the San Francisco, Chicago, and Philadelphia markets. Though I had to give him credit for trying, I turned his offers down flat. I suggested, instead, that Brian think hard about my earlier, albeit somewhat open-ended, offer. But don't take too long thinking about it, I warned him, because the clock is ticking.

I exuded confidence in talking about the MediaOne transaction publicly. But privately I had some concerns. Brian was working the phones like crazy trying to round up a partner to come back with a counter-offer. Unfortunately for us, he was having some luck. AOL was interested. So was Paul Allen, the software billionaire, and Microsoft. Greg Maffei, Microsoft's chief financial officer, had even flown to New York to talk through the possibilities with Brian. (In private, Mike used to jokingly refer to these various suitors as his "Barbarians at the Gate.") Just to make a point, presumably to AT&T, Brian and Greg went to a Knicks basketball game together at Madison Square Garden, where they were sure to attract attention. They did. Just the thought of Microsoft teaming up with Comcast gave me a big headache.

Microsoft was trouble. It had enormous cash reserves. Microsoft could easily write a check for several billion dollars and never miss it. If AT&T had to take on Microsoft in a bidding war, we'd lose. I had to convince Microsoft to bug out. Bill Gates, Microsoft's chairman, had been trying for years to push his Windows operating system onto the cable TV industry. The move made a lot of strategic sense for Microsoft. For all its software might, Microsoft's business triangle was terribly out of whack. It had loads of great technology and tons of branded products—but no real access to homes. (Read: distribution.) Hoping to hook a ride with cable operators, or at least gain a sympathy vote, Microsoft invested $1 billion in Comcast in 1997. Wall Street saw the investment as a huge validation of the promise of cable. Cable stocks, which had been treading near all-time lows, shot up almost overnight.

Cable operators were generally grateful to Microsoft for the investment. But they were also wary. The cable industry continued to keep Microsoft at arm's length. Microsoft kept writing checks, hoping. From Microsoft's perspective, it only made sense. TV sets were in 98 percent of U.S. households, while PCs were in just slightly more than half of all homes. If Microsoft could persuade cable companies to commit to deploying its technology in a really big way, the upside potential could be huge. The way I saw it, the cable industry's reluctance to commit to Microsoft was just the opening I needed.

Paul Allen was less of a threat. Paul was technically the "cofounder" of Microsoft, but he bailed out so early as to render him a footnote in the company's history. Bill Gates was the one who slogged it out, and he is rightly credited with turning Microsoft into the technology colossus that it is today. Even so, Paul was worth billions thanks to his Microsoft holdings. With that kind of wealth, Paul could make or break almost any deal he set his sights on. My gut instincts, however, told me Paul wasn't particularly interested in taking us on. He already had his hands plenty full. Paul was a big believer in the "Wired World"—his term for an advanced Information Age. Paul shelled out billions of dollars in the late 1990s to buy a string of cable systems, with an eye on turning his Wired World concept into reality. Paul was still nowhere close. To turn his cable systems into ones that could support high-speed Internet access, interactive video, and other digital services, he'd have to spend billions upon billions. For all these reasons, I didn't fear Paul. But given the short timetable I was on, I also didn't have a lot of time to mess around with him, either.

Because of my well-known fondness for Amos Hostetter—and my equally well-known dislike for Chuck Lillis, the MediaOne CEO—I didn't deal directly with the MediaOne negotiating team. Dan Somers, AT&T's chief financial officer, served as the liaison between our two companies, leaving me to deal with Brian and Amos. To his credit, Mike Armstrong, AT&T's CEO, gave me a very free hand to wheel and deal. He was also quite supportive, even when MediaOne started complaining that I had violated our "confidentiality" agreement by talking to other potential bidders. (Confidentiality agreements are aimed at keeping business discussions private.) MediaOne was hoping for an expensive bidding war to break out. When it became apparent that this wasn't going to happen, MediaOne started rattling the sabers. At one point, it even talked about suing. MediaOne didn't do that, of course. A lawsuit would have thrown a big wet blanket over the company's stock price, which was skyrocketing thanks to running speculation that a bidding war was about to break out.

Deal frenzy was in the air. Every day the newspapers were filled with stories speculating about new bidders coming into the fray—America Online, Time Warner, Disney, you name it. The whole drama even inspired a bumper sticker that soon appeared in Denver, MediaOne's headquarters city: "Honk if you want to buy MediaOne." By the end of April, everybody was on pins and needles. Nobody was feeling the pressure more than Brian Roberts of Comcast. He had to decide if he was going to stand his ground and risk a bidding war with AT&T, or relinquish his MediaOne prize and walk away. It was a Hobson's choice, and I didn't envy him. But I also had a job to do, and I intended to do it.

MediaOne formally accepted AT&T's offer about two weeks after it was submitted. That event triggered a countdown on the clock: Comcast had just four days to come back with a counter. If Comcast didn't counter, the MediaOne board would proceed with AT&T, and Comcast would be out in the cold for good. In anticipation of the final showdown, we—meaning

Brian and his associates, and me and my associates—all moved to AT&T's attorneys' office in midtown Manhattan to hash things out. That's when the fireworks began.

The adrenaline was off the charts. Brian and I, accompanied by our respective negotiating teams, were holed up in a conference room on one floor. Greg Maffei, Microsoft's chief financial officer, was in an office a few floors down. Bill Savoy, Paul Allen's longtime go-to deal guy, was standing by in a nearby office building. Paul was waiting by his phone in Seattle. Everybody's future, to a certain extent, hinged on Brian. I was about to burst. All Brian had to do was pick up the phone and I was dead meat. I had the Philadelphia trump card—Lenfest Communications. But it still wasn't mine to barter. Gerry and I still hadn't agreed on his buyout price. Fortunately, Gerry was still in the dark about my plans to flip Lenfest to Brian. The problem, for me, was that Gerry thought he had all the time in the world to hash out terms, and the slow pace of our progress reflected that. I knew better, of course. But I couldn't let on to Gerry that I was in a rush, otherwise I might blow my cover.

Time was running out. I could see by the look in Brian's eyes that he was edgy and probably a little flustered that we were trying to take MediaOne away from him. AT&T had everything to lose and nothing to gain by stringing this out. If I waited too long to make my move, I was afraid other companies might step forward to help out Brian. America Online and Disney were circling. This deal was already royally complicated, and getting more knotted up by the hour. Something had to give.

I excused myself from the negotiating table and put in an emergency call to Mike Armstrong and John Petrillo, AT&T's top strategic officer. I told them, in the strongest terms possible, that we needed to make our move immediately. I asked for their permission to offer Brian Lenfest Communications in exchange for walking away from MediaOne. Mike and John were understandably concerned. If I couldn't work out terms with Gerry, the whole thing could be a disaster. That won't happen, I pushed back. I promise I'll work things out with Gerry. But we have to pull the trigger on Brian—*now*. Reluctantly, Mike and John gave me their approval.

I hurried back into the conference room where Brian was waiting. After weeks of tough talk on both sides, the moment of truth arrived. I looked Brian dead in the eye and told him we'd sell him 2 million cable subscribers, including the Lenfest customers in Philadelphia, but only if he promised—right then and there—to stand down on MediaOne. About half of the 2 million I was offering would come from Lenfest; the balance would come from other markets that we'd work out later. If Brian took the deal, he'd wind up with a total of 8 million subscribers. That would immediately catapult Comcast to the No. 3 position in the cable industry behind AT&T and Time Warner. Brian would move into the cable big leagues, just as he'd always dreamed about. As part of the deal, I also wanted Comcast to agree to a big phone deal with AT&T along the same lines as Time Warner.

Brian pushed back. He'd take the cable deal, including Lenfest, but he'd only agree to a phone deal on one condition: AT&T had to get one other big unaffiliated cable operator besides Time Warner to agree to a phone deal. Once we had those two phone pacts in hand, Brian said Comcast would offer AT&T-branded phone service in all its markets on an expedited basis. Since we already had Time Warner in the bag, I readily agreed. Brian and I shook hands to seal the deal, giving me my first real sigh of relief in weeks.

Though Brian and I had been talking about prices and other details for a few days, he knew I couldn't give him a final purchase price on Lenfest because I was still working out terms with Gerry. In the end, Brian agreed to pay me whatever I agreed to pay Gerry. That price, in turn, would be applied to the other cable properties that we sold to Comcast. So if Gerry agreed to sell for, say, $4,000 a head, then that's what Comcast would have to pay for all the other cable systems we sold him. Brian, perhaps sensing that something was up, didn't ask about Gerry. I took that as a good sign and shifted my guns to my next two targets: Paul Allen and Microsoft.

Paul was relatively easy. Though he had made some threats about buying MediaOne outright and adding it to his growing cable empire, I didn't take him all that seriously. Paul, as I mentioned, had already dropped a bundle on cable and would have his hands full for years getting in shape for Wired World services. I also didn't think Paul had the stomach to cough up the $65 billion or so he would need to take MediaOne away from us. Even for a multibillionaire, $65 billion is a lot of money. But I also couldn't afford to be cavalier. Given his resources, Paul could, if he set his mind to it, upset my deal in a heartbeat. I also wanted to be respectful. Paul, after all, had spent serious money to buy his way into the cable industry.

Like most cable entrepreneurs, Paul had a "wish list" of markets he hoped to consolidate over time. I knew that St. Louis and Los Angeles were both important to Paul. Charter Communications, Paul's cable TV company, was headquartered in St. Louis, but only controlled half the market there. Paul also aspired to become a major presence in Los Angeles, one of the best media markets in the country. Fortunately for me, AT&T would have systems in both markets that I could use as bait. I quickly offered Paul our half of the St. Louis market and MediaOne's systems in Los Angeles in exchange for Paul's Fort Worth cable system. I also told him I wanted Charter to give us a phone deal in Los Angeles along the same lines as Time Warner. Paul agreed, and that was that.

I next moved on to Microsoft. Greg Maffei, Microsoft's chief financial officer, had the resources to blow me out of the water and we both knew it. Greg was starting to worry me. By then he knew that we had a handshake agreement with Comcast to stand down. But Greg wasn't backing down one whit. If anything, he was turning up the volume on his threats. Forget Brian, he told me, we'll just buy MediaOne for ourselves outright. I really didn't think he'd go that far. Microsoft, after all, was a technology development company. It had never expressed an interest in owning cable systems outright; it just wanted guaranteed access to cable TV lines to get its new broadband products into the hands of consumers. Still, I didn't want to test Greg's resolve, given that big war chest he was sitting on.

Greg had me over a barrel. To be honest, I would have been quite amenable to a lot of things right then just to get Microsoft off my back. Want a role in our long-term cable partnership with Time Warner and Comcast? Sure. Want guaranteed access to our cable TV lines for the next twenty years? We can definitely talk about it. But instead of getting creative and going for the gold, Greg defaulted to a familiar place: set-top boxes. In exchange for backing down on MediaOne, Greg told me he wanted a box deal. Specifically, he wanted AT&T to install Windows C/E, a Microsoft operating system that enables interactive entertainment and information services over the TV, on the first 10 million advanced set-top boxes we deployed.

I considered Greg's offer, then pushed back with a counter: AT&T

would do "five firm and five with an option," meaning AT&T would buy 5 million units up front, with an option to buy another 5 million units over time. But I told him the deal had to be on a "pay," not a "take," basis. That meant AT&T would promise to *pay* for the 10 million Windows C/E units, but we wouldn't be obliged to necessarily deploy them in the field. The point was a fine one, but key. If AT&T decided for whatever reason that Windows didn't jell with its long-term digital strategy, we wouldn't be obligated to actually use it. Greg pushed back again, arguing in favor of a "take" deal. If AT&T didn't actually deploy the C/E boxes, the deal could wind up being a washout for Microsoft. But I couldn't worry about Greg's strategic goals right then—I had my own to worry about.

Our deal was contingent on Microsoft making a big investment in AT&T. We wanted Microsoft to invest around $5 billion for a 2 to 3 percent stake in the company. Microsoft wouldn't get any control over AT&T or its deployment plans for C/E. But it would become a major strategic partner, putting it in a prime position to push AT&T to accelerate deployment of the boxes sooner rather than later. Greg also figured the deal might give Microsoft an inside track on broadband in general. I wasn't so sure about that, to be honest. But I was sure glad to get that $5 billion. The Media-One deal was going to leave AT&T more than just a little cash-strapped, so every billion we could get our hands on helped.

The deal, from a financial perspective, was practically pocket change for AT&T. C/E would only cost us about $14 per unit. That worked out to just $70 million for the first 5 million units, and $140 million for the full 10 million. I was ecstatic. For somewhere between $70 million and $140 million, I had just managed to take a legitimate threat to our $62 billion MediaOne deal off the table. I would have been plenty happy with just that, to be honest. To get $5 billion in cash on top of that was just the icing on the cake. I was puzzled that Greg hadn't played his hand a little more aggressively. But I certainly wasn't going to argue with the free card he was handing me, either. Greg, for his part, didn't seem to care about any of this. He was just happy to finally have a set-top deal with AT&T. So I guess you could say it was a win-win for both of us.

With Microsoft off the table, I had just one hurdle left, and it was a big one—Gerry Lenfest. I had the equivalent of a blank check (sort of) from Brian, who had agreed to pay me whatever I agreed to pay Gerry. But I couldn't just capitulate to Gerry's demands. After butting heads with

Gerry for months over his buyout price, if I suddenly got agreeable he might become suspicious. Also, Brian wouldn't pay the moon for Lenfest, so I had to make sure the final price was reasonable. But I had to figure out how to get the deal done fast—AT&T by then was set to announce the Comcast deal the next morning. Unfortunately, I still was nowhere close to a final agreement with Gerry. With time running out, I resorted to my only remaining option: I'd have to bluff the hell out of Gerry.

Racing the clock, I called up Gerry and told him I was sick and tired of dealing with him, and if he didn't agree to a deal with me that very night I would never do a deal with him—ever. I'd never buy, I'd never sell, I'd never leave the partnership. He'd be stuck with me forever. Gerry was taken aback at my tirade. I can't say I blamed him. I must have sounded like I was at the absolute end of my rope. And in truth, I was. At that very moment, AT&T's entire future, as well as a $62 billion deal, hinged on the next words out of Gerry's mouth. If he agreed to sell, AT&T's master plan could finally move forward. If he didn't, AT&T was looking at almost certain failure.

Gerry bought my act. After months of screaming at each other and butting heads, Gerry agreed that night to sell his 50 percent stake in Lenfest to AT&T for about $4,500 a subscriber, or about $5.6 billion. That was a lot more than what those systems were worth. But it was a lot less than what I would have been willing to pay to move forward on MediaOne. Gerry agreed to sign deal papers that night, as I had insisted. And then, just when I thought my nightmare was over . . . Gerry threw me a curveball. At the last minute, Gerry decided he wanted to discuss his decision with his children, who also owned a piece of Lenfest. Gerry instructed his lawyer to hold his final signature in escrow until his children—two sons and a daughter—had given their formal approval. The biggest deal of my life, not to mention AT&T, was now riding on the whims of Gerry's *children*. Great. My first reaction was to get on the phone and chew out Gerry. But I knew I had pushed Gerry about as far as I could without raising his suspicions. Having no alternative, I did the one thing that I hate more than anything in the world—I kept my mouth shut and did absolutely nothing.

I stayed up all night waiting by my phone and the fax machine. Dawn came, and still there was no word from Gerry. With no sign of the needed signatures from Gerry's children, we had to push back our Comcast announcement. I was starting to wonder if Gerry had finally caught on to what I was up to. If he backed out now, the Comcast deal was dead and so was I—I'd be right back to square one again. I was going crazy just thinking about it. Just when I thought the tension in the room was going to break the windows, our office fax machine clicked on—and the signatures started coming in. At around 10:00 A.M., the third and final signature page arrived. As soon as it was pulled off the fax and verified, we announced our deal with Brian to flip 2 million cable subscribers his way. Simultaneously, Comcast said it was abandoning its plans to buy Media-One. The deal of the century—the latest one, anyway—was done.

Gerry went through the roof. Though the Lenfest systems in Philadelphia weren't mentioned specifically by Comcast or AT&T, it didn't take Gerry long to figure out what had happened. Gerry was on the phone to me within minutes. He was absolutely livid that I hadn't told him of my plans to flip Lenfest over to Comcast. I heard him out. (Translation: I let him curse and yell at me.) After pulling the wool over his eyes for so long, I figured I owed Gerry that. I could certainly understand why he was so upset. But I didn't feel bad about it. Quite the contrary, I was hugely relieved. Thanks to the Lenfest transaction, AT&T could proceed decisively with its big phone plans and Comcast could walk away with its head held high. And Gerry? All his griping aside, Gerry was going to personally walk away with about $2.3 billion in AT&T stock.

The reaction of investors was overwhelmingly positive. The stock prices of all four companies—AT&T, MediaOne, Comcast, and Microsoft—rose a ton that day. That alone suggested we'd done the right thing. Even Gerry, whose net worth was tied up in AT&T stock, had to be happy about that. The fact that there happened to be a trailing transaction that Gerry didn't know about should have been a moot point. And I suspect it would have been a moot point if I'd sold to anybody other than Comcast.

With MediaOne in the bag, I immediately started lining up other cable operators for big phone deals. Our agreement with Time Warner would serve as the model for all the others. Before we could do that, however, we first needed to get a signed definitive agreement with Time Warner. That was the only way that other cable operators could be assured that our deal with Time Warner was real. Though we'd announced the Time Warner phone pact in February, we still didn't have a final agreement in hand. We did have a detailed letter of intent, which spelled out the broader terms.

But LOIs, as I've said before, aren't binding. We needed to have a final agreement in hand before we could proceed in earnest.

By then it was early May. I wasn't overly concerned about the definitive agreement. Jerry Levin, Time Warner's chairman and CEO, was firmly committed. He had publicly declared—over and over again—that the phone deal with AT&T was a huge win for both companies. So I had no doubt whatsoever about Jerry's commitment. Though it hadn't been announced, Jerry, with AT&T's blessing, had already tapped John Billock, a highly respected HBO executive, to serve as CEO of the phone venture. As soon as the definitive agreement was signed, the plan called for John to leave HBO and immediately start working on rolling out AT&T-branded phone service across the country. AT&T was making similarly aggressive plans on its end.

June started out normally enough. The national cable convention was held that month in Chicago. The annual show, hosted by the National Cable Television Association (NCTA), is considered a must-attend event for cable CEOs. It would be Mike Armstrong's first show. As the soon-to-be new owner of MediaOne, Mike was on his way to becoming a major force in the cable TV industry. Mike was scheduled to give the important keynote address. I was NCTA's chairman at the time, and would introduce him. A lot of cable executives at that point had never met Mike, and they were curious to hear what he had to say.

Jerry Levin and Dick Parsons, Time Warner's much-respected president (who later succeeded Jerry as CEO) also attended the show. Like everybody else, they were also interested in what Mike had to say. Because of Time Warner's impending twenty-year phone pact, Jerry and Dick had some fairly specific issues they wanted to discuss. We agreed to meet in Chicago, since we were all going to be there anyway.

At this meeting, Jerry got right to the point. Jerry wanted to talk about AT&T's intentions with respect to Time Warner Entertainment (TWE), a cable and entertainment partnership that was 25.5 percent owned by MediaOne. Time Warner owned most of the rest. TWE included most of Time Warner's cable TV systems—about 10 million subscribers—as well as HBO and Warner Bros., the big Hollywood movie studio. AT&T would inherit the MediaOne stake in TWE once the merger closed.

Jerry's interest was understandable, given TWE's long and tortured history. In the early 1990s, U S West, the former parent of MediaOne, had invested $2.5 billion in TWE in exchange for a 25.5 percent stake. Time Warner, which was strapped for cash, agreed to share control of the cable business equally with U S West. That meant Time Warner couldn't make any major decisions affecting cable without U S West's approval, and vice versa.

Veto power probably wouldn't have been such an issue if Time Warner and U S West had gotten along. But they didn't. It was a classic case of opposites . . . that don't attract. U S West was a regional Bell with a bureaucratic pedigree that dated back to the days of Alexander Graham Bell. Time Warner, by comparison, was a Hollywood power with a growing cable and entertainment business. Right out of the gate, things bogged down. Just when everybody thought things couldn't get any worse—they did. MediaOne, U S West's cable arm, got spun off as a separate company. MediaOne wound up with the TWE stake. MediaOne's CEO, Chuck Lillis, was a relative novice at cable. But that didn't stop Chuck from blocking Jerry on everything from proposed cable transactions to executive appointments. Jerry, trying to get out from under Chuck's thumb, desperately tried to restructure TWE. But the two sides—surprise, surprise—could never agree on terms. For Jerry, it was a special kind of hell to be chained to Chuck like that.

Jerry wanted to know what we intended to do about MediaOne's veto rights. The TWE partnership agreement didn't permit either partner—Time Warner or MediaOne—to acquire cable systems outside TWE. AT&T would have to surrender those rights in order to get regulatory approval for the MediaOne merger. So it wasn't a question of if we'd surrender veto rights, but when. Mike and I were both grateful to Jerry and Dick for signing a big phone pact with AT&T so early. As a good-faith gesture, and because we wanted to move the MediaOne deal along quickly with regulators, Mike said he would ask MediaOne to terminate its veto rights as soon as possible. That, of course, was exactly what Jerry and Dick wanted to hear.

Jerry also had some concerns about America Online. AOL at the time was spending a lot of time and money trying to force through regulatory changes that Jerry considered counter-productive for the cable industry. AOL wanted regulators to force cable operators to lease out their high-speed cable lines to AOL for free, or for greatly reduced prices. AOL argued that this type of "open access" was critical to its long-term viability.

Time Warner and other cable operators considered this approach nothing more than "forced access," and were vigorously resisting. AOL's public market capitalization was nearly twice that of Time Warner at the time. Jerry said he didn't think it was out of the question that AOL might try to stage a hostile takeover of Time Warner, using its soaring stock price as deal currency. Rumors to that effect had been swirling around.

Given the fact that we were about be joined at the hip on phone-over-cable services for the next twenty years, Jerry thought it was important for AT&T and Time Warner to be vigilant about AOL. He also thought it was important for us to keep each other posted about our respective dealings with AOL. Mike and I agreed. In addition to the pending phone deal, AT&T and Time Warner were the de facto leaders of the U.S. cable industry. So it only made sense to forge a united front. After talking it over, we agreed to never negotiate with AOL without the other company's prior knowledge and consent. I deliberately repeated our pledge to each other out loud as we shook hands just to make sure there would be no misunderstandings later.

Progress on the other phone deals proceeded swiftly. With MediaOne's cable systems as trade bait, and Time Warner and Comcast on the line for phone deals, other cable operators were quick to pledge their support. Even smaller operators wanted a piece of the action. By July, I had a dozen deals, all of them tied to cable "swaps" and phone deals, firmly in place. (In swaps, no money—just cable systems—changed hands.) In a presentation to the AT&T board that month, I laid out our master plan. I had cable-phone deals lined up with Cox Communications, Charter Communications, Adelphia, Cablevision, and, of course, Comcast and Time Warner. I also had a few deals with some smaller operators, including Falcon, Bresnan, and Chambers. Once all the deals were executed, AT&T would have access to more than 80 percent of U.S. phone customers. That was more than enough to make a run at the Bells' $100 billion local phone market. After years of talking about it, AT&T's local phone dreams, by all indications, were about to turn real.

Though things were shaping up on paper, I was getting a little worried. The Time Warner phone deal had been announced six months earlier, and we were still nowhere close to signing a definitive agreement. Talks with Time Warner, in fact, had practically ground to a halt. That was potentially a huge problem. All the phone deals, including my deal with Comcast, hinged on our ability to deliver Time Warner as a committed phone partner. If Time Warner backed out, all the other phone deals would collapse.

The holdup wasn't Time Warner. It was AT&T. By then, AT&T was quietly trying to convince Time Warner to redo the financial terms of the phone agreement. In the months since it had announced the phone deal, AT&T had concluded that it had underestimated the cost of rolling out phone service over Time Warner's cable systems by several *billion* dollars, hence its need to redo the terms. Jerry and Dick, of course, said no dice. A deal's a deal. AT&T also wasn't so happy with the technical terms. AT&T's original phone deal, you may recall, called for it to roll out traditional "circuit-switched" phone service over Time Warner's systems. By the summer, AT&T was trying to come up with a far more expansive definition for phone, one that could carry it into the next decade and beyond. That's when things *really* bogged down.

AT&T was pushing Time Warner to agree to dense technical standards and descriptions that God couldn't understand. I'd already gotten a taste of the problem firsthand. On a number of occasions I had sent out documents to AT&T's technology department that spelled out aspects of our phone deal. These documents were usually no more than a few pages in length. By the time I got them back, however, they'd be forty to sixty pages long and include all sorts of appendices, attachments, and footnotes. I'd read the thing and have no earthly clue what AT&T was talking about. You'd have sworn everybody at AT&T was on serious drugs.

The problem, in a nutshell, was "phone service," or rather how to define it. AT&T's technical people, as I would soon learn, were trying to precisely define "phone" and "phone service." In order to do that, AT&T had to try to figure out the evolution of phone service twenty years hence, and in the process they were getting bogged down in mud up to their headlights. One big area of concern was videoconferencing. The technology, which has been kicking around in one form or another for years, had never really caught on in the residential market. But that didn't stop AT&T from trying to figure out—and then technically define and describe—how an advanced form of videoconferencing might be used to make phone calls. There were about a thousand other blue-sky issues like that.

Trying to define "phone service" twenty years from now is like arguing about how many angels can dance on the head of pin. It can't be done.

It reminded me of the Pentagon and the crescent wrench. Remember that? The Pentagon some years ago wanted to make a bulk purchase of crescent wrenches. But instead of just saying that outright, they sent out a lengthy RFP (request for proposals) in which they described, in excruciating detail, the precise specifications and functionality of this particular device. Vendors drove themselves crazy trying to figure out what the Pentagon wanted.

By September, I was really worried. AT&T was still haggling with Time Warner over the meaning of "phone service," and neither side showed any signs of relenting. The warm good feelings that had been so evident in February when the phone deal was first announced had all but dissipated. Mistrust, fueled by armies of lawyers on both sides, had taken over. Publicly, the two companies continued to say that talks were proceeding well, but the handwriting on the wall suggested otherwise. The one point of leverage we did have with Time Warner—the TWE management rights—was gone. MediaOne, at our request, had signed those rights away the previous month, turning MediaOne into a passive investor.

Other cable operators were still on board with phone deals, but they were starting to become suspicious. None of the operators was willing to sign a phone deal until we had a definitive agreement locked down with Time Warner. I continued to assure cable operators that our phone deal with Time Warner was on track. But I was starting to sound hollow. I tried to not let on that I was concerned. Privately, however, I was sweating bullets. The success of AT&T's phone strategy was wholly dependent on the Time Warner phone deal. Though I didn't want to admit it, even to myself, AT&T's phone strategy was starting to look like a carefully constructed house of cards.

The first card fell away later that month.

Mike Armstrong, the AT&T CEO, was growing incredibly frustrated over the lack of progress with Time Warner. Wall Street and the press were starting to ask questions. The landmark deal that had been hailed in February was starting to look like a sham. It was also turning into a pressure point for Mike, who was being asked about it constantly. Mike thought we should try to sign final phone agreements with the other cable operators, with the understanding that their deal terms would be adjusted later to comport with the Time Warner terms. I wasn't that hopeful, given the growing concerns in the cable industry. But I told Mike I'd do the best I could.

I'd already agreed on the framework of a phone agreement with Cablevision, the big Long Island–based cable operator, so I thought I'd start there first. The base term of Cablevision's agreement—five years—wasn't nearly as long as I had hoped. Time Warner's deal, after all, would let AT&T have access to Time Warner's cable systems for twenty years. But it nonetheless would give AT&T the opportunity to establish a phone partnership with Cablevision and work up from there. AT&T at the time owned one-third of Cablevision but had no voting control over company matters. Still, as a big partner I thought Cablevision might be amendable to Mike's plan. I asked Chuck Dolan, Cablevision's founder and chairman, if he'd consider signing early so we could move things along. I told him AT&T, and Mike in particular, would consider it a huge favor. Chuck said okay, with one caveat. He didn't like AT&T's rather dense technical definition of "phone." Like Time Warner, he thought of "phone service" in the more conventional sense and wasn't really open to trying to define its evolution twenty years down the road. The good news, however, was that Chuck was agreeable to executing his phone deal immediately.

I relayed my conversation with Chuck to Mike the next day. I was pleased at Chuck's response and was expecting some favorable feedback. I was wrong. Mike wasn't pleased at all. In fact, he was perturbed. "Tell Chuck Dolan to do it our way or we'll overbuild him with fixed wireless," Mike instructed. I was dumbfounded. Fixed wireless was an unproven wireless technology for the home that most people considered lame beyond belief. Not only that, if AT&T tried "overbuilding" Chuck—competing with Cablevision head-on inside its franchise area—Cablevision would never do business with AT&T. Chuck was a tough-as-nails cable pioneer who didn't take kindly to anybody, even the chairman of AT&T, issuing threats in his direction. Chuck also happened to control the prime markets in New York surrounding Manhattan. It could be a great platform for showcasing AT&T-branded local phone service. There was no way I was going to deliver that message to Chuck, and I told Mike as much. "You don't *tell* Chuck Dolan to do anything," I informed Mike. "You *ask* him, and you ask him really politely." If Mike wanted his message delivered to Chuck, he'd have to do it himself, I told him.

I was so shaken by the exchange that after I left Mike's office I headed directly back to mine to write down, word for word, his directive to "tell Chuck Dolan . . ." AT&T had committed more than $100 billion to buy cable with the dream of turning its larger phone aspirations into a business reality. AT&T needed unflagging cooperation from the U.S. cable industry to be successful. By jamming cable operators like Time Warner and Cablevision, AT&T's whole phone strategy was in serious risk of failure. Didn't he understand that?

I got my answer in September. I was at a speaking engagement at Trinity College in Hartford, Connecticut, late that month. A reporter in the crowd lobbed me a question: Is AT&T in talks with AOL? At the time, rumors were swirling that AT&T was in discussions to sell @Home's Excite portal to AOL. Even though I normally wouldn't answer such a question, I felt it was important to dispel that notion given the handshake promise that Mike and I had extended to Jerry Levin and Dick Parsons earlier in the year. (Remember: In Chicago Mike and I pledged to keep Time Warner informed about any dealings with AOL.) Since I was CEO of AT&T's cable unit and knew nothing about such talks, I issued a flat denial. I was unequivocal in my response because I was sure that Mike would never break such an important promise. And he certainly wouldn't do it without consulting with me first.

I was dead wrong. I got a call very early the next morning from a harried AT&T attorney informing me that Mike had, in fact, been holding secret talks with AOL. The lawyer was understandably upset. Under securities laws, officials of publicly traded companies can't knowingly mislead the public about a company's plans or activities. (After all, investors make decisions based on such comments.) Those who do can get into hot water real fast with the Securities and Exchange Commission. The attorney informed me rather heatedly that as a result of my public denial, "we" now had a big problem. No, I corrected him, *you* have a big problem. I was livid that Mike would dare withhold such important information from me, especially given our pledge to Jerry Levin and Dick Parsons in Chicago. AT&T later put out a short, cryptic statement suggesting that AT&T had, indeed, been talking to AOL.

By then, Mike and I had been butting heads for a while on a variety of management and business issues. And I was tired of all the crosscurrents. Before the dustup on AOL, AT&T had suggested that I had committed to buy up to $1 billion in set-top boxes from General Instrument (later acquired by Motorola) without getting proper authorization. That was despite the fact that I had sent a half-dozen or so memos to Mike and other top AT&T executives that said otherwise. AOL was the last straw. When I saw Mike the following Monday in his office, we had it out. I told Mike that his decision to hold secret talks with AOL had put me in an untenable position with Time Warner and placed AT&T's entire phone strategy at risk. By breaking his word to Time Warner, he had broken the bond of trust between our two companies, maybe irrevocably. Mike didn't have a lot to say. He just couldn't believe that Time Warner would dare turn its back on AT&T. To Mike's way of thinking, Time Warner and the other cable operators needed AT&T as much as AT&T needed them. He was living in fantasyland, of course, and I told him as much.

When we were done yelling at each other and the room was finally quiet, Mike collected himself and said something along the lines of "We probably shouldn't work together anymore." I told him that was fine by me. Mike said he didn't want me to leave AT&T right away, though. He asked me to stick around long enough to get the Time Warner phone deal done. I promised to try, even though I knew there wasn't a snowball's chance in hell that Time Warner was going to come through.

I hoped—I prayed—that I could hold on to Time Warner. I called up Dick Parsons, Time Warner's president, right away and told him I'd been fired. Trying to sound chipper, I assured him that I'd stick around long enough to get our big phone deal done. Dick was as nice as he could be, but he also made himself crystal clear. He told me that I could come over and see him and Jerry any time—"We love you," he told me. But he said I should also know that Time Warner *probably wasn't going to do the phone deal after all.* Dick didn't offer a specific reason for Time Warner's pullout. But then again, he didn't have to. AT&T had blown it in every way possible. Not only had Mike backpedaled on the terms, he'd just reneged on a handshake promise on AOL. I knew the deal was dead as soon as the AT&T attorney told me Mike had been talking to AOL on the sly. By the time Dick and I hung up, the knot in the pit of my stomach felt like a cannonball.

My impending departure from AT&T was announced two days later, on October 6. In one of my last official acts as CEO of AT&T Broadband, I wrote a memo and expressed my concerns about the future of AT&T's

phone strategy. In the memo, dated October 12, I also told Mike that AT&T's big phone plan was doomed if we didn't wrap up an agreement with Time Warner by December 31, at the very latest. I also reminded Mike that AT&T's $100 billion bet on cable had never been about buying cable per se. It was about getting the support of the U.S. cable industry so that AT&T could gain access to the 50 million or so homes that were controlled by Time Warner, Comcast, and other big cable TV operators. As for fixed wireless, I pointed out that the technology "is not an alternative in the truest sense of the word—rather, it is simply the best response to a failed preferred course of action." It was a not-so-subtle reference to Mike's empty threat to use fixed wireless to overbuild Cablevision and other cable operators that didn't cooperate on phone-over-cable services. I sent copies of my memo to John Malone, who was by then an AT&T board member, and to Amos Hostetter, who would join the AT&T board once the Media-One deal closed.

Even as I wrote the memo, I already knew the outcome. The pullout of Time Warner was a fatal blow to the heart of AT&T's big phone strategy. Time Warner was key to everything. Without Time Warner, there would be no Comcast, which meant there would be no Cox, Cablevision, or Adelphia, or almost anybody else, for that matter. Cable operators had agreed to commit to long-term phone deals on the understanding that Time Warner was on board. To prove Time Warner's commitment, AT&T had to secure a signed definitive agreement. But Time Warner would never sign such an agreement. That meant nobody else would, either. Time Warner was gone, and we had no way to bring them back to the table. After months of battling the odds, AT&T was flat out of bargaining chits, flat out of leverage—and flat out of luck. For all practical purposes, AT&T's $100 billion phone-over-cable strategy was officially dead.

LOOKING BACK

So what did MediaOne teach me? Humility, for one thing. It was an exhilarating feeling, both personally and professionally, to have all those phone deals in hand and ready to go. We worked like maniacs to achieve something that almost everybody said was impossible—we convinced virtually the entire U.S. cable television industry to rally around AT&T's big phone strategy. Then to have to stand by and watch it blow up over cold feet and a throwaway meeting with AOL—a meeting that went exactly nowhere, I might add—was one of the most frustrating experiences of my life. In the process we also broke the hearts and trust of the AT&T shareholders and employees who had believed in us so faithfully. That is something I will always regret.

We'll never know for sure if things would have worked out as planned. But it's a tantalizing "what if" to think about. Instead of struggling for its very survival, AT&T today might be offering AT&T-branded local phone service to 80 percent of America. The Bells, instead of handily dominating the local phone business, might be fighting to hold on to customers. Customers might be enjoying better service, better value, and, for once in their lives, a real choice of local phone carriers. Too bad for consumers, and too bad for AT&T.

THE WEAKEST LINK

In snatching MediaOne away from Comcast, we didn't just have to refuel a Boeing 747 in midair—we had to fix the engine, change the oil, and rotate the tires. The sheer complexity of trying to deal with Comcast while simultaneously fending off Microsoft and Paul Allen and secretly negotiating with Gerry Lenfest was challenging, to say the least. It was also a testament to the strength of our teamwork and a stellar example of Rule 4: You're only as good as the men and women around you. Our teamwork on this deal was, in a word, superb. Working against impossible odds and crushing deadlines, we accomplished virtually everything we set out to do.

But at the end of the day, it didn't matter. A negotiating team is only as good as its weakest link. As I've said before, the best deal team in the world can't save you from the unintended consequences of freelance decisions. While those decisions may be quite well intended—and I have no doubt that Mike had the best interests of AT&T in mind—they can lead to outcomes you don't want and never envisioned. (For more on the vagaries of unintended consequences, see Chapter 8.) My message here is clear but simple: Row in the same direction as your teammates, and you'll be a lot less likely to capsize later.

DETAILS, DETAILS

Details can kill you, particularly if you let them overrun a deal like so much kudzu. AT&T's experience in trying to negotiate the Time Warner phone pact is an example of how taking your eye off the ball can just slay you at the negotiating table.

In trying to define "phone" and "phone service," AT&T allowed itself to get bogged down in details that, quite frankly, didn't make that much difference, and probably wouldn't for years. I give AT&T credit for trying to anticipate the evolution of communications technology. As a communications leader, AT&T is obliged to look ahead so that it can better anticipate the needs of customers. But for crying out loud, why did they have to use the Time Warner phone deal—a deal that was vital to the long-term success of the larger phone strategy—to score points on that? Engineers can concoct a world where you and I make phone calls off our television sets. But are we ever going to do that? Probably not. Do we want to do that now, or even it the foreseeable future? No. It was a classic violation of Rule 8: Don't keep score on things that don't matter.

For lack of a precise definition of "phone," AT&T, ironically, lost the best phone opportunity it ever had—or ever will have. As this is being written, David Dorman, Mike Armstrong's successor, is racing to salvage AT&T. Dave is smartly doing everything he can to restore the luster to AT&T's vaunted brand name, while trying to slow down the dramatic erosion in AT&T's core long-distance business. The recent belly flops of WorldCom and Qwest should help. (At least they won't hurt.) In any event, I wish Dave and the employees of AT&T the best as they try to resuscitate the company, which has been a part of America's landscape—and heartbeat—for more than a century.

WALK TALL

Thanks in large part to the courage and cool head of Brian Roberts, Comcast's able young president, we were all able to walk away from the negotiating table as huge winners. Brian showed an enormous amount of grace and leadership in deciding to walk away from MediaOne. It wasn't an easy call. Brian's deal with MediaOne created a lot of buzz for his company. He was also emotionally committed to it. By the time AT&T busted in on his party, Brian was already working hard to sell the deal to Wall Street and to his own employees. In his heart, and in his head, Brian was going to do that deal. Brian's dad, Ralph, of course, was backing him up every step of the way.

Once AT&T showed up, all bets were off. The knee-jerk reaction would have been to reload for bear and come back with a counter-bid. But Brian, to his credit, didn't do that. Even though he really coveted the MediaOne prize, he carefully considered his options and possible outcomes. A bidding war is never an attractive option—everybody tends to wind up bloody. Taking on a big partner such as Microsoft can have other unintended consequences. In the end, Brian did the right thing—he took the deal that would most benefit Comcast as well as the cable industry. In doing so, he exemplified Rule 5: Learn how to walk away. As I've said before, walking away from a deal that you really want can be incredibly tough. By standing down on MediaOne, Brian demonstrated that he was willing to be a partner with AT&T, and with the cable industry at large.

As we all know today, Brian's gamble to walk tall served him well. In 2001, Brian made an unsolicited bid for AT&T Broadband, the cable and Internet arm of AT&T. He eventually prevailed, putting him in charge of the TCI and—yes—all those MediaOne cable TV assets that we took away from him in 1999. When his deal closes, Brian and Ralph will be the undisputed leaders of the U.S. cable industry.

GERRY LENFEST

Gerry Lenfest to this day still complains about the fact that I bought his 50 percent stake in Lenfest Communications without letting him know that I planned to flip it to Comcast. Let's set aside, for a moment, the fact that the deal turned Gerry into a billionaire. (In exchange for his stake, Gerry got 43 million shares of AT&T stock, which at the time was worth about $2.3 billion.) Let's also set aside the fact that Lenfest's cable systems weren't even close to being worth that much. The only reason I was willing to pay $4,500 a subscriber was that *Brian* was willing to pay that much.

Let's instead go straight to Rule 7: Read the fine print. In this case there was no mention of, and certainly no prohibition of, trailing transactions in my agreement with Gerry. Once he sold the systems to me, I was free to sell them to anybody I darn well pleased. Gerry said his big fear in selling to Comcast was that his senior managers might lose their jobs. If Gerry had been that concerned, he could have shared a bigger part of his $2.3 billion payday with them. Gerry set aside just $60 million for his senior managers and other employees, some of whom had been with him for more than twenty years. I personally thought they deserved and earned a bigger cut. But that obviously wasn't my call. Even so, I will always be grateful to Gerry for selling Lenfest Communications to me when he did.

AMOS HOSTETTER

If you ever doubted the importance of not making enemies, look no further than Amos Hostetter.

Like a lot of successful entrepreneurs, Amos is incredibly intelligent, hard-driving, and relentless when it comes to getting what he wants. These are the exact attributes you *don't* want in an enemy. As I've pointed out before (Rule 6: Have adversaries if you must, but don't have enemies), enemies are prone to act in unpredictable ways, particularly ones like Amos with a sharp axe to grind and the means to do it.

In strong-arming Amos, Chuck Lillis of MediaOne succeeded in one small way: He was able to get Continental out of Boston and consolidate it with MediaOne's other operations in Denver. But Chuck's heavy-handedness also got him something he hadn't bargained for—an avowed enemy. Amos despised Chuck for breaking his promise, and he had it in for Chuck from that day forward. So did a lot of other cable guys. That wasn't because Chuck moved Continental to Boston, mind you. If a company spends billions of dollars to buy an asset, as Chuck's company did, the buyer can darn well move it anywhere he wants. The cable industry turned against Chuck because he was disrespectful. Amos had thirty years of his life wrapped up in Boston and in Continental, and Chuck basically told him to take a hike if he didn't like it. That was the part that offended so many people.

One final footnote on the Chuck-Amos blowup. It was unfathomable to most of us in the cable industry that Chuck would even think about reneging on his handshake promise to Amos. But let's be honest: Amos was the one who really dropped the ball. He also classically violated Rule 7: Read the fine print. Amos, unfortunately, never bothered to put his

Boston requirement in writing when he sold Continental to MediaOne. So Chuck was free to move it anywhere he pleased, whenever he pleased. So do yourself a favor and learn to yell before, not after, you sign on the dotted line, and you'll save yourself a lot of upset later.

COMCAST'S DEAL STRATEGY

Fast-moving deals like MediaOne don't give you a lot of time to navel gaze once they get going. The trick is to anticipate the possible responses of competitors so that you have a fast comeback if you need it. All of which leads me back to Rule 3: Do deals as fast as possible . . . but no faster.

As a basic point of planning on the MediaOne deal, Brian should have checked in with Amos. Sheer decorum would have told you that. Brian didn't have to give him chapter and verse. But he could have reached out in a courteous way. If he'd done that, I suspect Brian would have won some serious brownie points with Amos. In the process, he probably would have gotten an earful about Amos's concern over the voting-control issue, allowing him to plan accordingly. Even more important, he would have deprived me of a critical deal ally.

Brian also should have reached out to me. By then rumors were rampant that AT&T was seriously interested in making a bid for MediaOne. Securities laws don't permit companies to talk too freely about their plans. But if Brian had called me up to hash things out, I would have found some way to get the message across that, yes, AT&T is serious. Brian would have been free to proceed with his plans, of course. But at least he would have known right away that he was going to have a fight on his hands and planned accordingly. In retrospect, I could appreciate that Brian was trying to work out a friendly deal with Chuck Lillis of MediaOne. If he'd clued in Amos, who despised Chuck, or me, who also despised Chuck, that could have added extra layers of complication to his life that he probably didn't want or need right then. But then again, that is the nature of successful dealmaking. The challenge—always—is to take complicated situations and turn them in your favor.

6

RUPERT MURDOCH—
SATELLITE STAR

NEWS CORP. chairman Rupert Murdoch is a media genius. That is the reason—the *real* reason—he scares the bejesus out of his competitors.

Rupert's sense of the audience is nothing short of remarkable. He has laserlike ability to zero in on what consumers want and turn it into must-see television—or must-have reading or must-have *something*. He also understands, maybe better than anybody on the planet, the connection between distribution and content, and he knows how to use it to his advantage. For all these reasons, cable operators practically tremble at the thought of Rupert entering the satellite TV business here in the United States. Rupert is just that good, and everybody knows it.

In comparison to other media giants, such as AOL Time Warner and Viacom, News Corp. is still fairly small. News Corp. recorded 2001 revenues of about $14 billion, less than half of AOL's $38 billion and a third less than Viacom's $23 billion. Still, the company is a formidable programming power, and becoming more so all the time. News Corp. is the quintessential business triangle, an almost perfect amalgam of content, technology, and distribution. News Corp.'s assets today include broadcast TV, cable television programming, satellite TV, a Hollywood movie studio, a string of newspapers, a big book publisher, and lots and lots of sports. Fox Sports Net, a twenty-four-hour cable sports network, is Rupert's answer to ESPN. The channel, which is sold on a regional basis across the country, has more than 70 million subscribers. Rupert even has his own baseball team—the Los Angeles Dodgers. Put it all together and what you wind up with is a highly capable news and entertainment machine that strikes terror in the hearts of competitors—and on three continents, no less.

One of Rupert's biggest claims to fame is satellite TV. Sky Global Networks, known simply as "Sky," is a worldwide network of satellite TV operations that beam programming directly to consumers via pizza-sized receivers. Sky is an all-digital service. So it delivers crystal-clear pictures, CD-quality sound, and, depending on the market, up to hundreds of channels, including dozens of movie, digital music, and pay-per-view selections. As of 2002, more than 85 million homes around the world had access to Sky channels in the United Kingdom, Japan, Asia, and Latin America. Sky's biggest operation is in the United Kingdom, where service is sold under the name British Sky Broadcasting, or "BSkyB" for short. BSkyB, which is considered the model for satellite TV, has attracted a loyal following thanks to its innovative programming, impressive channel lineup—more than 240 channels in all—and creative use of technology. One popular service, called Sky Sports Active, permits viewers to select which camera angle they see and call up replays on whim. Playercam, another innovative service, lets viewers follow the movements of a particular player around the field or court. Another service, Sky News Active, lets viewers control how and when they view the news twenty-four hours a day. As of 2002, BSkyB had more than 10 million viewers, and was continuing to add subscribers at a steady clip.

Rupert for years has longed to extend his Sky family into the U.S. satellite TV market. After years of eying the market, Rupert in 2000 made a serious bid to buy DirecTV, the No. 1 satellite TV operator in America. DirecTV, controlled by General Motors, had more than 10 million customers. Needless to say, U.S. cable operators weren't too happy about the prospect of having to do head-to-head combat with Rupert. Though DirecTV had done pretty well on its own, it had never seriously challenged the U.S. cable industry. In the hands of a programming master like Rupert, however, some cable operators fretted, DirecTV might double or even triple its subscriber base. Cable operators didn't say much publicly about Rupert's campaign to buy DirecTV. But there was an awful lot of hand-wringing behind the scenes.

Then the unexpected happened: EchoStar, America's No. 2 satellite

TV provider, came in at the last minute with a competing bid for DirecTV. Rupert, who was within reach of DirecTV, was devastated. Cable operators were ecstatic. Charlie Ergen, EchoStar,'s CEO, had almost no sense of programming, or so little that it's a waste of time to even talk about it. Cable operators, for that reason, had never really considered EchoStar a major threat. EchoStar had about 7 million customers. Many of those customers were located in rural markets that cable operators didn't care about. Charlie eventually beat out Rupert to get DirecTV (at least on the first pass, but read on). And cable operators couldn't have been happier.

The cable industry's big sigh of relief was quite understandable. Rupert's ability to dream up clever programming and killer distribution plays—over and over again—drives competitors up the wall. Look at Fox Broadcasting. Nobody in the United States had ever started a national television network from scratch. The Big Three networks—ABC, NBC, and CBS—were created in the 1940s in a spotty fashion and evolved from there. (ABC was actually formed out of NBC's "red" and "blue" networks; Edward Noble, founder of Life Savers candy, and ABC started broadcasting under that name in 1943.) When Rupert boldly announced plans in 1986 to build a new network from scratch, everybody laughed and said it couldn't be done—because, in fact, it had never been done before. Rupert, being Rupert, put his head down and got to work. At one point it looked as if the whole project might collapse over foreign ownership rules, which prohibit non-Americans from owning U.S. broadcasting properties. To get around the problem, Rupert, a proud Australian, became a U.S. citizen. Extreme? Of course. Unpredictable? Always. Successful? You bet. Fox went on to become America's fourth network, just as Rupert predicted, providing News Corp. with a formidable distribution outlet for its ever-expanding libraries of top-notch programming.

Rupert is always confounding critics. When Rupert agreed to pay $1.6 billion to take away CBS's NFL football broadcasting rights back in 1993, he was practically a laughingstock. Conventional wisdom at the time held that Rupert was paying way too much for a franchise that was rapidly declining in value. Younger viewers, the Holy Grail of Madison Avenue, were increasingly tuning in to ESPN and extreme sports, not traditional football. A lot of people predicted Fox couldn't possibly live up to the broadcasting standards set by CBS, which had been televising NFL games for years. Rupert, as usual, soldiered on. In the hands of Fox, football got

a much-needed facelift—and viewers tuned in by the millions. Fox's ratings and ad revenues shot up. Adding insult to injury for CBS, a bunch of
TV stations, many of them CBS affiliates, defected to Fox.

Rupert, first and foremost, is a programmer. Over in the United Kingdom, Rupert isn't in the BSkyB business—he's in the U.K. *programming*
business. The distribution vehicle just happens to be satellite TV. In Rupert's world, distribution, preferably fortified by lots of advanced technology, is a mere commodity, a means to get his content into the hands (or
living rooms) of consumers. Rupert is basically agnostic about which platform he uses—broadcast, satellite TV, cable, the Internet, you name it. He
uses them all, and in as many combinations as possible. Look at Sky Active, a BSkyB service that lets viewers send e-mail through their televi-
sions. (You can also place bets on sporting events and send messages to
cell phones.) That's a good example of Rupert using the interactive technology inherent in satellite TV to enhance his programming.

Rupert's not selling interactivity, per se, mind you. My guess is that a
lot of his customers don't even think about the technological implications
of Sky Active, which is actually a fairly sophisticated service. Same goes
for Playercam, which allows viewers to track the movements of a particular player. Yet both services are targeted, quite deliberately, to a mass audience. That's pure Rupert, who's always believed that media are about
finding ways to appeal to the largest common denominator—not the least
common denominator. In a nutshell, that's what makes Rupert so successful as a competitor in the marketplace.

A lot of cable operators try to cover up their fear of Rupert by paint-
ing him as an unfair competitor. The biggest gripe you hear is that Rupert
blocks other programmers from getting carriage on his satellite TV systems around he world. That's simply not true. Rupert, as a matter of principle, is *always* on the lookout for more and better content. All you have
to do is look at his channel lineups around the world to see that. The argument that Rupert discriminates also ignores the basic physics of satellite TV systems. Unlike conventional cable TV systems, satellite TV can
accommodate hundreds of channels. So by definition they tend to be far
more democratic.

Despite all the vitriol you hear, Rupert has actually been quite a good
friend to the U.S. cable industry. Though most cable executives don't like
to acknowledge it, much less talk about it, back in 1997 Rupert almost sin-

glehandedly saved the cable industry from financial ruin. In doing so, Rupert added more value to cable operators than almost any individual before or since. The episode spoke volumes about the fair-minded nature of Rupert Murdoch. Unfortunately, it also spoke volumes about the rather monopolistic mind-set of some cable operators, who, as I see it, repaid Rupert by stabbing him in the back as soon as they got the opportunity. I personally consider this little-known piece of business history to be quite illuminating, which is the reason I am sharing it now.

Our story begins in 1995. Rupert was already a satellite star overseas thanks to his growing network of Sky satellite TV ventures. In the U.K., British Sky Broadcasting, better known as BSkyB, was a huge hit. Rupert was also becoming a major influence in the United States thanks to Fox Broadcasting, which against all odds had become America's fourth major TV network alongside ABC, NBC, and CBS. That year, MCI, then America's No. 2 long distance company, invested $2 billion for a 13 percent stake in News Corp. The two partners subsequently invested almost $700 million to buy slots for "direct broadcast satellites," also known as DBS, in the United States. The name of the new venture announced in 1996 was ASkyB, short for American Sky Broadcasting. Over time, the two partners hoped to grow ASkyB into a formidable U.S. complement to News Corp.'s other Sky ventures around the globe.

Cable operators yawned. They figured it would take Rupert and MCI years to build a satellite TV venture from scratch. If anything, the betting was that MCI, a rank newcomer to video, would slow down Rupert. On top of that, Rupert didn't have anything even approximating a business plan. All he had was a new telecom partner and a general idea about what he hoped to accomplish over time. As far as cable operators were concerned, Rupert was sort of like the ten-year-old kid who wakes up one day and proudly proclaims that he wants to become president of the United States when he grows up. Nice idea, kid, but get back to me in a few years.

Rupert was ready to plant his flag in yet another media beachhead: cable news. Thanks to Fox TV, News Corp. was already a rising star in broadcasting. But News Corp. was a basically a nonstarter in cable TV. Not that Rupert hadn't tried. In 1994, News Corp. launched FX, a general entertainment cable network, to tepid reviews. Unfortunately, FX never really took off, and by 1996 only had about 27 million subscribers. Big established cable networks like ESPN, Discovery, and CNN, by comparison, were available in more than 60 million cable homes. To make his mark in cable, Rupert decided he needed to do something dramatic.

And thus the Fox News Channel was born. The twenty-four-hour cable news network, known as FNC for short, would compete head-on with CNN. Like the CNN network it was modeled after, FNC would feature live coverage from news correspondents based in far-flung bureaus around the globe. The move was risky, even for Rupert. During its twenty-year reign, no other cable news channel had ever come close to challenging CNN's dominance. That was no accident. Ted Turner, the legendary creator of CNN, was also its chief protector. Ted had always made it clear that he didn't think the cable industry needed another twenty-four-hour cable news network—it had CNN, and that was enough. Given Ted's larger-than-life status in the cable industry, Rupert knew it might be tough to convince cable operators to buck Ted and carry FNC. Still, Rupert wasn't that worried. After all, he'd beaten the odds many times before.

By then it was the summer of 1996. Rupert set an October launch date and started soliciting cable operators on their interest in carrying FNC. I was one of the first people he approached. At the time I was CEO of Inter-Media Partners, a San Francisco–based cable TV operator. We had about 1.4 million cable subscribers at the time, making us the ninth-largest cable operator in America. I soon agreed to carry FNC and offered to help him convince other cable operators to also pick it up. By then I'd known Rupert for a few years. Our paths had first crossed in the early 1990s not long after I founded InterMedia. I tried to help Rupert get his hands on KRON-TV in San Francisco and some other broadcast assets that were owned by my former employer, Chronicle Publishing. Things didn't work out on KRON, but Rupert and I hit it off and emerged from the whole process as friends.

My decision to carry FNC, however, wasn't just based on friendship. Rupert was offering cable operators a bundle to carry it—a minimum of $10 a head a month. At the time, most programmers were paying no more than $5 a head, so Rupert's offer was generous, to say the least. Rupert also had a track record of delivering innovative programming that consumers liked. So any way you looked at it, I figured FNC didn't represent much of a risk. As a favor to Rupert, I told him he could announce his carriage deal with us before we had actually finalized terms. By doing that, Rupert and I hoped other cable operators would be encouraged to follow InterMedia's lead and pick up FNC. In exchange, Rupert generously agreed to give InterMedia the same terms as Tele-Communications, Inc. (TCI). The favor wasn't insignificant. In the cable world, programming deals are based on bulk—the more eyeballs you can deliver, the sweeter the terms. TCI at the time was the biggest cable operator in America with 7 million subscribers, plus another 4 million from its affiliates. TCI got the best terms that Rupert was offering, $13 a head.

John Malone of TCI also stepped up in a big way. John believed the world needed a more conservative news channel to balance out CNN. John had been encouraging Rupert for years to come up with an alternative to CNN, which was very much a reflection of Ted's liberal political leanings. Rupert, of course, was a Republican, just like John. (I was also a Republican at the time, as John likes to remind me. I eventually saw the light, however, and became a Democrat in 1997.) John even met with Rush Limbaugh, the conservative talk-show host, to try to convince him to join FNC. That didn't pan out, but that John would get out and beat the bushes for Rupert like that said a lot about how strongly he felt about FNC. It probably didn't hurt that Rupert was offering $13 a head. At the time, you might recall, TCI was in a bit of a financial bind. (John also got an option to buy up to 20 percent of FNC later. He ultimately took a pass.)

Bresnan Communications and Falcon Cable, both of them midsized cable companies, quickly signed up for FNC. Continental, the big Boston-based cable operator controlled by Amos Hostetter, was also on board. Everybody else said no. And they kept saying no—for months.

Rupert, being Rupert, kept pushing. He just couldn't believe that cable operators would turn a blind eye to FNC, especially given the attractive terms he was offering. It was like trying to push down a brick wall. Cable executives gave News Corp. every excuse in the book. But the real reason was this: Nobody wanted to risk offending Ted. A few openly wondered why anybody would want to disrespect Ted by stealing viewers away from CNN. Cable operators also had the bowling balls to ask for more money. Never mind, apparently, that the $10 a head was already precedent-setting.

Perplexed News Corp. executives tried to point out the obvious: that FNC would represent a fresh alternative to CNN, which had dominated cable news for almost twenty years. Given its pedigree, FNC also promised to be an innovative network that would break new ground. News Corp., after all, had a track record of delivering programming that consumers liked. Cable operators weren't having any of it. Most of them turned a deaf ear. The message was clear: The U.S. cable industry wasn't interested in any cable news network that Rupert had to offer—not then, not ever.

Time Warner, America's No. 2 cable operator, tried to play its hand close to the vest. Jerry Levin, Time Warner's CEO, had a ticklish political situation on his hands. He was trying to get regulatory approval for his pending acquisition of Turner Broadcasting, which included CNN. Jerry couldn't afford to annoy Rupert too much, lest he appeal to regulators and hold up the merger. But Jerry also couldn't afford to upset Ted Turner, Turner Broadcasting's founder and CEO, who would become a major Time Warner shareholder and board member once the merger closed.

Ted, who has a tendency to demonize all his enemies, or perceived enemies, I should say, hated everything about Rupert—his conservative politics, his Australian heritage, and his sprawling media empire. More than anything else, though, Ted hated the idea of Rupert ripping off CNN. That's why Ted went so crazy about FNC. In Ted's mind, Rupert wasn't just declaring war on CNN—he was declaring war on Ted and all that he stood for. And nothing Jerry or anybody else could say would ever convince him otherwise.

Rupert plowed ahead. He launched FNC in October as scheduled, but with a pitiful number of subscribers—around 20 million. (The number was even less if you didn't count contributions from satellite TV.) That was far less than the 40 million or so cable subscribers Rupert had been banking on. I was stunned at the lack of interest, especially given the rich terms that Rupert was offering. Rupert was offering cable operators $10 per subscriber up front to carry FNC. For a cable operator with just 2 million customers, that worked out to an extra $20 million. And it wasn't as if FNC was junk. FNC featured eye-catching graphics, aggressive reporting, and live news updates from around the globe. Rupert was understandably frustrated at the sorry reception he was getting from cable operators. But true to form he kept banging on doors.

By early 1997, the cable industry's standoff with Rupert was still going strong. I felt bad for Rupert, but by then I had my own drama to contend with. That February I left InterMedia and moved to Denver to become president of TCI. My career switch was totally unexpected, but for me it was a labor of love. John Malone, TCI's CEO, was a friend and business partner and needed my help. TCI's founder and chairman, Bob Magness, had just passed away, so John would have to take over as chairman. John asked me to come on board as TCI's president to help turn around the company, which, as I mentioned, was having a rough time. Customers hated TCI. So did regulators. And Wall Street, and just about every other constituency you can think of. All the pain was reflected in TCI's stock price, which was near an all-time low of about $10. As if all that wasn't bad enough, I had just broken my arm in several places and was trussed up like a Thanksgiving turkey. About the last thing I was thinking about was Rupert Murdoch and FNC. That was about to change.

I had been at TCI just a few weeks when Rupert detonated the cable equivalent of a nuclear bomb: He announced plans to combine ASkyB, his nascent and largely formless U.S. satellite TV operation, with EchoStar, the No. 2 satellite TV operator in America. The new company, which would be called Sky, would be a satellite colossus. It would have access to 75 percent of the United States by the end of 1998, and offer five hundred channels within a year. Since Sky would be an all-digital service, pictures would be crystal clear and the audio would be CD quality. In addition to all the cable staples like CNN, ESPN, and Discovery, Sky would also offer News Corp.'s full panoply of programming, including Fox for Kids, regional Fox Sports channels and, of course, FNC. Rupert, to his credit, had finally found a way to sidestep U.S. cable operators and get FNC into as many living rooms as CNN. And he intended to do it using one of the most sophisticated distribution platforms in the universe—satellite TV.

I thought I was going to have a heart attack. Most cable TV systems at the time only offered thirty-five channels. And forget about national sports. If it wasn't on ESPN or local TV, you were basically out of luck. Most cable systems were still plugging along on the same old "analog" technology they'd been born with thirty years earlier. The technology, which uses electrical waves to transmit video signals over cable lines, was regarded as pretty nifty in the 1970s when a lot of cable systems were being constructed. But analog had fallen woefully behind the technological curve. TCI was particularly vulnerable. Customers already hated the company because of its lousy service and expensive rates. If Rupert's new Sky service showed up in TCI's markets, literally hundreds of thousands of customers might bolt.

Wall Street immediately grasped the gravity of the situation. Cable stocks plunged 30 percent just on the prospect that the cable industry, with its tired, channel-limited technology, was about to be competed against by a digital platform in the sky. ASkyB, Rupert's satellite partnership with MCI, had always been just a fuzzy concept. Thanks to the EchoStar deal, the guy who brilliantly understood the connections between content and distribution was about an hour away from getting his hands on a national platform that was *already in the sky*. The same U.S. cable operators who had so gleefully frozen out FNC were suddenly looking down the barrel of a double-barreled shotgun—and Rupert's finger was firmly on the trigger.

Cable operators had a right to be petrified. Satellite TV, after all, is the only distribution platform that is truly national in scope. It goes from the Indian reservations of South Dakota to the skyscrapers of New York City, and everywhere in between. Satellite TV, as I said, is "all digital, all the time," so pictures and sound are exceptional. It's also customer-friendly in the extreme. Satellite TV is fundamentally a self-installed service. All you have to do is go to a Circuit City (or some other electronics retailer) and pick up the satellite equivalent of a McDonald's Happy Meal—everything you need is right there in the box—then go home and follow the instructions. To fire up the service, all you have to do is call an 800 number and—boom—you're on.

Cable operators immediately branded Sky the "Death Star," and turned to regulators in Washington for help. The cable industry argued that Sky would give Rupert too much control over the media in the United States. News Corp. already owned twenty-two TV stations at the time. With the EchoStar deal, Rupert would wind up with a majority of satellite slots that covered the United States. Regulators basically shrugged. If anything, they were glad to see cable operators squirming. Customer service in the cable industry, led by TCI, had deteriorated so badly that they were happy to see almost anybody come in and shake things up. So much the better if that somebody happened to be Rupert Murdoch, a media titan who had the resolve and the means to hang in there for the long haul.

I thought TCI was doomed. I knew I could eventually fix TCI to be competitive with Sky. But I couldn't fix it fast enough to stop the competitive bleeding that was going to occur if Sky, with its slick marketing, digital format, and hundreds of services, showed up in my markets any time soon. That could be the fatal shot through the heart from which TCI might never recover. I had to figure out a way to take out Rupert fast, or I was one dead duck. With the clock ticking and my back against the wall, I decided I only had one option—I would have to try to cut a deal with Rupert.

I called up Chase Carey, the senior News Corp. executive who had introduced me to Rupert some years earlier, and asked him to meet me in San Francisco the following weekend. Chase, who was the CEO of Fox Television, was based in Los Angeles. I was in Denver. I asked him to come alone and said I would do the same. We didn't talk much on the phone right then. That was understandable. Rupert had just announced his deal with EchoStar, so Chase was in a ticklish situation. By then I'd talked over my game plan at length with John Malone, TCI's chairman. Though it was a long shot, we agreed it was at least worth a try.

Chase and I met the following weekend, as scheduled, in my old InterMedia office in downtown San Francisco. I closed the door and got right down to business. Had Rupert ever thought about doing a merger with Primestar? I asked him. Primestar was a satellite TV company that was jointly owned by the biggest cable TV operators in the United States—TCI, Cox, Comcast, Time Warner, and MediaOne, which had just bought Continental. Primestar had been launched as a competitive answer to EchoStar and DirecTV. But it only served the rural markets that weren't of much interest to cable operators. Chase listened patiently but didn't say much. That was understandable. Primestar was merely a complement to, not a competitor of, the U.S. cable industry. As such, it held little interest for Rupert, who had big national ambitions.

But I wasn't done. Rupert had a well-known sweet spot: FNC. So I tacked on another hypothetical. In addition to making Rupert a full-fledged partner in Primestar, I asked him, what if all these cable operators also agreed to carry FNC? That got Chase's attention. Just to sweeten the pot, I threw out another hypothetical. Rupert had been trying for years to pump up the distribution of FX, his general entertainment cable network, but had never had much success. What if cable operators also agreed to expand carriage of FX? I didn't elaborate, but then again, I didn't have to. The implications of what I was saying were crystal clear: If Rupert agreed to lock arms with Primestar, he would have a pathway for getting FNC and FX into 65 million cable homes. That, of course, was Rupert's Holy Grail.

Under these circumstances, I pressed, do you think Rupert might consider a deal with us?

The room suddenly got very quiet. Chase's wheels were turning. So were mine. Though I obviously had the cable industry's interests in mind, I also thought the plan was a good one for Rupert. EchoStar only had about 450,000 subscribers at the time. Most of those customers were located in smaller rural markets, not the big lucrative urban markets that Rupert longed to tackle. I had no doubt that Rupert could turn Sky into a huge success. But Chase and I both knew it wouldn't be easy or cheap. There was also the ticklish issue of Charlie Ergen, EchoStar's CEO. Charlie was supposed to become CEO in the merged company, reporting to Rupert. Charlie and Rupert were like oil and water. I had picked up rumblings that the two were already butting heads over all sorts of issues. No surprise there. Rupert was a true visionary who thought globally about absolutely everything. Charlie always had a hard time seeing beyond the four corners of EchoStar. One area of friction was technology. Charlie favored EchoStar's platform, which he claimed had superior security features. Rupert favored another technical standard that was more popular in Europe. They also differed on how to deal with the cable industry. Charlie for years had adopted a David versus Goliath mentality toward cable operators. Charlie, of course, was the "David" in that drama. Rupert, a media Goliath in his own right, genuinely aspired to develop a constructive relationship with the U.S. cable industry. By his way of thinking, competitors could—and should—work together cooperatively, not antagonistically.

The two also differed in their management styles. Charlie for years required executives traveling on business for EchoStar to share hotel rooms. Charlie used to bunk up, as well. Charlie's frugality, unfortunately, showed up in his handling of some ASkyB executives. Charlie, true to his word, did extend job offers to a couple of ASkyB executives. But his offers, in some instances, represented pay cuts of 50 percent—with no employment contracts or even moving expenses thrown in. Adding to the agitation in the air, Charlie wasn't including News Corp. executives in some high-level meetings related to Sky. I didn't let on to Chase that I knew any of this, of course. Chase, being the good poker player that he is, also didn't tip his hand to me. By the end of our meeting, Chase said he'd think over my proposal and get back to me. I knew right then that I at least had a shot. Just the fact that Chase didn't turn me down flat told me that.

I got a call from Rupert the following week. He let me know that he was intrigued with my proposal. Go ahead and give it a try, he told me. If I could really convince the Primestar partners to link arms with him, we might have something to talk about. I hung up the phone feeling jubilant, sort of. To kill off the EchoStar deal, I'd have to convince cable operators to do the one thing that many had sworn they'd never do—give a helping hand to Rupert Murdoch. In asking cable operators to support Rupert, I'd be asking them to set aside a lot of strong feelings about a programmer they truly feared and in at least one case (Ted Turner) truly detested.

Some of their fears were pretty rational. Rupert, after all, was a global player who had never made any bones about his desire to become a major player in the U.S. cable industry. Over time, I had no doubt that Rupert would be successful in that quest. Given his global ambitions and News Corp.'s ever-growing collection of assets, it was inevitable, in fact. But so what? My immediate concern was Sky. Its arrival in the market would spell certain ruin for many U.S. cable operators, including, most notably for me, TCI. After all he'd been through on FNC, if Rupert was willing to turn the other cheek and try to work collegially with the cable industry, I was going to do everything within my power to make sure the cable industry delivered.

I put in emergency calls to the Primestar partners and laid out my cards. I told each of the CEOs what they already knew in their guts and in their hearts: The only way to derail the EchoStar deal was to join forces with Rupert. Take your pick, I told them—refuse to invite Rupert into Primestar and suffer the competitive consequences now, when you are least prepared to respond. Or you can take my deal and delay, at least for a while, the day when you have to compete head-on with one of the most potent programmers on the planet. You're not going to stop Rupert, I told them. Nobody can ever *stop* Rupert. But if you take my deal you can at least buy some time to prepare for that day.

To be honest, Primestar's cable partners weren't too wild about my plan. Right off the bat they didn't like the idea of Rupert becoming a partner in Primestar, which had always been a cable-only owned and operated venture. The biggest gripes by far, however, were about carriage of FNC and FX. Some cable operators argued that my proposal was a straight quid pro quo: They would be offering to carry FNC and FX in exchange for Rupert walking away from Sky. That really annoyed me. As far as I was concerned, the cable industry's own arrogance—not Rupert's—had created Sky. Now it was up to the cable industry to do the right thing and make it go away. Was I trying to use carriage as a carrot with Rupert? Sure. But that didn't negate the fact that Rupert had good programming, and he deserved to have it carried. Cable operators had always publicly espoused an interest in carrying good programming. The cable industry, in fact, was based on that premise. I also pointed out that TCI, Continental (by then owned by MediaOne), and InterMedia had all agreed to carry FNC long before Sky was even an issue. So don't talk to me about "quid pro quo," I pushed back. Carrying FNC wasn't a quid pro quo—it was simply the right thing to do.

Gordon "Gordy" Crawford was a huge help. Gordy, who is senior vice president of Capital Research and Management, has been a major investor in media companies for years—and he has a reputation for calling things right, and early. Gordy, who owned stock in all our cable companies, was convinced that my plan was the right way to go. If we didn't take out Sky, Gordy believed, cable stocks had the potential to fall straight through the floor. But if cable operators pulled together as an industry and supported my plan, he was confident cable stocks could recover their post-Sky losses, and then some. All the Primestar cable owners sort of sat up straight when they heard that. Coming from Gordy's mouth, that sort of glowing prediction meant something.

Cox and Comcast soon gave me a thumbs-up on the plan, or so I thought. To be sure, both companies had questions about the particulars. But in concept, at least, I felt they were on board (but read on). Time Warner was a tougher sell. The company was still trying to get its merger with Turner Broadcasting approved and refused to commit. Ted Turner was still adamantly opposed to Time Warner carrying FNC over its cable systems. When Jerry Levin, Time Warner's CEO, pressed him on it, Ted didn't budge an inch. "Over my dead body," he told Jerry. Ted's resistance was a significant political problem. Ted was in line to become vice chairman of Time Warner and get a seat on the board. Once the merger closed, he would also become Time Warner's largest individual shareholder. The fact that Ted opposed FNC wasn't just Jerry's problem, however. It was quickly becoming the entire cable industry's problem. If Time Warner didn't go along with my Primestar-FNC plan, Rupert would probably proceed with Sky. And if Rupert proceeded with Sky, that meant the U.S. cable industry, Time Warner included, was right back where it started—with a loaded shotgun to the temple and Rupert's finger squeezing the trigger.

Ted's argument—that he opposed anything that competed with CNN—was completely irrational. Ted was just upset that Rupert had the temerity to suggest that there should even be an alternative to CNN. Since FNC didn't seem to be a subject that Ted could discuss with any degree of objectivity, I didn't even try to take up the issue with him directly. Instead, Gordy and I went straight to Jerry Levin to plead our case. Jerry was sympathetic, but he said Ted had him over a barrel. "I just can't say no to Ted," Jerry told me. "I just can't do it." I could appreciate that Jerry's back was against the wall. But I had TCI and the rest of the cable industry to worry about. I was hopeful that Jerry would do the right thing for the industry once the Turner merger was approved. Until then, I'd have to figure out another way to get around Time Warner.

Other Primestar cable partners were still queasy about linking arms with Rupert. But they were far queasier about the prospect of having to compete against Sky. In the end, I got enough votes to make Rupert a minority partner in Primestar. In exchange, Rupert agreed to give Primestar access to the orbital satellite channels News Corp. and MCI controlled, along with satellites and other related facilities that were under construction. We all knew from the outset that there was a possibility that the Justice Department might turn down the Primestar merger on competitive grounds. The U.S. satellite TV industry had only a handful of players. Our deal would eliminate one of them—ASkyB. That was bound to raise a red flag in Washington. Still, we all agreed to press ahead and do the best we could under the circumstances.

Our agreement with Rupert on FNC was handled separately. Both sides agreed to handle everything related to FNC and FX carriage on a handshake only. Even so, as far as I was concerned, our verbal agreement was ironclad. Even if regulators turned down the Primestar merger, all the Primestar cable partners would still be obliged to carry FNC and FX—no ifs, ands, or buts. To the uninitiated, it might have appeared that the cable industry was paying off Rupert with carriage to get him to walk away from Sky. But nothing was further from the truth. In agreeing to carry

FNC and FX, the Primestar partners were simply doing something that they should have done much earlier. It was simply the cable industry's way of finally doing the right thing by Rupert, and the right thing by customers. Just to make sure there would be no misunderstandings later, I called up each and every cable CEO and talked through their respective carriage obligations on FNC and FX.

I was pleased and relieved. In just thirty days I'd managed to take out a potentially huge threat to the cable industry. But I also felt a huge rush of personal obligation toward Rupert. He had agreed to work with the cable industry—an industry that had repeatedly spurned him and dragged him through the dirt. I was humbled by his willingness to turn the other cheek. I was also grateful for his confidence. Most of all, I was impressed with his civility. Given his awful treatment at the hands of cable operators, I wasn't even sure we deserved it.

In April 1997, amid much finger-pointing on both sides, Rupert's deal with EchoStar collapsed. Officially, the deal died after News Corp. insisted that EchoStar adopt a satellite decoder system favored by News Corp. EchoStar balked, setting off a back-and-forth with News Corp. that would wind up, eventually, in court. The blowup occurred just a few days before the Sky deal was scheduled to close. Charlie Ergen, as you might expect, hit the roof. By then, some industry estimates were saying that Rupert was going to have to spend $3 billion—at least—to turn the Death Star into reality. News Corp.'s stock price had taken a beating on the mere speculation that Rupert might have to resort to creative financing to pull it off.

A few weeks later, the other shoe dropped. Rupert announced that he was merging ASkyB into Primestar, marking the first serious collaboration between Rupert and the U.S. cable industry. Just as Gordy had predicted, cable stocks shot up on the news that the Death Star no longer had its guns pointed in the cable industry's direction. That good news was followed by still more good news. In a string of carefully orchestrated press releases, cable operators, led by TCI, announced aggressive upgrades on their cable systems. The implicit message was clear: The cable industry would never again be caught off guard by competitors like Sky. Not only had the cable industry dodged a bullet called Sky, it managed to send a message to the world that cable operators could work together collegially. Not long after that, a couple of cable executives sent me a tiny shipwreck for the big fish tank in my Denver office. A plaque on the side was simply inscribed: "Death Star." The point wasn't lost on anybody: The Death Star was officially dead.

When the time came for cable operators to proceed with the second agreement, to carry FNC and FX . . . they were nowhere to be found. Once Rupert was neutralized and Sky was no longer a competitive threat, the Primestar cable operators developed what I can only describe as a collective case of amnesia. All of a sudden, cable operators had a totally different recollection of their bargain with Rupert. *Carriage for FNC? I never agreed to that—I just said I'd consider it.* It was wild—and so was I. Our agreement with Rupert was clear (at least to me)—carriage for FNC and FX as soon as possible. At the request of the cable operators, I had served as the main contact with Rupert. After the fact, Cox and Comcast tried to argue that they couldn't be held accountable for agreements in discussions that they had never actually participated in. I about hit the ceiling when I heard that.

In fact, I did hit the ceiling. After I peeled myself off, I started making phone call after phone call to remind everybody—in the strongest language possible—of their carriage commitments on FNC and FX. Most responded by shrugging shoulders and dragging feet. Brian Roberts, the president of Comcast, insisted he never agreed to carry FNC. Gordy Crawford begged to differ. Gordy, who happened to be listening in on one of Brian's "you-misunderstood-me" explanations, interrupted to point out that Brian had, indeed, offered to carry FNC. And the reason Gordy knew this, he said, was that he had heard it with his own two ears. (Unbeknownst to Brian, Gordy had been listening in via phone when Brian made the offer.) Brian to this day says he doesn't recall the exchange.

Jim Robbins, the CEO of Cox, was no better. When News Corp. approached him to work out carriage arrangements for FNC, Jim protested that all he had ever agreed to do was give FNC "a fair hearing." A fair hearing? What planet was he on? John Malone worked the phones just as hard as I did. John got the same story. He later said it seemed to him that cable operators were "weasel-wording" on their FNC commitments. That was putting it nicely.

Carriage deals for FNC and FX that should have taken days got strung out for months or even *years*. Comcast and Cox both dribbled out their agreements on a market-by-market basis and didn't sign the last ones until 1999. In Cox's case, it took a blowup during the climax of the regular football season to push things to closure. Rupert, unfortunately for Jim, owned the TV station in Washington; Cox owned the cable system. Rupert got so fed up with Jim's empty promises on FNC that he finally jerked the TV signal off Cox's cable system just as the Washington Redskins were heading to the playoffs. Rupert pulled the plug on the last regular-season game and made it clear he'd continue the blackout through the Super Bowl, if necessary. Needless to say, everything hit the fan when Rupert did that. Cox promptly accused News Corp. of using dirty tricks to get its way. As far as I was concerned, the whole thing was Jim's fault. If he'd just gone forward with our agreement, Rupert never would have felt the need to bang him over the head like that. Time Warner finally agreed to carry FNC, but only after a year of trading lawsuits and public barbs with Rupert.

Rupert eventually got widespread carriage for FNC and FX. As of 2002, FNC and FX were available in more than 78 million cable homes. But that was only because Rupert pushed and prodded. After reviewing the proposed merger of ASkyB and Primestar for more than a year, the Justice Department rejected it. Regulators decided the combination would have resulted in less competition in the satellite TV industry, making it an unattractive proposition for consumers. So in the end Rupert got nothing out of the Primestar deal, and nothing timely out of his handshake carriage deal. What he did get, unfortunately, was a hard lesson in the ways of the U.S. cable industry.

LOOKING BACK

Sky was a seminal event for the cable industry. In retrospect, it was the wake-up call that we all needed. As a result of the Sky crisis, TCI ran itself better; so did the cable industry as a whole. We treated our customers better. We began working with each other and with regulators in a more positive and productive manner. Because of Sky, quite literally, we rallied as an industry. That caught the attention of big outside investors, including Bill Gates, Paul Allen, and AT&T. All three wound up investing heavily in cable, which in turn affirmed the value and promise of our industry.

Perhaps none of this would have happened if it hadn't been for Rupert Murdoch. If he hadn't been willing to work with us to redefine the cable industry, I suspect many cable operators, including TCI, wouldn't have survived for long. That's why, to this day, I get so incredibly annoyed whenever I hear cable operators complain about Rupert's "unfair" and "discriminatory" business practices.

The cable industry's propensity to label News Corp. a competitive threat while turning a blind eye to the growing influence of America's own media giants is also quite disturbing. As a marketplace competitor, News Corp. is certainly daunting—but it's no more daunting than our home-grown giants, most notably AOL Time Warner and Comcast. All three are "vertically integrated" in that they control vast amounts of "content" as well as "distribution." All three exert a lot of influence in the marketplace. And all three have global aspirations.

The only difference? News Corp. is an Australian-based company headed by an Australian media maverick, while the other two are U.S.-based companies that are charter members of the old cable guard. Don't get me wrong: I'm a huge fan of AOL Time Warner and Comcast. Both companies have made enormous contributions to the media industry through their leadership and high-quality programming. But so has Rupert. And he should be commended—not castigated—for his continuing efforts and accomplishments.

THE CABLE CLUB

One of the worst-kept secrets in the cable industry is that cable companies that own content as well as distribution are often interested only in their *own* content, which is to say programming in which they have a vested financial interest. As Rupert's experience on FNC showed, cable programmers who don't own their own cable systems can get squeezed out in a hurry.

As you may recall, I experienced a version of this myself in launching the YES network (see Chapter 4). I succeeded in getting all the cable TV operators in the New York market to carry the service, with the exception of one: Cablevision of Long Island. Cablevision had been broadcasting Yankees games for many years, then lost the rights in a bitter dispute with the Yankees organization. I was CEO of YES, so I had the rather unpleasant chore of having to go back to Cablevision, hat in hand, and try to negotiate carriage rights for YES. The whole episode was quite unfortunate. For me, personally, it was also a real eye-opener about the dangers encountered by unaffiliated programmers. To be sure, I'd heard programmers complain about the problem for years. But until I actually experienced it myself, I never realized how scary and truly awful that situation could be.

Not everybody has Rupert's resolve. Some years ago, Group W, the cable arm of Westinghouse, tried to launch a news service to compete with CNN. Cable operators locked arms—and turned Group W down flat. After months of trying to get carriage for the service and getting nowhere, Group W finally shut the whole thing down. Rupert, as we now know, also got the cold shoulder. But unlike Group W, Rupert refused to take no for an answer. Instead, he resorted to Rule 9: Hang in there. By refusing to accept defeat, Rupert eventually got what he wanted—full distribution for FNC and FX. He also broke the logjam on CNN, paving the ways for others to follow. And for that we should all be grateful.

TED TURNER

I love Ted. He's brilliant, passionate, and visionary. Ted has done more to validate the cable TV industry as a multichannel provider than almost any human being alive. His concept of twenty-four-hour news turned broadcast news on its proverbial ear and changed the way we all thought about the world. It's almost hard to imagine life today without CNN, one of the truly revolutionary creations of the twentieth century.

But Ted was dead wrong in trying to keep FNC off the dial. Not only was it bad for the cable industry, it was bad for consumers. Even if Ted didn't think Rupert deserved carriage, consumers had a right to see FNC and draw their own conclusions. In an ideal world, Ted might have recognized that CNN was bound to generate copycats and simply accepted the compliment (Rule 10: Learn to keep your mouth shut). But then again, dear Ted didn't earn the nickname the "Mouth of the South" for nothing.

I will give him credit for one thing, though. Unlike some Primestar partners, at least Ted was emotionally honest. He was also consistent. Ted despised Rupert before FNC threatened CNN's lock on cable news, and he despised him even more after.

WEASEL-WORDING

By obfuscating and stalling on FNC, cable operators only turned Rupert into an even more aggressive competitor (Rule 6: Don't have enemies).

Rupert for years was basically agnostic about the U.S. cable industry. Not anymore. After his mauling on FNC, Rupert saw cable operators as a grabby bunch of dissemblers who can't be trusted. Who could blame him? Cable operators gave every indication that they planned to carry FNC. I guess John had it about right. They were weasel-wording.

While cable operators might have won the battle on Sky, they hardly won the war. After Sky folded, Rupert tabled the idea of trying to get into the satellite TV business in the United States—but he certainly didn't table it for good. As you may recall, Rupert tried to buy DirecTV in 2000. Rupert got beat out at the last minute by Charlie Ergen of EchoStar. But he didn't get beat out for long. As this is being written in the fall of 2002, regulators have turned down EchoStar's bid to buy DirecTV on anticompetitive grounds. The action paves the way for Rupert to circle back around and buy the company. Should Rupert prevail, cable operators will be facing a far more formidable—and determined—competitor. Ask me then who won the war.

7

VIACOM—IF AT FIRST YOU DON'T SUCCEED . . .

T HE Viacom cable deal stands as one of the most controversial chapters of my dealmaking career. It's also a good reminder of a simple but inescapable truth: In business, as in life, sometimes the best plan is an alternate plan.

The Viacom transaction, on its face, was fairly straightforward: The entertainment giant wanted to sell its cache of cable TV systems to my company, InterMedia Partners, for about $2 billion. Sounds simple enough, I know. It wasn't. Before it was all over, Congress would do everything it could to kill the deal, the Federal Communications Commission would do everything it could to save the deal, and the White House would scramble hard just to stay out of the line of fire. As if all that wasn't enough, I'd also wind up in the middle of a nasty legal face-off between (Viacom chairman) Sumner Redstone and (TCI CEO) John Malone that was threatening to blow up everybody. Given all the twists, turns, and surprises that we encountered, it's a miracle the deal survived at all.

To understand and appreciate the three-ring circus that ultimately became the Viacom deal, you have to back up almost a decade to 1986. At the time I was chief officer of planning and finance for The Chronicle Publishing Co., a big media company based in San Francisco. Chronicle Publishing owned a string of broadcast TV stations and newspapers, including the *San Francisco Chronicle*. The company also owned a few cable TV systems, and was interested in buying more. With that objective in mind, I started scouting around for investment opportunities.

I happened to read an article in a newspaper about special tax breaks for companies that sold media assets to minority-owned firms. These special tax breaks were available through a federal program that was administered by the Federal Communications Commission. The article was laced with quotations from one of the country's foremost experts on the program, Frank Washington, an African-American who had been at the FCC when the program was conceived in the late 1970s. The name—Frank Washington—caught my eye. I didn't know Frank personally at the time, but I knew him very well by reputation. Frank was a vice president at McClatchy Newspapers, a small publisher down the road in Sacramento that also owned cable, radio, and cellular phone properties.

I called up Frank right away and introduced myself. Frank, as it turned out, knew everything there was to know about minority tax breaks. A lawyer by training, Frank had worked as an advisor to the Carter White House on telecommunications during the 1970s. It was during that time that Frank, working with the Carter administration, devised the concept of offering tax breaks to companies that sold media assets to minority-owned businesses. President Carter's goal was an honorable one: to increase minority ownership of radio properties. The Carter White House believed and hoped that the civil rights movement, particularly in the South, which was President Carter's home territory, might be enhanced if there were more black-owned radio stations. Frank later worked at the FCC, where he helped draft the rules for the actual tax breaks. These tax breaks later came to be known as "minority tax certificates."

The more Frank told me about the FCC's program, the more intrigued I became. In practice, minority certificates worked pretty much like the tax breaks that had been extended for years to homeowners. As most homeowners know, you can sell a house and not pay capital-gains taxes on the sale so long as you buy another house within a specified period. Once the second property is sold, however, capital-gains taxes become due immediately. Under the FCC's program, a company selling media assets to a minority-owned firm could defer paying capital-gains taxes so long as it reinvested the proceeds in another media property within two years. Once the reinvestment assets were sold, however, capital-gains taxes would become due immediately. Qualifying companies literally received a piece of paper from the FCC that spelled out these terms and conditions—hence the name "tax certificates."

The FCC program, as I said, had been developed with the worthy and rather specific goal of encouraging minority ownership of broadcast properties. The problem was that the actual language that set out the rules of the program was quite broad. Some of the rules, to be honest, were open to fairly loose interpretation. Under the FCC rules, for example, a company was considered to be "minority owned" so long as a minority investor owned at least 20 percent of the company—period. Did that mean that a nonminority investor could build a "minority" company from scratch by merely recruiting a minority investor who was willing to take a 20 percent stake? The FCC also said nothing about financial risk. Could financial risk of the minority-owned concern be borne solely by the nonminority investor? Or did the minority investor-partner also have to have real money on the line? There was also the question of what type of media properties might qualify for tax certificates. The FCC's policy had been written with radio-related deals in mind. Yet, its general language seemed to leave the door open for TV stations and cable TV assets, as well. And if that was true, then why couldn't the FCC's program be leveraged into related areas such as cable "content," or programming? After all, "cable TV systems" and cable TV "content" were related properties—one really couldn't exist in the market without the other—so why not? The more Frank and I talked, the more it became apparent to me that the FCC's program just might be the goose with the golden egg.

When Frank and I hung up after that first conversation, my head was buzzing. Though the FCC's rules didn't say you could use tax certificates for cable properties, they also didn't say you couldn't. Most tax certificates up until then had been issued for radio-related deals. Nobody had ever tried using a tax certificate on a major cable deal. I figured it was at least worth a shot. Chronicle Publishing, a family-owned and -operated media empire, wasn't exactly the "minority" investor the FCC had in mind. But the rules were what they were—and in my eyes they were a treasure trove of tax breaks just waiting to be tapped.

I had no way of knowing how the FCC might respond. I also didn't know if sellers would be game. There was only one way to find out. I'd have to put my hunch to the test using an actual cable deal. I already had a test case in mind. I'd been eying some cable properties in Florida that were owned by the Buford family of Texas. The Bufords, who owned a handful of smaller cable systems in mostly rural markets, wanted to sell the Florida properties and use the proceeds to buy some other cable systems right away. In order to qualify for a minority tax break, a seller had to reinvest sale proceeds into another media property within two years. So on paper, at least, the Bufords were ideal guinea pigs for my experiment.

I called up Frank Washington, who was still working at McClatchy, and explained the situation. I asked Frank to come in as my minority partner on the sale. Frank agreed to accompany me to Texas to explain how the FCC's tax-certificate program worked. If the Bufords went for it, Frank agreed to leave McClatchy to become Chronicle Publishing's full-time minority business partner. Frank was excited at the prospect. So was I. If things worked out, Chronicle Publishing could wind up getting the Florida cable systems at a good price, while Frank could get a new career trajectory that could earn him millions. Frank and I shook hands to seal the deal. Though we didn't know it right then, our handshake marked the beginning of the end of the very program that Frank had labored so hard to create.

Frank and I flew to Tyler, Texas, to meet with Bob Buford, the family's patriarch, to pitch him on the deal. Frank gave Bob a tutorial on the history of tax certificates, offering him a detailed explanation of how the Bufords, who were white, could legitimately use the FCC's program to their benefit. Frank also explained how the application process worked and highlighted all the pertinent rules and regulations. When Frank was done, I gave Bob a term sheet that outlined the applicability of the FCC's program to his cable TV systems. The term sheet showed, step by step, how we planned to set up a separate minority-owned partnership, with Frank as the general partner. It also explained a new tax-sharing arrangement I had dreamed up. For every $100 in deferred tax savings off the sale, we wanted the Bufords to lower their selling price by half that amount, or $50. I thought the arrangement was only fair given that the Bufords would be deferring millions of dollars in taxes. That was as good as money in the bank to the Bufords.

I could tell that Bob's wheels were turning. Bob, like many people, had never heard about the FCC's program. The fact that he might be able to take advantage of a minority tax break was intriguing, to say the least. Bob listened intently to our presentation. When we were done, Bob asked

Frank and me to step outside so he could make a few calls in private. After thirty minutes or so, Bob emerged from behind his office door and informed us that he really liked our plan. Even so, Bob said he wanted a few days to think over our offer. Bob asked if he could hold on to our term sheet while he mulled things over. I didn't think much of it at the time, and readily agreed. Frank and I flew back to California that afternoon to await his call.

After a few days Bob called to let us know he had, indeed, decided to do the cable deal using tax certificates—with another buyer. As it turned out, Bob didn't need the extra time to think about our proposal. He just needed our term sheet so he could entice another investor to step into our shoes and bounce us out of the deal. Another buyer ultimately wound up acquiring the Bufords' Florida cable systems, marking the first time that the FCC had ever issued a tax certificate for a straight cable TV deal. I was quite disappointed at how Bob Buford handled the whole thing, to be honest. But—to continue to be honest—I was also happy to finally get the confirmation I'd been looking for. My gut feelings about minority tax certificates weren't just hunches anymore.

I left Chronicle Publishing about a year and a half later to start my own cable company, InterMedia Partners. My goal was to become the leader of the small-to-mid-sized cable TV operators, just as John was the leader of the big cable operators. The first cable property I set my sights on was Hearst Cablevision, a 65,000-customer system located in the South Bay of San Francisco. The system was owned, as the name might suggest, by the Hearst publishing empire. I had known Hearst's CEO, Frank Bennack, for years through my association with Chronicle Publishing. I called up Frank and told him I wanted to buy the system. I also told him I was prepared to pay well for it, $180 million. That worked out to about $2,800 a subscriber, which at the time was the top end of the going rate for cable systems. Frank didn't hesitate. He told me he'd be happy to sell—but couldn't because the tax bite for Hearst would be too vicious. On a $180 million deal, Frank pointed out, he'd owe more than $70 million in taxes. I had anticipated that response, and had my counter-punch ready: What if I could tell you how you could sell the systems to me and not pay *any* taxes? Under those circumstances, I countered, would he be willing to sell? Frank was definitely interested.

My magic tax antidote? A minority tax certificate, of course. There was just one snag. Frank didn't want to buy any more cable properties. The Bufords had been an ideal test case because they wanted to sell cable and buy more cable. (Under the FCC's rules, a seller had to agree to reinvest sale proceeds in another broadcast asset within two years.) Frank's situation was different. He wanted to dump his cable systems, but he didn't want to buy any more cable systems to replace them. But there was one media asset out there that piqued Frank's interested: RJR Nabisco's 20 percent stake in ESPN, the cable sports network. (The other 80 percent was owned by ABC.)

I had a ready answer for that, too. The FCC's rules, as I mentioned, were quite ambiguous about what constituted a "broadcast" asset for purposes of reinvestment. According to the rules, "broadcast" was virtually anything that involved the transit of electronic signals through the air. *Bingo.* If a radio station was the same as a TV station was the same as a cable system—and the FCC had said as much in the Buford case—why couldn't *programming* on cable systems also qualify as a "broadcast" asset? After all, the only way to receive ESPN, Discovery, and other cable TV networks was to beam the signal over a satellite and tune in via cable TV. So long as I met the four corners of the rules, as written, I figured the agency couldn't say no. It was just a hunch, mind you, but I figured it was worth a shot.

The FCC bought my argument. Ray Hernandez, a lawyer I knew through TCI, served as my minority partner on the deal. Thanks to Ray, I got the Hearst cable systems for about $150 million, which was $30 million less than the systems would have sold for on the open market. I paid around $2,300 per subscriber, which was about $500 less than the going rate at the time. Ray earned more than $1 million for his participation. Frank Bennack made out best of all. He turned around and used his net proceeds to buy RJR's 20 percent stake in ESPN, which went on to become one of the hottest and most profitable cable sports networks on the planet. As of 2002, Hearst's 20 percent stake in ESPN was worth around $2 billion. (Disney, which later bought ABC, inherited ABC's 80 percent stake.) Even better, Hearst would never have to pay a dime in capital-gains taxes so long as it held on to ESPN. (Those taxes will be due if and when Hearst ever sells its stake in ESPN.)

By the time the Hearst deal was done, I knew as much about tax certificates as anybody in America, with the possible exception of Frank

Washington. I was also pretty comfortable using them as a deal instrument. I had demonstrated rather conclusively that they could be used for media transactions in general, not just radio or pure broadcast deals. I did, however, have one nagging question: How big a tax break would be too big for the FCC to swallow? The average tax deferral granted under the FCC's program, at that point, was about $38 million. I was already pushing the edge. Hearst got a tax break of more than $60 million. Nobody at the FCC batted an eyelash. Would a $100 million tax deferral cause the FCC to blink? How about a $500 million break? The FCC's rules were deliciously silent on the subject. It was anybody's guess when, or even if, the FCC might balk. But one thing was for sure: Wherever that invisible line was, I hadn't yet crossed it.

I next set my sights on Cooke Cablevision, the cable TV business owned by Jack Kent Cooke, the media billionaire and former owner of the Washington Redskins. Cooke Cablevision owned cable systems in Arizona, Georgia, South Carolina, and Tennessee. Altogether, the systems had about 800,000 subscribers, which was more than enough to put InterMedia on the map. Cooke Cablevision technically wasn't for sale. But I knew from reading the newspaper that Mr. Cooke was ready to bail out of the cable business. He'd been quoted in some newspapers as saying that he wanted to sell Cooke Cablevision, and even said how much he wanted for it—about $2.5 billion. That was about $1 billion more than his systems were actually worth. But I was glad to hear he wanted to sell all the same.

I had never actually met Mr. Cooke personally. Like most billionaires, he tended to be rather reclusive. But I knew him very well by reputation. Mr. Cooke owned three high-profile properties: the Chrysler Building in New York City, the Washington Redskins, and Cooke Cablevision. Like most men of wealth, Mr. Cooke loved a bargain. I figured he would jump at the chance to use a tax certificate once I clued him in on all the financial advantages. But I'd also learned my lesson in Texas. To make it difficult for him to bounce me out of the deal or, worse yet, gin up a bidding war, I decided to team up with other cable operators and bid for Cooke Cablevision as a group. Once we had the company, we could parcel up the systems by region among the various cable operators. It only made sense. If I went in solo, I'd have to sell off some of the systems anyway.

It didn't take me long to round up some bidding partners. In addition to InterMedia, five other cable companies participated: TCI, Adelphia,

Falcon, TCA, and Chambers. We all agreed to adhere to a sort of Muske-
teers' pact: It would be one for all, and all for one. Mr. Cooke would have
to sell Cooke Cablevision to us as a group, or he couldn't sell to us at all.
Mr. Cooke, who is now deceased, wasn't too pleased at this tactic. He tried
picking us off one by one. It took him a while to figure out that this tactic
wasn't going to work. It took us a while to figure out exactly what Cooke
Cablevision had by way of cable assets so we could settle on a fair purchase price. (As you may recall, he tried to count hospital and prison beds
in his franchise areas as "cable homes." Nice try, anyway.) All in all, it took
us more than a year to put the deal together. When it was done, it was
quite a beauty.

In the end, we had six buyers, three tax certificates, and three minority partners. So the deal structure, to say the least, was quite complex.
Under terms of the deal, InterMedia would get 300,000 of Cooke Cablevision's 800,000 cable subscribers. The remaining 500,000 subscribers were
divvied up among the five other buyers. Frank Washington, who by then
had left McClatchy to form his own cable television investment company,
served as my minority partner. Adelphia and Falcon, which also used tax
certificates, recruited their own minority partners. All three of us followed the blueprint that I had created for the Buford deal. TCI, TCA, and
Chambers didn't use tax certificates for various reasons, so their respective deals were fairly straightforward.

Despite its size and complexity, the Cooke deal sailed right through
the FCC. About $600 million of the overall $1.6 billion transaction was
covered by tax certificates, pushing up, yet again, the high-water mark on
tax certificate deals. Mr. Cooke got to sidestep about $250 million in capi-
tal gains taxes for two years. He was pretty happy about that. So was
everybody else. My cable partners and I all got attractive prices for some
prime cable systems. Our minority partners all walked away with a few
million dollars to do with as they pleased. By the time we wrapped up the
Cooke deal, I was a really big fan of tax certificates.

By now it was 1992, and InterMedia was on a roll. Thanks largely to
the Hearst and Cooke deals, we had 650,000 subscribers in some great
markets, including San Francisco, Nashville, and Atlanta. But I was itching to get even bigger. I already had my next target in mind: Viacom Cable. The company was named after its parent, Viacom, the entertainment
giant controlled by Sumner Redstone. Today Viacom's investment in cable

is confined to its cable TV networks, principally MTV, Showtime, and Nickelodeon. But back then it was also a prodigious owner of cable TV systems. Viacom Cable had 1.1 million cable TV customers, making it the tenth-largest operator in America. Most important for me, those customers were located in markets where I already had a growing presence.

I considered Viacom Cable to be crucial to my long-term business strategy. I was a big believer in "clustering" cable systems, which is the concept of owning whole markets, not just pieces of them. Clustering allows operators to run their cable systems more efficiently. It's simple math, really. The more customers you have in a particular market, the more you can spread your costs around. An operator can roll up billing, customer service, and marketing functions, among other things, which in the end saves everybody money. Clustering also creates bigger competitive battlegrounds, making it easier to hold the line against rivals.

Fortunately for me, Sumner Redstone, Viacom's chairman, had little interest in the "distribution" business at the time. When he bought Viacom in 1987, Sumner inherited Viacom Cable as part of the package. Sumner's real passion was "software," his pet name for anything related to content. Right after he bought Viacom, Sumner made it clear that his focus would remain on software. As far as Sumner was concerned, that was the best way to ride the home entertainment boom into the next millennium. Sumner's laserlike focus on content, unfortunately, left Viacom's business triangle terribly out of whack, which was one reason he later got religion and decided to merge with CBS. In owning CBS, Viacom also picked up a valuable distribution outlet—all those CBS-affiliated TV stations across the country. But that wouldn't happen until much later.

Sumner was an old hand at the media game. He'd made a fortune in the movie-theater business before deciding to switch gears and pursue the home entertainment market, which is what brought him to Viacom's door. Sumner, confident that content was king, poured in millions to shore up MTV and Viacom's other cable TV networks. Every dollar spent on MTV, of course, was a dollar that *didn't* go into development of the distribution side of the business. Absent strong funding and management support, Viacom's cable systems group soon got relegated to Siberia status—and there it sat. For me, the biggest question wasn't if Sumner wanted to sell Viacom Cable—it was just a matter of when.

The "when," unfortunately, was anybody's guess. By then I'd been making runs at Viacom Cable for more than four years. I'd first approached Viacom about buying its San Francisco–area systems in 1988 right after I founded InterMedia. I was still new to the cable club, so I didn't know Frank Biondi, Viacom's CEO, personally. But I knew Frank quite well by reputation. Frank was practically a legend in the media world. He'd worked his way up through the ranks at HBO and became its CEO in 1983. Frank later jumped to Coca-Cola, where he oversaw Columbia Pictures and Columbia Pictures Television. He was chairman and CEO of Coca-Cola Television when Sumner recruited him in 1987 to become Viacom's CEO.

In 1988, I got Frank on the phone and told him I wanted to buy Viacom Cable. Frank didn't know me at all, but he was as nice as he could be. Frank said Viacom wasn't particularly interested in selling its cable systems, at least not right then. He explained that Sumner had just bought Viacom and was still doing inventory, so to speak. Frank left the door open for me to check in with him later, though.

By the fall of 1992, big changes were in the air. Congress had just passed legislation that put the entire cable TV industry under strict new price regulations. The move was Congress's way of punishing cable operators for years of perceived rate abuses. Overnight, the era of double-digit rate increases that consumers had been screaming about came screeching to a halt. Consumer advocates cheered; cable operators groaned. Right off the bat, there was talk that cable rates could get slashed by up to 20 percent. The FCC, at the behest of Congress, immediately began studying how much to roll back rates. In the meantime, strict limits on the prices that operators could charge were imposed. To raise rates above the cap, cable operators had to submit voluminous filings to state regulators justifying their actions. Even then, approval wasn't assured. With no assurance that they could increase rates, cable operators turned cautious. Expensive upgrades on cable systems, essential for keeping pace with new technology, ground to a halt. Cable operators also started taking a hard line on rate increases for programming. That, in turn, put the squeeze on programmers like Viacom, which are wholly dependent on cable operators for their livelihood. Cable stock prices and overall valuations plummeted as skittish investors pondered the industry's future and tried to figure out which companies would survive—and which ones wouldn't.

The other shoe dropped a year later. On September 23, 1993, Viacom filed an antitrust lawsuit against TCI. The suit's language, which Sumner

Redstone himself had helped draft, made it clear that this lawsuit wasn't going to be a run-of-the-mill legal action. "In the American cable industry, one man has, over the last several years, seized monopoly power. Using bully-boy tactics and strong-arming of competitors, suppliers, and customers, that man has inflicted antitrust injury on plaintiff Viacom and virtually every American consumer of cable services and technologies. That man is John C. Malone." The suit further accused John of using his control over the cable industry to "extract unfair and anticompetitive terms and conditions from cable programmers, including Viacom." As a result, Viacom charged, "the consumer has paid—and will continue to pay—a monopoly tax to John Malone."

John fired right back. In equally stinging language, TCI accused Viacom of stooping to a "cynical misuse" of the legal system in an effort to "chill fair competition, to seize an unfair advantage over its competitors, and to prejudice public opinion and regulatory and enforcement agencies" against TCI. The cable giant also belittled Viacom's vitriolic language, suggesting Sumner was simply trying to gain an advantage in his continuing public battle to buy Paramount Communications. The Viacom suit "is replete with inflammatory but entirely unrealistic and untrue accusations and innuendoes. . . . While a complaint that smears competitors may further Viacom's strategy to gain . . . an unwarranted edge in the vigorously competitive marketplace, as well as in the bidding for Paramount, Viacom's drafting tactics have made a proper response by [TCI] needlessly time consuming and difficult."

Sumner's lawsuit was ostensibly aimed at forcing John to change TCI's business practices. But the real burr under the saddle, as TCI pointed out, was Paramount Communications. Sumner had announced plans to buy Paramount only two weeks earlier. The deal marked a pinnacle in Sumner's dealmaking career. In getting Paramount, Viacom would inherit Paramount Pictures, TV stations, theme parks, a Hollywood film library, Madison Square Garden, and Simon & Schuster, the venerable book publisher. (Free Press, the publisher of this book, is a unit of Simon & Schuster.) Sumner was rightly proud of the deal. At that point, he'd been chasing Paramount for four years.

Sumner's warm glow over Paramount would be short-lived. Even as the deal was being announced, Barry Diller, the head of QVC, was hatching plans behind the scenes to take Paramount away from him. Barry recruited a number of backers, including John Malone, then lobbed an aggressive counter-offer for Paramount. Barry's counter was $80 a share, representing a rich premium over the $69 a share that Sumner had offered. Barry's surprise offer killed Sumner's deal and set off a spirited bidding war for Paramount. Sumner was livid. He was forced to scramble just to stay in the running. The timing of the legal action raised eyebrows. Some felt Sumner was using the suit just to get John to back off.

Tension between Sumner and John had been building for years. A lot of it stemmed from TCI's attempts to horn in on Sumner's programming turf. John fired the first shot in 1991, when TCI launched a pay TV channel called Encore that competed head-on with Viacom's Flix. Even as the whole Paramount mess was melting down, John was preparing to launch a suite of pay TV channels that would compete with Viacom's other pay TV services, notably Showtime and The Movie Channel (TMC). Viacom accused TCI of dropping Showtime in some markets and replacing it with Encore. (John always denied this.) Viacom said TCI was also taking a hard line on Viacom's requests for rate increases. At the time, TCI was exploring the possibility of teaming up with Bertelsmann Music Group, the big European music publisher, to launch a music video channel that would compete against MTV. That, of course, annoyed Sumner even more.

Needless to say, by the time John butted his nose into the Paramount deal, Sumner was locked and loaded. Even though I understood Sumner's frustrations with John, I was quite concerned. Sumner's lawsuit was Mutually Assured Destruction (MAD) for the cable television industry. MAD is a term created by the theoreticians of nuclear strategy. It's a guarantee, so the theory goes, that when both sides have nuclear weapons neither is willing—or stupid enough—to fire off on the other, lest they both get incinerated. It has been described as two guys fighting in a phone booth with hand grenades. If Sumner and John started lobbing grenades at each other, I was sure they were both going to die. And they wouldn't die alone. TCI, as I said, was InterMedia's biggest investor. TCI also had partnerships with dozens of other companies throughout the cable television industry. If John went down, there was a good chance he'd take a lot of innocent bystanders with him. Sumner, a mighty programmer in his own right, was also at risk. If the Justice Department took the bait laid out by Sumner, it was going to examine the entire cable TV industry, not just

TCI. In trying to protect the weak, trustbusters would also look at the power of the strong—and Sumner was right in there.

Sumner had a reputation for using litigation as a negotiating tool. Sometimes his legal tactics backfired. In 1989 Viacom filed an explosive antitrust lawsuit against Time, Inc. The $2.4 billion suit, which grabbed headlines across the country, accused Time of refusing to carry Showtime/ TMC on its cable TV systems as part of a conspiracy to protect their own pay-movie channels, HBO and Cinemax. Viacom accused Time of engaging in predatory and abusive practices designed to put Showtime out of business. Time fired right back. In a counter-suit, it accused Viacom of using Nickelodeon, the popular children's channel, to "coerce" cable operators to carry MTV and VH-1. The accusation, unfortunately for Sumner, resonated with a lot of cable operators. Nickelodeon by then was considered a must-have service. MTV and especially VH-1 weren't. Viacom priced the services such that cable operators had to carry MTV and VH-1 to ensure that they could get Nickelodeon for anything even resembling a reasonable price. Time also accused Viacom of stealing trade secrets.

The legal tirades, which went on for more than two years, were captivating and awful to watch. Viacom and Time were both industry bigfoots. They both had the resources and legal firepower to carry on their fight for years. Most important of all, perhaps, both companies were certified industry insiders. So they both knew where the bodies were buried. The only question was whether they were willing, when push came to shove, to help federal investigators dig them up. Fortunately, it never got that far. Viacom and Time finally came to the conclusion that it probably wasn't so smart, given the stakes on the table, to be airing their dirty laundry like that. The two companies reached an out-of-court settlement in 1992, and both suits evaporated.

Many of the same issues that had boiled to the surface in the Time suit were being raised again in Sumner's latest suit against TCI. I was afraid the cable industry might not be so lucky this go-round. Sumner and John were both tough guys. Tough guys, unfortunately, always want to find out who's tougher. Sumner claimed John was using his distribution power to keep Showtime and Viacom's other pay TV services in check. But what if John decided he wanted to talk about Viacom's misuse of power on the programming side? Viacom routinely sold its cable networks as a bundle to cable operators, forcing them to pay higher fees if they tried to buy à la carte. Cable operators had privately complained about the practice for years. Time had raised the exact same issue in its counter-suit against Viacom in 1989. If anything, Viacom had only become more emboldened in its pricing practices since then.

And what about Sumner's cherished MTV? For all practical purposes, MTV had a monopoly. Small programmers that had tried to break into the music video niche over the years routinely complained of MTV strong-arming. True? Not true? I had no idea. But I did know that once the federal investigation got going it could wind up delving into practices and places that we, as an industry, simply didn't want to contemplate. The cable industry was already struggling under the weight of federal price regulation. There was no telling what kind of regulatory remedy the Justice Department might recommend once it got done investigating the accusations of Sumner and John. I watched from the sidelines and hoped for the best. But the knot in my stomach kept telling me the worst was yet to come.

In 1994, Viacom finally decided to sell Viacom Cable. Two years of price regulation had ravaged the cable industry. Making matters worse, the FCC had recently rolled back cable rates by a whopping 20 percent. The size of the reduction left many cable operators gasping. Even the biggest cable operators, such as TCI, felt the pain. The dire turn of events helped convince Viacom that it no longer wanted to be in the distribution business. I was thrilled. By then I'd been waiting six years for Viacom Cable to be placed on the auction block. But I was also worried: I knew Sumner would never sell Viacom Cable to me so long as he and John were at war. TCI owned 31 percent of my company, making John my biggest investor. At the same time, I knew there was no way I was going to sit by and watch somebody else waltz in and buy those systems, not so long as I was still breathing, anyway.

A truce between John and Sumner was the logical answer. But egos—Sumner's and John's—were raging. Their legal war had been going on for a year and showed no signs of slowing. If anything, the vitriol was only getting worse. Months of public bickering had caused positions on both sides to harden. I wasn't too crazy about the idea of voluntarily inserting myself into the middle of that emotional minefield. But something had to give. Not only was their legal fight threatening the long-term vitality of the cable industry, now it was affecting me directly and personally. I wasn't sure if I could bring peace between them. I wasn't even sure if I was the right guy for the job. But for the good of the industry and, to be honest, my own self-interest, I decided I at least needed to try.

I put in an urgent call to Philippe Dauman, Sumner's right-hand man and general counsel. When I got him on the phone, I laid it out for him. We need to settle this lawsuit, I told him, and we need to settle it now, before the Justice Department investigation progresses beyond the point of no return. Philippe listened. Instead of trying to kill each other in court, I offered, why don't we do a massive deal using—you guessed it—minority tax certificates, then make the whole thing contingent on settlement of all outstanding legal issues on both sides? That way, Sumner could finally get resolution to his many outstanding issues with TCI, and I could walk away with cable systems that John and I considered important to the long-term success of InterMedia. Best of all, Sumner and John could call off the dogs and get back to running their respective businesses.

The way I looked at it, this could be the mother of all tax certificates. Assuming Sumner agreed to sell Viacom Cable for around $2 billion, Viacom could qualify for a tax break of more than $600 million. Under the FCC rules, Viacom would be obliged to reinvest that $2 billion in another media property within two years. On paper, at least, capital-gains taxes would become due whenever the reinvestment property was sold. Realistically, however, Viacom would *never* have to pay those taxes. Why? In a word: Hearst. You may recall, Hearst indefinitely deferred its tax payment by reinvesting its proceeds in ESPN. I figured Viacom could get the same benefit (read: pay no taxes) by simply reinvesting proceeds from the sale of Viacom Cable in Showtime or another Viacom cable service. By merely investing in its own programming, then, Viacom could indefinitely defer more than $600 million in capital-gains taxes. That was as good as money in the bank to Viacom. Philippe loved the idea.

I had a few concerns in the back of my head. Officially, the FCC didn't put a limit on the size of minority tax breaks. But common sense suggested there was an invisible line beyond which the FCC would simply go bonkers. There were also intangibles to consider. After the Cooke deal was approved, Congress, the press, and others criticized the FCC for not being tougher on us, given the size of the tax break involved—about $250 million. If we proceeded on Viacom, we would be asking the FCC to approve more than double that amount—and for a traditional media conglomerate, no less. The fact that there were two battling billionaires involved probably wouldn't help. Would the Viacom deal be too big, too star-crossed— too *white*? Would this be the deal that finally crossed the FCC's invisible line? I had to wonder, if only to myself.

We started drafting the deal that summer in secrecy. Given the size of the deal, I felt it was important to be extremely careful. I called in my old partner Frank Washington, who knew every twist and turn of minority tax certificates. Frank by then had formed his own investment company, Mitgo. Using tax certificates as a funding vehicle, Mitgo had acquired interests in cable systems that served about 440,000 cable subscribers. Most of those subscribers were owned in partnership with InterMedia, which had about 650,000 cable subscribers overall.

For Viacom, we would use the same deal structure we had used on so many other transactions. InterMedia and Mitgo would set up a separate partnership to buy the actual cable assets. Mitgo would serve as the general partner and own a 21 percent stake. The balance would be owned by InterMedia, which would become the limited partner. (Under the FCC rules, you may recall, a minority partner had to own at least 20 percent of a partnership for it to qualify as "minority owned.") Frank and I labored over every detail of the transaction. We wanted to make sure that it complied in every respect with the FCC's requirements. In some cases, we deliberately exceeded the FCC's requirements. Under the FCC rules, minority investors were only required to hold on to a media property for one year. Frank agreed to stay involved in Viacom Cable for at least three years. Our caution was a reflection of the high stakes on the table. If everything went our way, Viacom could walk away scot-free on a $600 million tax bill. If things went haywire, however, the whole thing could turn into a Pandora's box the size of Mount Everest.

As work on the deal progressed, Viacom and TCI declared a legal cease-fire. Lawyers for the two companies stopped shooting at each other and finally got to work on a settlement. I was thrilled that the two companies were finally engaged in constructive conversations. But it was also obvious that the wounds inflicted by Sumner's caustic lawsuit would take a long time to heal. Talking to one reporter, John said it felt funny to be doing a deal with Sumner, given the personal nature of some of his charges. "It's like Stalin selling guns to Hitler," John quipped. It wasn't clear from John's comment who was Stalin and who was Hitler, but it didn't really matter. What did matter was that the two were once again talking to each other.

By January 1995, word began leaking out that a landmark tax certificate deal was in the works. Stories about the deal soon started showing up in the press. Speculation was all over the map about how large Viacom's tax break might be, with guesses ranging from a low of $200 million to more than $400 million. We said nothing publicly. Most of the estimates were far lower than the actual figure, which was just north of $600 million. Since corporate tax return information is private, we figured we would never have to disclose the actual figure, anyway. As it turned out, that was just a lot of wishful thinking on our part.

Republicans, who had always hated the idea of minority tax certificates, suddenly smelled blood in the water. Since its inception in 1978, Republicans had viewed the FCC's program as a way for Democrats to curry favor with minorities. Buzz was especially strong in the Republican-controlled House. Congressman Bill Archer, a Republican from Texas, was the new chairman of the powerful House Ways and Means Committee— and he was out to score points. Before long, Representative Archer was vowing to hold hearings to review the FCC's minority tax certificate program. Right out of the chute, he said repeal of the program was a possibility. Not only that, he said any changes to the FCC's program might apply *retroactively* to tax certificates issued on or after January 17. That, of course, would affect us. If we were lucky, we'd wrap up the Viacom deal in time to announce it by the end of the month.

Though I could hear the tom-toms, I wasn't overly concerned. After all, the FCC's program had been a fixture in Washington for seventeen years. Minority tax certificates had a lot of supporters, both in the minority business community and in Congress. Before any changes could be enacted, I figured they'd have to be thoroughly vetted and debated. That could take months. Even if Representative Archer did succeed in killing the program—which we considered a long shot—we figured he'd never be able to do it retroactively. Congress rarely killed programs retroactively. Turning back the clock on programs like that was so antithetical to this country's legislative history as to be practically un-American. If anything, we thought Congress might revise the program to eliminate obvious loop-holes. There was also talk of imposing a cap on the dollar amount of qual-ifying deals. Our deal notwithstanding, that probably made some sense.

On January 20, 1995, we formally announced the Viacom deal. In a press release, we said RCS Pacific L.P., a new minority-owned partnership, would buy Viacom's cable TV systems in a deal valued at $2.3 billion. Mitgo would become the general partner on the deal. InterMedia would be the limited partner, but would retain the right to buy out Mitgo's stake after three years. TCI, a longtime InterMedia investor, would provide $600 million in financial backing. The balance would come from a variety of investors, including the pension funds of Chrysler and General Motors and the Bank of America. Frank, independently, would also contribute some money. We didn't specify how much.

We were all genuinely proud of the deal. In addition to its sheer size and visibility, the Viacom deal would turn Mitgo into a major force in the cable industry. Mitgo was already sizable, with about 440,000 cable sub-scribers. Once the Viacom subscribers were folded it, that number would ratchet up to 1.5 million, making Mitgo the largest minority-owned cable company in America. Frank, as the sole owner and president of Mitgo, would become one of the most important African-American voices in me-dia. That event would mark a personal capstone for Frank, who had spent most of his career trying to expand and promote minority ownership in the media world.

The deal also marked—fortunately—the beginning of the end of Sum-ner's lawsuit against John. Once the transaction closed, Viacom said it would withdraw its antitrust lawsuit against TCI. Viacom didn't elaborate on its rationale for dropping the suit so abruptly. But then again, it didn't have to. Sumner had filed the suit in a fit of rage over a programming dis-pute with John. Now that Sumner had what he wanted and understand-ably needed—long-term financial security for Showtime and for his other cable networks—there was simply no need to continue the legal fight. Thanks to the peaceful resolution, both sides could refocus their energies where they belonged—on their respective businesses.

The deal, for me personally, marked the end of a six-year odyssey to buy Viacom Cable. I couldn't have been more pleased at the outcome. The transaction would leave InterMedia with close to 1.8 million cable sub-scribers, significantly enhancing our distribution capability in key markets across the country. To make maximum use of that access, InterMedia would spend $300 million to upgrade Viacom's cable systems to handle high-speed Internet services, movies-on-demand and other digital services. By the time we were done, all three legs of InterMedia's business triangle (product, technology, and distribution) would be significantly improved.

Viacom was also a huge winner. In announcing the deal, Viacom said it planned to use proceeds from the sale to pay down the $10 billion in debt it had taken on to buy Paramount Communications. What Viacom didn't say, however—and what nobody asked—was how it planned to *record* those proceeds on its books for tax purposes. The short answer: Viacom planned to record the $2.3 billion as an investment in Showtime and some other media assets. By going that route, Viacom could technically meet the FCC's reinvestment rules while delaying indefinitely its obligation to pay capital-gains taxes. To all appearances, we were well on our way to pulling off the biggest tax-certificate deal in history.

Even as we were touting the deal, we were bombarded with questions about Representative Archer's upcoming hearings. I tried to take the high road. Given the size of the deal, I said, I wasn't especially surprised that the transaction was resulting in some close scrutiny. But I also made it clear that the transaction complied precisely with the FCC's rules, and therefore we expected speedy approval for a tax certificate. As for Frank, I pointed out what I believed to be the obvious: He was a veteran cable executive who was deeply committed both to the cable industry and to the minority tax-certificate program. Some critics tried to make hay out of the fact that Frank had helped create the very program that he was now trying to use to his benefit. My answer: So what? Frank was exactly the kind of minority entrepreneur the FCC's program had been created to encourage. The fact that Frank was astute enough to foresee a consolidation trend in cable and was trying to personally participate was something for which I felt he should be praised, not castigated.

Representative Archer's January 27 hearing, as expected, was rough. Republican lawmakers were openly hostile. Some referred to the FCC's program as "corporate welfare" for white-owned companies. There was also a lot of sniping about the FCC. Admittedly, some of the FCC's rules had rather large loopholes. But that wasn't really the FCC's fault. The agency had tried to tighten up some of the rules in the late 1980s but got blocked by Congress. Democratic lawmakers were concerned that the Reagan administration might use the opportunity to cut back the program. After it was revealed that Viacom's tax break would be around $600 million, there was a lot of sniping about the U.S. Treasury being robbed. All in all, the hearing was the political equivalent of a public stoning.

Two weeks later Representative Archer moved in for the kill. He introduced a bill to repeal minority tax breaks, saying it would save the U.S. government more than $1.4 billion over a five-year period. He tied his bill to a popular provision that would allow self-employed workers, including farmers, to deduct their health-insurance costs. Lawmakers said the $1.4 billion in savings from the FCC's program could be used to help offset the cost of the insurance benefits. Representative Archer argued that it was important to pass the bill quickly so self-employed workers could take advantage of the new benefits before April 15, when federal tax returns were due. Therefore, Archer asked that the bill be made effective retroactively to January 17.

The House action ignited a spirited debate among senior African-American lawmakers. Some Democrats viewed the bill as a blatant attempt to turn back the clock on affirmative action. Congressman Charles Rangel, a Democrat from New York, was positively fuming. He basically accused lawmakers of holding Frank to a different standard just because he was an African-American. Using some choice words, he said Frank's windfall was no reason to kill the FCC's program. Other African-American lawmakers agreed. They said it was clear the FCC's program needed an overhaul, but took issue with killing the program outright. It didn't do any good. Despite stiff opposition and a lot of finger-pointing, Representative Archer's bill was approved a few days later. By then the bill had picked up a new nickname that made all of us wince: the Viacom Bill.

Frank was devastated. As an original architect of the FCC's tax certificate program, he genuinely believed in its goals and ideals. Now the program, which represented one of the biggest accomplishments of his life, was about to get killed because of a business transaction that Frank himself had helped put together. Frank was understandably upset. He'd created the rules, played by them hard—then got penalized when he dared to take advantage of a program that was developed for people just like himself. In one interview, Frank openly challenged the fairness of it all.

Speaking to reporters, he wondered aloud why Congress would permit such an offensive and controversial bill to be jammed through so quickly. "Is this America?"

The White House tried to help, sort of. President Clinton, a longtime supporter of affirmative action programs, proposed modifying the FCC's program to make it more palatable to critics. One suggestion was to raise the financial threshold for participating minorities. The FCC's rules only required minority partners to own a 20 percent stake. The rules were silent, however, about how much actual capital the minority partner had to contribute. Taken to the extreme, a minority-group member could own 20 percent of a company but contribute zero capital and still qualify as a minority partner. President Clinton supported the insurance deduction, which was attached to the Viacom Bill. Since he wasn't willing to entertain an outright veto, and everybody knew it, his suggestion went nowhere.

The Senate was our only hope. Lawmakers there were also anxious to extend the health deduction for self-employed workers. But they were queasy about assaulting minority rights retroactively. The Senate Finance Committee held a hearing on the bill in March. Frank and I both testified. If the Senate didn't like the FCC program as written, we urged, just change it—but don't kill it outright. I also challenged the fundamental fairness of crafting tax policy on a retroactive basis. I pointed out that our deal, which had taken months to negotiate, met the FCC's rules as written at the time. I argued it wasn't fair to hold us to a standard that hadn't existed when our deal was being put together. Bill Kennard, the chairman of the FCC, also urged lawmakers not to kill the program. Bill, who is an African-American, went so far as to call the program the "cornerstone" of the federal government's effort to expand minority ownership in media.

None of it did much good. Senator Bob Packwood, the committee's chairman, said he had serious doubts about the program. Among other things, Senator Packwood said he wasn't convinced it encouraged minority ownership of media assets. Senate Majority Leader Bob Dole, picking up the pace, said it was hard to sympathize with a company (Viacom) that was about to walk off with a $600 million tax break. The committee, as feared, voted to adopt the House bill that repealed the FCC's minority tax break. The full Senate followed a short time later. The law repealing minority tax certificates was officially enacted on April 11, 1995, forever ending the FCC program that had aided minority businessmen and women for more than seventeen years. Enactment of the law, as expected, was made retroactive to January 17. The Viacom deal was officially dead.

I felt awful that Republicans had been able to use our deal as a club to beat the FCC's program to death. I felt especially bad for Frank. He not only lost a big deal that was important for Mitgo, he lost something that was important to him on a deeply personal level. But right then I couldn't fret over the FCC's program or Frank—I had $2 billion in cable assets that were about to walk out of my life forever unless I came up with a miracle fix really fast. If Viacom found another buyer, I would never get my hands on those cable systems. That meant I would never control San Francisco, Nashville, and a lot of other markets that were important to InterMedia.

There was also the matter of Sumner's lawsuit. If the Viacom deal unraveled, so did the settlement with TCI. That meant John Malone, my dear friend and business partner, was right back where he had started—in the legal trenches slugging it out with Sumner. If those two started firing missiles again, the cable industry—to say nothing of InterMedia—was bound to get caught in the cross fire. I couldn't let that happen. I *wouldn't* let that happen. With time running out, I only had one option left: I'd have to come up with new deal. I'd have to move fast. By then, Viacom had already put out an announcement saying that it was exploring other ways of selling off its cable TV systems. Time, for me, was clearly running out.

I started throwing body blocks everywhere I could. I put in an emergency call to Philippe Dauman, Viacom's general counsel, and pleaded my case. If he'd delay bringing in another buyer, I promised to come up with a deal structure that would duplicate, from a tax perspective, the plan that Congress had just killed. Just give me a little time, I pleaded. I *promise* I'll make this happen. To be honest, I didn't have a clue how to duplicate my original plan. It was a one-of-a-kind, you might say, based on an aggressive interpretation of an obscure federal program with loopholes big enough to drive a dump truck through. But I couldn't worry about that right then. I had to get Philippe's commitment, otherwise everything was going to blow apart at the seams.

I called up John Malone, who has one of the most adroit minds on the planet when it comes to figuring out financial problems. I also called in Pete Zolintakis, a Pricewaterhouse partner and my longtime tax attorney. The three of us basically shut ourselves in a room and brainstormed on ways to save the deal. Back in New York, Viacom was also cramming. Alfred Youngwood, a talented tax attorney, took the lead for Viacom. Our mutual goal was simple but challenging: to approximate the same tax savings for Viacom as the original transaction, while also realizing financial benefits for InterMedia from a purchase price perspective. We obviously couldn't use the minority tax break, which was gone forever. We'd have to peruse other parts of the U.S. Tax Code for possible solutions. Day after day we pored over the tax code and hashed things over among ourselves. Like college kids jamming for finals, we pulled all-nighters and drank lots and lots of coffee. When we all finally came up for air about a month later, we had our plan.

And what a plan it was. The deal structure was geared to meet Section 355 of the U.S. Tax Code, which sets out the criteria for tax-free spin-offs. Needless to say, it was incredibly complex. The deal involved twenty-seven steps, including two spin-offs, one of which was the financial equivalent of a partial initial public offering. Under the new plan, TCI would actually buy Viacom Cable, then flip the cable systems to InterMedia. Viacom would receive a slightly lower price—$2.25 billion instead of the original $2.3 billion—but it would also wind up paying slightly less in taxes over the long haul. TCI, in turn, would pay slightly more in taxes, but that would be offset by the slightly lower selling price. The transaction would leave InterMedia with 1.4 million cable subscribers. That was 400,000 less than the 1.8 million we would have wound up with under the original deal. But I really couldn't complain. After our spectacular crash and burn during the first go-round, I was just glad to be back in the game at all.

We unveiled our plan on July 25. In a press release, Viacom said the latest version of the deal would "unlock the value of noncore assets"—referring to Viacom Cable—while reducing Viacom's corporate debt load by $1.7 billion. Sumner, in a carefully worded statement, said the deal would also enhance Viacom's position "as the world's premier content-driven media company." The statements were mostly aimed at the IRS. For this to qualify as a tax-free transaction, Viacom would have to prove that the deal was being done for valid business purposes. (Sumner's interest in lightening his tax load obviously wouldn't qualify.) Viacom said nothing about the size of its tax break. The omission was quite deliberate. If everything went according to plan, we expected Viacom to walk off with a permanent tax deferment of about $800 million, which was nearly a third more than it would have gotten under the first version of the deal.

There wasn't much lawmakers could do. Section 355 of the U.S. Tax Code had been in place for years. Unless lawmakers planned to go after the IRS itself, we were home free. Even so, the complicated structure of our plan invited a lot of criticism. Many tax experts openly bet that the IRS would turn us down. Some people predicted the IRS and the Treasury Department would eventually ask Congress's help in changing Section 355. (Nobody talked about the probability of anybody trying to change Section 355 *retroactively,* but I'm sure some people at least thought about it.) We said nothing publicly. Having learned our lesson the hard way during the first go-round on the Viacom deal, we weren't about to give our critics any more ammunition.

True to form—for this deal, anyway—it was a white-knuckled rollercoaster ride right up to the bitter end. The IRS wasn't exactly singing praises of our plan. Philippe Dauman, the Viacom general counsel, spent a lot of time down at the IRS trying to convince the agency that our plan was, indeed, legal. After a lot of convincing and, yes, even pleading, the IRS finally gave its blessing. Many tax experts were dismayed. (So dismayed, in fact, that an analysis of the IRS's Viacom decision in *Tax Notes,* a trade publication for the tax community, began simply: "Did Aliens Kidnap IRS Lawyers?")

It would appear that the IRS wasn't as convinced as everybody thought, however. Two days after it approved our plan, the IRS quietly published a notice killing a key element of our twenty-seven-step plan. The move effectively prevented anybody from ever following in our footsteps. As for us, we were just thankful the IRS didn't try to make the change retroactive.

LOOKING BACK

The IRS action marked the end of one of the most remarkable, even improbable, deals of my career. John, in talking about the Viacom deal, later said he thought it was "as close to perfect" as he and I had ever done. Considering how things could have turned out, I can't say I disagree.

The Viacom deal is a prime example of why mental agility is so important in the context of dealmaking. By all rights the Viacom deal should have died when Congress killed the minority tax break. The only thing that saved the Viacom deal—and I mean the *only* thing—was the utter refusal of a handful of committed people to give up. (Remember Rules 4 and 9: You're only as good as the women and men around you and Hang in there.) Instead of folding our tent and going home, as many people had expected us to do, we rallied. We took one step back, considered our options—then brainstormed like crazy to come up with an alternate plan. As I've said before, and as the Viacom deal shows, the ability to hang tough and think fast isn't just important for successful outcomes—it's absolutely essential.

MINORITY TAX CREDITS

The FCC's minority tax certificate program was established in 1978 with the honorable goal of encouraging minority ownership in media. Did our attempt to use the program constitute an abuse of the program, as some charged at the time? The answer, to be honest, is yes and no.

On a purely personal level I strongly support and advocate diversity in media. I fundamentally believe that more diversity ultimately translates into stronger and more informed media. It's just an inherently good idea. But how to bring about that change? The minority tax break, for starters. Some people dumped on the program because it appealed, more or less, to rich white-owned corporations looking for a tax break. But so what? In many ways the minority tax break was no different from the time-honored tax deduction for charitable contributions. Rich people use it all the time to make contributions to worthy causes, but nobody ever seems to complain about that. The FCC's program offered benefits to rich, white-owned corporations. But again I say—so what? The program also encouraged minority ownership of media. Between 1978 and 1995, the FCC granted slightly more than three hundred certificates, all with the aim of expanding diversity in media. Though some big corporations received tax breaks, no doubt, a lot of minority businessmen and women also benefited.

Social aims aside, the FCC's rules on minority tax breaks were what they were. And in 1995 they were wide open to interpretation by anybody with a serious business agenda to push. Did we know that we were pushing the envelope by trying to squeak through a $600 million minority tax certificate? Absolutely. But we were also strictly abiding by the rules as written, which at the end of the day was all we were obliged to do. I suppose you could make an argument, as some did at the time, that we violated the *spirit* of the FCC's program. The agency obviously had higher ideals in mind than simply deferring taxes for media conglomerates. But again, the agency's written rules—not the spirit of the rules—were the only legal road map we had to follow. Even the FCC agreed with us on that. The agency let us know later that it would have approved a minority tax certificate for Viacom if Congress hadn't intervened. So criticize me for walking on the edge, if you must, but don't accuse me of stepping over the boundary, because that just didn't happen.

GODZILLA VERSUS KING KONG

I am a huge fan of both John Malone and Sumner Redstone. Nobody knows the cable television business as well as John; in the programming world, Sumner is an absolute master. As businessmen, they are smart, aggressive, and insightful. They have inspired us all with their visionary thinking. But like all mortals, Sumner and John have their shortcomings. And one shortcoming they share is this: They're both hotheads. The characteristic isn't that uncommon among top dealmakers. (I've been accused of being fast on the draw, myself.) I guess it only stands to reason that people who are adept at making decisions quickly would also be prone to fly off the handle more quickly, as well. The problem with Sumner and John, however, is that they have the resolve and resources to follow you to the Gates of Hell if they get mad enough.

When Sumner and John went after each other, it was the equivalent of Godzilla going after King Kong. They were determined to fight to the end, even if it meant everybody around them got crushed. Their accusations and counter-accusations could have put the future of the entire cable industry—distributors and programmers alike—on the line. Fortunately, Sumner and John settled their differences before any great damage had been done. There was one silver lining, however. Sumner and John emerged from their legal battle with a renewed sense of respect for each other. That, in turn, led to a more productive working relationship between their two companies, which ultimately had a positive effect on the entire cable industry.

Sumner and John could have gotten to that peaceful spot a lot sooner, however, if they had just minded Rule 6. (Have adversaries, if need be. But don't have enemies.) Sumner and John had legitimate beefs with each other. Sumner was angry with John for putting the financial security of his cable networks at risk; John was upset with Sumner's equally heavy-handed tactics on Paramount. Sumner eventually got Paramount, but it cost him an extra $2 billion thanks to the last-minute arrival of Barry Diller and John. Sumner was understandably upset at the intrusion, but that's how it goes sometimes on big deals. Until the last document is signed, sealed, and delivered, anything is possible.

In the end, Sumner and John did what they should have done at the beginning, which was to find common ground and reach a truce. To be sure, sometimes that isn't possible (see chapter 4). But if both sides are willing, as John and Sumner demonstrated, positive outcomes are achievable. No matter how thorny the situation, both sides can emerge as winners. Even better, they can emerge as friends. My message here is simple but clear: Learn to turn the other cheek. If Sumner and John can do it, I have to believe *anybody* can.

REGRETS

John Malone and I used to joke that it took an act of Congress to kill one of our deals, and even then we still prevailed. But in truth we both felt terrible that Congress was able to use the Viacom deal as an excuse to kill a program that had been assisting minority businessmen and women for more than seventeen years. Lawmakers didn't have to go that far. The program could have been modified in any number of ways to tighten up the rules and eliminate abuses, or perceived abuses. But I believe House Republicans chose not to do that because the real issue wasn't Viacom—it was affirmative action. Republicans never liked the premise of affirmative action. That had always been a decidedly Democratic notion, one that dated back to the days of President Lyndon Johnson. In repealing minority tax breaks, Republicans managed to further chip away at the crumbling foundation of affirmative action in general.

My second regret concerns my longtime friend, Frank Washington. Like me, Frank is a successful businessman. Unlike me, Frank is an African-American. So for him the Viacom deal wasn't just business. It was also deeply personal. Frank fundamentally believed in the social ideals associated with the FCC's tax certificate program. Frank was rightly proud, both as a businessman and as an African-American, of his role in developing the FCC's program. To suggest later, as some lawmakers did, that Frank's commitment to those social ideals was less than sincere was an affront to him both personally and professionally. Frank did nothing untoward in teaming up with us and with Viacom. He was just a smart businessman who had learned his way around the system, and he was legitimately trying to put that knowledge to work for his company.

Frank literally cried when Congress killed the FCC's program. He not only lost a big deal that was important to his company, he also lost a bigger fight for higher social ideals. I cried right along with him. Like Frank, I believed then, as I believe now, in the social ideals of affirmative action. As an active Democrat, I hope that some form of the FCC's program will one day be resurrected, albeit with more thoughtful, precise, and tempered rules. As a nation, I think, we would all benefit from that.

8

USA NETWORKS: OPTIMAL OUTCOME

U NINTENDED consequences. In business, they're like the plot twist endings of horror movies: If you're not careful, they can reach out and grab you by the throat out of nowhere.

If you're lucky, unintended consequences reveal themselves fairly quickly. If you're not, they don't. They fade into the woodwork and don't become apparent for years, usually at some incredibly inopportune moment. That's about the time you find yourself smacking your forehead and muttering, "Oh, right." For a dealmaker, surprise endings of that sort are the absolute worst. By then the game is over. Everybody's gone home, leaving you to face the consequences that you yourself helped put into play. All you can usually do is plant your feet, brace yourself, and take it across the jaw. Sometimes things work out. Sometimes they don't.

The most inconsequential things can trigger reactions that you never intended or, worse yet, never expected. When Microsoft bought a small stake in Road Runner, the high-speed Internet service, some years ago, it insisted on inserting a clause that gave it the right to approve—or reject—the first CEO. Road Runner's partners, Time Warner and MediaOne Group, basically shrugged and said okay. When Time Warner and MediaOne finally got around to naming a CEO for Road Runner a few years later, they picked an outstanding one: Greg Maffei, Microsoft's chief financial officer and top dealmaker. The selection was roundly applauded by everybody—except Microsoft, that is. Bill Gates, Microsoft's chairman, was none too pleased at the prospect of losing a valued member of his senior management team to Road Runner. Invoking his veto rights, Bill promptly nixed Greg as Road Runner's first CEO. Greg was quite upset, but there wasn't much he could do about it. The irony? *Greg* was the one who had insisted on inserting the veto clause in the first place.

For a CEO, anticipating the unintended consequences of his or her actions in the marketplace is an integral part of the job. Most deals, particularly the larger ones, are akin to skipping a rock across the surface of a lake: They're going to cause ripples. The trick is to figure out ahead of time if any of those ripples have the potential to develop into riptides, and plan accordingly.

When Carly Fiorina, the CEO of Hewlett-Packard, launched an aggressive campaign to save her proposed merger with Compaq, I have no doubt that she truly believed the merger was in the best interest of shareholders. Initially, Carly's campaign was focused solely on Wall Street, which didn't like the deal right off the bat. Analysts were concerned that it would leave H-P too exposed to the eroding personal computer business. Walter Hewlett, an H-P board member and the son of H-P cofounder Bill Hewlett, soon made it clear that he also didn't like the deal and planned to wage a proxy fight to defeat it. The Packard family, representing H-P's other cofounder, Dave Packard, soon joined forces with Walter. Carly, formerly a star saleswoman from Lucent, seemed genuinely stunned—and responded by stepping up her save-the-deal campaign even more. The more critics pushed, the more Carly pushed back. Before long, Carly was engaged in a coordinated campaign to save the Compaq deal that was worthy of George Patton. Then the mud started flying in all directions. Investors, stunned by the down and dirty tactics, starting picking sides and issuing their own statements. So did customers, employees, and even ex-employees.

By the time of the H-P shareholder vote on March 19, 2002, H-P's wounds were so deep and so ugly that it didn't really matter how the vote turned out. Either way, H-P was going to take years to heal. The final H-P vote was a squeaker. Slightly more than half of the company's common shares were voted in favor of the deal, while slightly less than half voted against it. (The vast majority of employees, however, voted their shares against the deal.) Carly won her grudge match with Walter Hewlett, for sure. But at what cost to H-P? I would submit that her victory was quite a hollow one, given the greater damage done to her company. Did Carly anticipate that the situation had the potential to turn so bitter? I doubt it. If she had, I have to believe that Carly would have done a far better job of reaching out early to Walter and to Wall Street.

In Carly's case, the unintended consequences of a particular course of action became apparent fairly quickly. In the case of Greg Maffei of Microsoft, it took a couple of years. Unintended consequences can also creep up on you bit by bit. By the time it finally dawns on you that, yes, you really are in a jam, it's usually too late to do anything about it. Consider the curious journey of USA Networks, the big cable TV network. Like any good tale with a surprise ending, this one began innocently enough.

Our story begins in 1995. Seagram, the big spirits maker controlled by the Bronfman family, plunked down $5.7 billion that year to buy an 80 percent stake in MCA from Matsushita, the Japanese electronics maker. MCA was a true Hollywood powerhouse. It owned Universal Studios, Universal theme parks, a growing television production business, extensive film and television libraries, and a couple of record companies. MCA also owned a 50 percent stake in USA Networks, a cable TV partnership that controlled USA Network and the Sci-Fi Channel. The other 50 percent of the USA partnership was controlled by Paramount Pictures, a division of Viacom, the entertainment giant controlled by Sumner Redstone.

Seagram's purchase of MCA rocked Hollywood. It also cast a spotlight on Edgar Bronfman, Jr., Seagram's youthful president and chief executive officer. Edgar had succeeded his father, Edgar Bronfman, Sr., as CEO just a year earlier. At the time, Edgar was just thirty-nine. Edgar Jr., a songwriter and onetime movie producer, had a rather audacious plan in mind: to turn the house of Absolut into a global entertainment power. But Edgar, and therefore Seagram, had a problem: Edgar knew next to nothing about the media business.

Despite his soft-spoken manner and lack of media experience, Edgar did have an important characteristic for success in business: He knew what he didn't know. He demonstrated as much in hiring Frank Biondi, the former CEO of Viacom, to head Universal. The fly in the ointment, however, was that Frank had recently been fired by Viacom, which also owned Paramount Pictures. Sumner's parting with Frank had been rather ragged, and he was in no mood to do Frank any favors. Viacom immediately protested the hiring, claiming that Frank's noncompetition agreement with Viacom prevented him from taking a similar job at Universal.

That set off a war of words with Edgar, who was determined to hold on to his new Hollywood star. After a lot of tough talk from both companies, Viacom finally released Frank from his noncompetition agreement in 1996.

About a week later, Seagram turned around and poked Viacom in the eye—this time over a long-simmering dispute involving the USA partnership. In a stinging lawsuit filed in April 1996, Seagram claimed Viacom's 1994 purchase of Paramount and its related assets violated the USA partnership agreement. Seagram said the agreement prevented either company from owning or launching cable TV networks outside the USA partnership. Seagram argued that Viacom's ownership of MTV and its other cable TV networks, as well as its launch of its then-new Nick at Nite TV Land network, constituted a breach. MCA had bitterly complained about the same issue when Viacom was in the process of buying Paramount, but never took legal action. Seagram asked the court to force Viacom to either dispose of MTV and its other cable TV networks or sell its 50 percent stake in USA Networks back to Seagram.

Sumner, caught off-guard by the legal assault, came back swinging. Viacom counter-sued, accusing Seagram of trying to "coerce" Viacom into selling its USA stake at a price far below market value. Viacom also argued that, because it had owned cable networks before it bought Paramount, those rules in the partnership agreement didn't even apply. For eighteen months, the legal tug-of-war dragged on. At one point Viacom offered to buy back Seagram's USA stake for $1.94 billion. Edgar, to his credit, hung tough. In rejecting the offer, Edgar said Seagram wasn't a seller. The soft-spoken CEO with a soft spot for the arts, as it turned out, had a backbone made of steel.

In September 1997, Edgar's patience and persistence finally paid off. A Delaware judge sided with Seagram, saying that Viacom had, indeed, violated the USA partnership agreement in buying Paramount. The ruling paved the way for Seagram to take 100 percent control of the partnership and its two cable TV networks, USA and the Sci-Fi Channel. Even better for Edgar, the court ruled that Seagram could retain a number of popular Universal-produced television shows, including *Xena: Warrior Princess* and *Hercules*. The turn of events marked a rare, hands-down legal defeat for Viacom, which took the loss in stride. Sumner characteristically claimed victory, then sold Seagram its 50 percent stake in USA for $1.7 billion.

Edgar suddenly had a huge—and totally unexpected—ace in his hand. Edgar had been the only studio head who didn't own a broadcast or cable television network outright. The USA partnership had given Universal an indirect vehicle for distributing TV programs and movies. But the arrangement had always been less than ideal because of Viacom's involvement. Now that Viacom was out, it was a whole new ballgame. Edgar suddenly had a chance to use USA Networks as a serious launching pad for Seagram's bulging film and television library.

That was the good news. The bad news was that USA Networks was a bit of a wreck. Kay Koplovitz, USA's CEO, had worked hard to turn the two cable TV networks, USA and Sci-Fi, into winners. USA, the larger of the two cable channels, reached about 67 million homes, so it had pretty good distribution. But the channel itself was eclectic and inconsistent. Kay had been trying to reposition the network as the place to tune in for compelling original shows and popular TV reruns. But she could never quite pull it off. USA televised everything from the Westminster Dog Show to *Baywatch*. The original content tended to be hit-or-miss and had never really resonated with audiences. Sci-Fi was even worse off. The channel, which only reached about 36 million homes, was ostensibly devoted to science fiction. But in practice its programming lineup was all over the map. The bulk of Sci-Fi's programming consisted of tired, old TV reruns, including *My Favorite Martian* and *Dark Shadows*. None of it hung together particularly well.

To turn USA into a winner, Edgar would have to do a serious overhaul of both channels. Edgar didn't have the expertise to do it himself, of course. He'd have to recruit new management talent. But who? Universal, as I said, didn't own any broadcast or cable TV assets on its own. Unlike the other big Hollywood studios, it didn't have an in-house talent pool it could dip into any time it needed a quick talent fix. Frank Biondi, the former Viacom honcho, would have been the logical choice to call in and fix USA. But Edgar wasn't so sure that Frank was up to the job. (Edgar eventually came to share Sumner's rather dismal view of Frank and fired him.) Edgar, once more, would have to take matters into his own hands.

That presented Edgar with a huge opportunity—and a huge risk. If Edgar chose wisely, USA could become a star vehicle for showcasing Universal's content, not to mention all its retail products related to its movies, theme parks, and the like. Edgar, who yearned to be taken seriously in

Hollywood, would rightly receive credit for having turned USA around. If Edgar bungled the effort, however, he'd get criticized for burning the free card that the court had just handed him. He'd be known as the guy who took a cable also-ran and made it even worse.

Edgar's dilemma was hardly a secret. His legal battle with Sumner and subsequent victory became a fixture on the pages of the business and entertainment press. After a while, laying odds on Edgar's next move became a favorite topic of discussion around the water coolers and power lunch tables of Hollywood.

On the sidelines, taking it all in, was Barry Diller.

Barry was practically a legend in Hollywood. He famously got his start working in the mail room of the William Morris Agency, the big talent agency that catered to all the top stars. A chance meeting at a party with Leonard Goldberg, then head of programming for ABC, led to an offer to become Leonard's assistant. By twenty-five, Barry was vice president of programming at ABC. Barry quickly demonstrated a knack for figuring out what resonated with audiences, particularly the younger audiences that advertisers craved. During his brilliant run at ABC, Barry pioneered the "movie of the week" and the "miniseries." Both concepts were a big hit with audiences—as well as advertisers—and quickly became industry staples. At thirty-two, Barry became chairman and CEO of Paramount Pictures, the fabled Hollywood movie studio. Under Barry's watchful eye, Paramount churned out such monster hits as *Saturday Night Fever,* *Raiders of the Lost Ark,* and *Flashdance.* Paramount TV, a division of Paramount, also hit its stride with such hit shows as *Happy Days* and *Laverne and Shirley.* Barry later jumped to Twentieth Century Fox. At Fox, Barry continued to burnish his image as a movie hit maker, turning out such popular hits as *Die Hard* and *Working Girl.*

Barry worked his magic again at Fox Broadcasting under Rupert Murdoch, the chairman of News Corp. Rupert was determined to turn Fox into America's fourth broadcast network alongside ABC, NBC, and CBS, a feat that had never been done before. Once more, Barry delivered impressively. Under Barry, Fox developed a string of megahit shows, including *Beverly Hills, 90210, The Simpsons,* and *Married . . . with Children.* The shows were creative, offbeat . . . and audiences loved them. So did advertisers. Fox's cachet on Madison Avenue skyrocketed, propelling Fox—and Barry—to fame. By the time Barry left Fox in 1992, the network was well on its way to becoming a certified hit. So was Barry. He even had his own catchphrase: "Diller Sizzle." It was a shorthand way of saying that whatever Barry touched turned to programming gold.

After leaving Fox, Barry hit the road in search of new opportunities. In December 1992, he found one. Barry shocked the Hollywood establishment by announcing plans to become the CEO of QVC, a dumpy little shopping channel based in West Chester, Pennsylvania, about forty-five minutes outside Philadelphia. Barry's backers at QVC were hardly Hollywood insiders. They included Comcast, a cable TV company based in Philadelphia, and Liberty Media, the programming arm of cable giant TCI, which was headed by John Malone. If Barry was disappointed, he didn't show it. Barry quickly agreed to invest $25 million for a 12 percent stake in QVC, then crowed that he planned to turn QVC into the gold standard of television commerce. Wall Street, which had always admired Barry's talent and bravado, pushed up QVC's shares by more than 30 percent within two weeks. By all indications, the "Diller Sizzle" was alive and well.

Barry's decision to hook his star to QVC struck some people as curious. Barry, after all, was a creative type who thrived on the excitement and glamour of Hollywood. One of his best friends was Michael Eisner, the chairman of Disney. Another good pal was Jeffrey Katzenberg of DreamWorks. Another close friend was Diane von Furstenberg, the fashion designer. QVC was a cultural backwater. The guy who defined Hollywood cool was suddenly sitting on top of a cubic zirconium empire. Barry never even bothered to move to West Chester, preferring instead to helicopter in each day from Manhattan. But no matter. In speech after speech, Barry described QVC as the perfect marriage of television and content. Not only that, he insisted QVC was the future of television, no small statement considering his programming pedigree.

It all sounded good, especially coming from Barry. But in truth, QVC was just shopping—and unexciting shopping at that. QVC had grown out of the infomercial tradition of the 1960s, and it hadn't changed all that much over the years. During every twenty-four-hour period, more than 150 items were "presented" to viewers by QVC's game-show-like hosts. Viewers dialed a toll-free 800 number to call in their orders. One of the biggest sellers was cubic zirconium jewelry. There was no glory in QVC. There was no glamour. It was just commerce.

But what QVC did have was a pristine balance sheet. You didn't have to be a rocket scientist to figure it out. Barry intended to use QVC as a launch vehicle to do big media deals. It was brilliant, really. QVC's balance sheet was flush with cash and practically debt free, making it an ideal currency for deals. Even better, QVC was privately held, so Barry didn't have the hassle of having to get approval from public shareholders. Comcast and Liberty were happy to let Barry grow QVC into a bigger media enterprise. And why not? If Barry benefited, so would they. On paper, at least, it looked like a real layup.

Soon Barry made a run at Paramount Communications, one of the biggest names in Hollywood. It was the ultimate content play: Paramount owned a treasure trove of entertainment assets, including cable, film and television libraries, a big book publisher, and, of course, Paramount Pictures, the Hollywood studio that Barry had once headed. Barry's timing, unfortunately, was a little off. By the time Barry lobbed his bid, Viacom already had a deal in place to buy Paramount for $8.2 billion. Paramount nixed Viacom's deal and said it would consider Barry's offer. Viacom soon found itself in the middle of a heated bidding war. Sumner was furious and promptly filed a lawsuit accusing Barry and John Malone, who had backed Barry's bid, of conspiring to put Viacom out of business. (See Chapter 7.) Sumner eventually prevailed, but he had to pay an extra $2 billion to claim his Paramount prize.

Barry rolled the dice again the following year. His target: CBS, one of the most storied news and entertainment organizations in America. The plan, hatched in the summer of 1994, called for QVC to be folded into CBS in a reverse merger, with CBS as the surviving entity. Barry, naturally, would have been in charge of the combined company. All the top CBS executives, including Howard Stringer, the CBS president, would have reported directly to Barry. Confident that the deal was in the bag, Barry, accompanied by Howard Stringer, flew out to meet CBS honchos in a series of private meetings. Press releases were being readied and CBS's board had convened to give its final approval when word came in that the deal . . . was dead. Comcast, which had blocking rights on big deals affecting QVC, balked at seeing its 18 percent stake in QVC diluted down to just 5 percent, with no votes and no board seat to boot. To get around a regulatory problem—cable companies couldn't own cable and broadcast TV assets in the same market—Comcast worked out a deal structure that would have permitted it to stay involved. Barry nixed that idea, telling

Brian Roberts flat out that he didn't want a partner. Barry, as promised, soldiered on by himself . . . then ran headlong into a brick wall. In the face of intractable opposition from Comcast, Barry had no choice but to pull the plug and walk away from the CBS deal. Barry resigned from QVC shortly thereafter.

Barry, it was clear, needed a creative platform he could truly call his own. Just one year after he crashed and burned on CBS, Barry made his move. In August 1995, Barry announced plans to spend $45 million for a 20 percent stake in Silver King, a group of twelve small UHF television stations whose sole purpose in life was to transmit the Home Shopping Network, the big cable TV network devoted to shopping. Silver King had been spun off from HSN a few years earlier, but was still closely aligned because of its dependence on HSN for programming. Barry's supporter on the deal? John Malone of TCI, his former ally on CBS and Paramount. TCI, through its Liberty Media programming arm, controlled both HSN and Silver King. As part of the deal, John agreed to give Barry 70 percent control of Silver King, thereby ensuring that he wouldn't run into another CBS fiasco. The way John looked at it, he was hiring Barry to run HSN for him. For Barry, the move marked a chance to finally revolutionize Internet commerce. If he worked it right, Barry could grow HSN into real media powerhouse.

Barry, who was already an advisor to HSN, soon starting pushing to bring Silver King and HSN back together. From Barry's perspective, it only made sense. Silver King was a pure distribution play; HSN was a pure content play. The two would be far stronger together than they could ever be apart. Using Silver King, Barry hoped to create the perfect "business triangle," if you will—a perfect blend of distribution, content, and technology. Silver King would represent the "distribution" leg of the triangle; HSN could provide content. Layer on interactive technology and other new innovations and Silver King could develop into an ideal platform for launching all sorts of services over time.

HSN, unfortunately, was a mess. The channel, which had zoomed to success in the 1980s hawking everything from cubic zirconium jewelry to exercise equipment, was awash in bloat and inefficiency. There were also nagging allegations of payoffs to vendors. Regulators had a lot of questions about HSN's business practices. So did the HSN board. (I should know, because I was on the HSN board.) John and I weren't so sure that

Barry could turn HSN into anything other than what it was—a relatively uninteresting shopping channel. But we were more than willing to let him try, particularly since Barry was offering TCI $300 million in newly issued Silver King stock in exchange for John's controlling stake in HSN.

Barry was a brilliant manager. But like all of us, he also had his blind spots. One of his biggest was an almost manic fear of being fired. At HSN, Barry insisted on inserting a clause that said he couldn't be fired—ever— by anybody under any circumstances. Employment contracts at the CEO level typically devote a lot of attention to the financial terms of separation in the event of termination (sometimes called the "golden parachute"). But to stipulate in writing that a CEO could *never* be fired under *any* circumstances short of criminal wrongdoing was practically unheard of.

Barry's paranoia seemed to date back to his days at Fox. As Barry's influence inside the Fox organization continued to grow, so did his tension with Rupert Murdoch. Rupert, who was stationed in New York at News Corp.'s U.S. headquarters, was pleased with the growth of the network under Barry. But he was a little worried about Fox's slow pace of expansion into other areas, such as sports. In 1992, Rupert moved to Los Angeles, where Fox is based. Saying he wanted to get more involved in day-to-day operations, Rupert moved into the office right next to Barry's and set up shop. The message to the troops was clear: Barry was no longer fully in charge. Barry also confided to some people that Rupert refused to give him a piece of Fox. Barry left Fox shortly thereafter.

The HSN board didn't care about any of this. As a practical matter, we figured the chances of Barry's screwing up were slim to none. Barry was an experienced manager with a passion for the business. Wall Street loved him. Even more important, so did John Malone. He implicitly trusted Barry's business judgment—and John doesn't trust too many people. (John once said there was nobody he trusted more with his money then Barry Diller. Coming from a guy who cares a whole lot about how his money gets managed, that's a strong endorsement.) The way the HSN board looked at it, we were lucky to get a person of Barry's stature and talents. So if Barry wanted an ironclad employment contract, we were more than happy to give it to him.

With Barry at the helm, HSN greatly improved. Barry, who always had a sharp pencil when it came to weeding out costs, quickly trimmed HSN's bloated structure. He brought in a lot of new managers and exerted tight control over day-to-day operations. Allegations about vendor payoffs soon evaporated. Confidence in HSN's long-term prospects soared. For all Barry's hard work, however, HSN was fundamentally the same—it was still a big, boring shopping channel. Barry, of course, had far bigger ambitions than just conquering shopping. He still had his eye on Hollywood.

Barry wanted to be the savior of Internet commerce, and by 1997 he was making some headway. Barry by then had emerged as a chief proponent of electronic commerce. He had assembled an eclectic but interesting collection of assets, including Ticketmaster and a budding e-travel site. But Barry's growing empire was still light on hard media assets. Years of consolidation had taken many of the best entertainment and media assets off the table. And forget about the big Hollywood movie studios. They were long gone. Time Warner owned Warner Bros. Viacom owned Paramount. Sony owned Columbia. Miramax, the movie fiefdom controlled by Harvey Weinstein and his brother, was firmly entrenched at Disney, which also owned ABC and ESPN. Barry did manage to buy one studio, Savoy Pictures, a tiny independent with four TV stations attached to it.

Barry's acquisition binge had left him with sixteen TV stations and a hodgepodge of e-commerce and shopping assets. That wasn't bad considering where Barry had started out just two years earlier—with no distribution, no programming, and no Internet assets. But the former media king was still a long way from the Hollywood big leagues. Barry didn't seem to care one bit. He just couldn't seem to say enough about the promise of Internet and video commerce. To hear him lather on about HSN, you'd have thought the last thing on Barry's mind was Edgar Bronfman, Jr. Nobody believed him for a second, of course.

Edgar Bronfman, Jr., Seagram's CEO, was under a lot of pressure. All you had to do was pick up a newspaper to know that. Thanks to his landslide victory over Viacom, Seagram was on a court-dictated pathway to owning USA Networks outright. That was good. But Edgar didn't have a rescue plan for USA, which was bad. Edgar was also taking a lot of heat for financing the MCA deal with Seagram's 24 percent stake in the chemical giant DuPont. To get funding for the MCA deal, Edgar sold the stake back to DuPont for about $9 billion, which was about $3 billion less than what it was worth on the open market. Adding to Edgar's pain, DuPont shares continued to gain in value, even as the entertainment stocks were slipping. Seagram by then was considered more of an entertainment play, so its stock price bounced off some lows along with all the others. Seagram's stockholders weren't too happy about all this, to say the least. And since a lot of those shareholders were members of the Bronfman family, neither was Edgar.

Barry, who has a nose like a bloodhound when it comes to sniffing out opportunities for himself, picked up the phone and called Edgar. Barry offered to help Edgar out of his jam by running USA for him. (To be fair, Edgar was actually the one who first proposed the idea of Barry coming onboard to run USA. Edgar had broached the subject over a private dinner at his home while the Viacom-Seagram court fight over USA was still going on. Barry, ever ambitious, agreed to think it over and get back to him.) With Barry's knowledge and Edgar's entertainment assets, the partnership was bound to be a win-win for everybody. Edgar was still interested, and why not? Barry, after all, was everything that Edgar aspired to be—a certified Hollywood insider. Barry consorted with the royalty of Hollywood. Heck, Barry *was* Hollywood royalty. The fact that Barry was CEO of a rather dowdy shopping channel in Tampa did nothing to change his top billing in Hollywood. Even though he'd been out of the limelight a long time by then, Barry was the real deal.

And Edgar? Though he had almost singlehandedly managed to transform a stodgy liquor company into a major entertainment powerhouse, Edgar was still a Hollywood novice. Sure, Edgar got invited to all the right parties and knew all the right people, at least by name and affiliation. But Barry—he automatically commanded respect. *Things happened* when Barry showed up. Edgar, with all his family history and connections, was still acquiring his own star power. To transform USA into something special, he'd need somebody like Barry in his corner. True? Not true? I had no idea. But I suspect that's what Edgar thought. And Barry, being a master of the Hollywood illusion, was probably happy to have him think it.

After he pitched Edgar, Barry called up John to deliver the good news: Seagram was interested in combining HSN with USA and Sci-Fi into one company. Barry, of course, would run the combined company. TCI would retain a hefty stake in the surviving entity. Universal Studios, unfortunately, wouldn't be part of the mix. But the combined company would have the full support of Seagram/Universal, which would retain a large stake. John and I were thrilled. Thanks to Barry, TCI was on the verge of turning a plain-vanilla shopping platform into a credible media player, one that could go toe-to-toe with the likes of Time Warner, Sony, and Via-com. It was almost a miracle, really. USA and Sci-Fi represented hard me-dia assets. HSN, to be honest, didn't belong in the same world. The only thing that made HSN even remotely interesting to investors and, I sus-pect, to Edgar, was the fact that Barry was willing to put his name on it. But if Edgar was willing to overlook the obvious, then so were we.

By then I had left InterMedia to become president of TCI under John, who had been elevated to chairman. Since I was still on the HSN board, I decided to poke around a little bit. I called up Bob Matschullat, Seagram's vice chairman and chief financial officer, to talk through the details of Barry's plan. Bob and I went way back. We'd graduated from Stanford business school together in 1971 and had remained friendly over the years. I told Bob that John and I were thrilled at the prospect of teaming up with Seagram. But I was also a little curious. Why not throw Universal Studios into the mix? The other big entertainment houses like Time Warner and Viacom were structured to allow for maximum cross-pollina-tion of the cable and movie properties. Why not do the same with HSN?

Bob was as nice as he could be, but he also made it clear that there was no way that was happening. The deal, if it went forward, would have to be structured to ensure that Barry's operations were completely separate—fi-nancially, managerially, and otherwise—from the rest of Seagram's media empire. The problem, in a word, was Barry. Like so many people in the en-tertainment world, Bob and Frank Biondi, the Universal chief, were well aware of Barry's penchant for power grabbing. There was also the matter of Barry's unique employment demands. Barry made it clear to everybody that he'd entertain no changes whatsoever to his existing employment contract. So even though Barry would technically be working for Edgar, in practice he'd have complete managerial autonomy. And he couldn't be fired—ever. That presented Seagram's with a Hobson's choice: agree to Barry's terms, but keep him penned up tight or reject his terms and watch one of the best management talents ever produced by Hollywood walk out the door.

Bob and Frank were understandably wary. They felt that if Barry got his nose under the Universal tent, Edgar would wind up as CEO in name only. Hollywood insiders knew about the power play that had led to Barry's departure from Fox. Edgar was a good, solid manager, but he was no Rupert. Bob didn't fear Barry, mind you. But he did recognize Barry for what he was—a brilliant, aggressive, domineering entertainment executive. To bring that sort of personality into the Seagram fold to stand side by side with Edgar, an understated and genteel executive, would have been a nightmare—for Edgar. Given Barry's bigger Hollywood ambitions, or at least *perceived* Hollywood ambitions, Bob said, that was the way it would have to be.

I tried to convince Bob to change his mind. I strongly argued in favor of throwing Universal into the USA mix. I used all the right buzzwords, including "Diller Sizzle," "creative synergy," and "teamwork." Nothing worked. Outwardly, I expressed disappointment. But in my heart I knew Bob was right. He was dead on the screws, in fact. If I'd been in Bob's shoes and had the responsibility of advising Edgar, I'd have given him the same advice. Bob was right: There was no limit to Barry's ambition. John and I knew it. In fact, we'd been counting on it. Barry, perhaps sensing the answer ahead of time, hadn't even bothered to ask Edgar about Universal. He later told John that he never had any interest in running the studio, anyway.

After seven weeks and a lot of back and forth, we had a deal. On October 20, 1997, we announced that HSN and Universal Studios were combining their cable and TV assets. The merger would leave Barry as chairman and CEO of USA Networks. The merger would take a series of transactions to effect. Technically, USA Networks would be merged into HSN, which would be the surviving entity. Upon closing, HSN would change its name to USA Networks. (We did it this way because HSN was the only publicly traded company of the bunch.) Under terms of the deal, Seagram/Universal would get $4.1 billion of total consideration in the form of a 45 percent stake in USA, plus $1.2 billion in cash. Barry would control 40 percent of USA; Liberty would wind up with 15 percent of the combined company, with the right to ratchet up to 25 percent over time. The combination of Barry's 40 percent stake and Liberty's 15 percent stake, for which Barry exercised voting rights, would leave Barry in full control of USA.

The new media partnership would control three cable TV networks—HSN, USA, and Sci-Fi—twenty-five broadcast stations, Ticketmaster, Universal's TV production and distribution business, and a small Internet shopping business. In announcing the deal, Edgar called Barry "one of the entertainment industry's most admired and effective talents." Barry returned the favor, saying he had "known, trusted, and respected Edgar Bronfman, Jr., for more than twenty years." Barry crowed that the new partnership, assisted by TCI and others, would enable USA Networks to grow into a "major enterprise." In a prepared statement, Ron Meyer, the president and chief operating officer of Universal Studios, offered that he was "delighted to become associated with Barry Diller." Ron, who was revered for his management of Universal Studios, described Barry as a "close personal friend and executive who enjoys the deepest respect of the entire entertainment industry." On the surface, at least, it was a real lovefest.

What nobody said outright, of course, was that Barry was penned in like a prize stallion in a padded corral. The one Seagram business that Barry perhaps lusted after the most, and for which his experience had best prepared him—Universal Studios—was strictly off-limits. By the time we announced the deal, there were so many walls in place to keep Barry boxed in that USA and Universal might as well have been in different businesses. They were like East and West Berlin before the Wall came down. If he was concerned, Barry didn't show it. After all, he had just managed to talk his way from the backwaters of Tampa into the pinnacle of the Hollywood power structure. Or so he thought.

By the time the USA deal closed on February 12, 1998, the consequences of this rather strained arrangement were already becoming apparent. Barry by then was trolling hard for media deals. It didn't take him long to come up with a big one: NBC. The deal was strategically compelling. The combination would fill in a lot of Universal's holes and also give it a high-profile distribution platform for TV shows, movies, and other content. Because of foreign ownership rules, Seagram, a Canadian company, technically wasn't allowed to own a broadcast network. (It could own cable, but not traditional broadcasting assets like NBC.) To be sure, foreign ownership wasn't an insignificant issue. But it was by no means a dealbreaker. What the board couldn't get around, however, was Barry. As the NBC discussions wore on, Barry made it clear he wouldn't cede any management control—not one iota, in fact. He wanted the same arrangement that he had with USA: namely, he would have 100 percent control over the company—with no chance of being fired or second-guessed, ever, under any circumstances.

Seagram really liked the deal and tried to come up with an arrangement that might satisfy Barry. Bob and some of the others on the Seagram/ Universal side played around with the idea of giving Barry 100 percent control over NBC for a period of time, but with the firm understanding that a sunset provision would kick in after a while. Barry refused to budge, however, and talk about the deal eventually died.

Barry, never one to stay down for long, kept pitching deals—and kept getting turned down. Since I was representing TCI's interests on Barry's board, I supported all of Barry's ideas, including his idea of starting a new movie production business. TCI was happy to extend Barry's reach as fast and as far as possible. After all, anything that added value to USA automatically added value to TCI. The board members from Seagram and Universal, as I said, had an entirely different agenda. The problem, from their perspective, was that any deal that transformed USA into a major Hollywood power would, by definition, expand Barry's management authority. That, of course, was something they had no interest in doing. Before long, the USA board turned fairly schizophrenic, with all the Universal-related directors routinely leaning one way, and all the non-Universal-related directors (including me) leaning another on development and expansion opportunities. It drove Barry nuts.

Barry and Seagram were suddenly living a version of "Pareto Optimality" gone bad. Pareto Optimality, an economic theory dreamed up by Vilfredo Pareto in the 1920s, is a state of affairs in which it is not possible to improve the economic lot of one side without making the other side worse off. Barry and Seagram were at a stalemate: If it let Barry out of his management box, Seagram felt, it ran the risk of diminishing its own media fortunes. But Barry felt he needed to expand his reach to make good on his greater promise to his shareholders and to himself—to turn HSN into a major media player.

Fortunately for Barry, fate came to the rescue. Vivendi, a French water utility company intent on becoming a global entertainment power, bought Seagram for $34 billion in 2000. The following year, Vivendi, now called Vivendi Universal, agreed to buy Barry's stake in USA (as well as the stakes held by Liberty Media and the public) for about $10 billion. That was more than double what these stakes had been purchased for just three years earlier in our USA deal. Vivendi agreed to install Barry as the head of Universal Studios, including the theme parks and, of course, the fabled movie studio. Barry also got a big title: chairman, Vivendi Universal Entertainment. The move marked—at long last—Barry's triumphant return to Hollywood. Barry, with his infamous "Diller Sizzle," had finally come full circle.

In announcing its arrangement with Barry, Vivendi pointedly noted that Barry wouldn't have an employment contract with Universal. Barry, to all appearances, would finally be working without a safety net—sort of. Barry's employment contract with USA would remain firmly in place, however. That meant Barry could stay at USA and oversee the cable assets, Ticketmaster, and all the other Internet commerce assets that he had assembled for as long as he pleased. But his service at Universal Studios, the real apple of Barry's eye, was totally at the pleasure of Jean-Marie Messier, then Vivendi's chairman.

Barry, always his own best spin doctor, characterized the omission as a big plus—for *him*. Barry was quoted in some papers as saying that, because he had no contract with Universal, he was free to walk away from Universal at any time. (As if.) The point was a fine one. Ron Meyer, who was still running Universal, was one of the most respected—and liked— executives in Hollywood. Under Ron's leadership, Universal had churned out a string of hits, including *The Mummy, Erin Brockovich,* and *American Pie*. Ron had also managed to turn Universal into a relatively collegial and pleasant place to work, at least by Hollywood's cutthroat standards. But no matter. Hollywood has always been a town of illusions. And nobody but nobody has ever been better at playing that game than Barry Diller.

LOOKING BACK

By one measure the USA deal was hugely successful in that it allowed TCI to turn a relatively uninteresting shopping channel, HSN, into a credible and valuable media asset. Seagram also didn't fare so bad. With Barry at the helm, Seagram's investment in HSN-USA soared more than two and half times, to about $7.5 billion. All that said, the deal structure didn't serve either side particularly well. Having Barry penned up like that didn't allow either side to take advantage of his prodigious talents or the natural synergies that are inherent in big media organizations. What we wound up with, as I said, was a version of Pareto Optimality gone bad. I suspect the strategic standoff would still be going on if Vivendi hadn't come along.

STAR POWER

Edgar might have been a Hollywood novice in comparison to Barry, but he was a Hollywood novice sitting on top of one of the best collections of media assets in the world at the time.

With all due respect to Barry, Edgar probably would have been better off taking a pass on Barry and finding somebody else to run USA. There were at least a half-dozen highly qualified entertainment executives who could have stepped in at the time and done a nice job. As it was, Seagram and Universal brought in somebody they fundamentally feared and didn't really trust. It was a terrible way to start a marriage. Just the fact that Edgar's own senior management team felt the need to protect him from Barry like that should have been a huge red flag to everybody.

I could certainly understand Seagram's interest in HSN. Consolidation had claimed most of the best assets, so there wasn't an awful lot left. HSN was basically the last girl left on the dance floor. All that said, I think Seagram should have taken a pass. HSN, after all, was just shopping. So it was an odd cow that was never going to fit in with the rest of Seagram's media assets. Plus, it was attached to Barry, who, as I said, had some complicated strings attached.

Don't get me wrong. John Malone and I loved the USA deal. It was only because of this deal that we were able to roll up HSN into Seagram, which, under Edgar, was fast on its way to becoming one of the most dynamic media organizations on the planet. TCI got a huge upside from that. But putting TCI's interests aside (with apologies to John), Edgar probably could have done a lot better by taking his marbles and trying his luck elsewhere. NBC versus HSN? You be the judge.

BE CAREFUL WHAT YOU ASK FOR . . .

As a CEO who has labored under, shall we say, challenging management situations myself over the years, I can appreciate the desire, if not the need, to create as much certainty as possible in the executive suite. But let's be honest here. Barry's "no-firing" demand eventually became a big stretch.

I could understand, to a point, why this particular requirement was important to him. In fast-growing and fast-changing companies like HSN, executives need the latitude and freedom to make decisions quickly and with impunity. My current contract with YES gives me similarly broad security. (And, in fact, I picked up some of my own employment contract language from Barry.)

But in the context of Seagram and certainly of NBC, asking for that kind of ironclad protection was, at least in my opinion, a tad excessive. When I was at TCI, I didn't even have an employment contract. By the time he got to USA, I think Barry's employment demands hurt him a lot more than they helped. How so? *Methinks thou dost protest too much.* By insisting that he could never be fired, Barry predetermined the limitations placed on him. And those limitations, as we've discussed, weren't insignificant. The irony is that nobody was ever going to fire Barry, anyway. For all his eccentricities and excesses, Barry was—and is—a brilliant executive. Seagram was rightly thrilled to have him. So in the end, not only was Barry's "no-firing" requirement a reach, it was also totally unnecessary. (Rule 8: Don't keep score on things that don't matter.)

I think Barry would have done himself and USA a huge favor if he had been a bit more flexible on his employment demands. If he had done that, he might be sitting in the CEO's office at NBC today. Maybe he could have revisited the question of CBS. Maybe he could have done a lot of things. As it was, it took a French water company intent on conquering the media world to set things straight.

Well, almost. In the fall of 2002, Vivendi tried to reduce its heavy debt load but ran into a brick wall. As it turned out, a thicket of restrictions buried in the merger agreement gave Barry all sorts of approvals over asset sales. Vivendi discovered that it couldn't sell off certain assets that were important to Barry, including USA and Sci-Fi, without his express approval. (Is this starting to sound familiar?) These same conditions also gave Barry a lot of sway over the future of Vivendi Universal Entertainment, the partnership that included Universal Music and Universal Studios. Now *that's* a plot twist ending that could only happen in Hollywood.

9

LOOKING AHEAD

So why write a book about big media deals, some of which are now five years old and counting? The short answer: because these deals will happen again.

The media world, as I said at the outset of this book, conducts itself according to a different set of rules. Take consolidation. Most industries in the throes of consolidation eventually do fully consolidate. Then there are no more deals—the chessboard is set. That was the experience of the railroad industry, the oil industry, the chemical industry, and the steel industry. In fact, that's been the experience of just about every major U.S. industry I can think of with one notable exception—media.

The media world never seems to find contentment. No matter how much it consolidates and reconfigures itself, the media world is never truly at peace. Not that a lot of CEOs don't try, mind you. As discussed in this book, media CEOs spend a lot of their waking hours thinking up new and clever ways to combine and recombine assets, all with the hope of engineering the ultimate media machine. That's one of the reasons the media world is in constant flux. Almost like clockwork, breathtaking deals emerge every few years and appear to settle the competitive chessboard. But any given chessboard only lasts until . . . the next breathtaking deal comes along.

There is no perfect media company, and maybe there's not supposed to be. When Henry Luce started Time, Inc., back in 1923, he had just one magazine—*Time*. Then *Life* came along and there were two magazines, and before you knew it there was a third and then a fourth. Today, the magazine division of Time, now called AOL Time Warner, publishes more than 140 titles around the globe. In addition to such gold standards as *Time, People,* and *Sports Illustrated,* AOL Time Warner also publishes *Rugby World* (United Kingdom) and *InStyle,* a frothy spin-off of *People* that features happy news about the lifestyles of the rich and famous. The little company that started out with one magazine in 1923 recorded revenues of $38 billion in 2001, making it one of the biggest media conglomerates on the planet. The magazine division accounted for just 12 percent of overall revenue, making it one of the smaller parts of AOL Time Warner.

The evolution of Time underscores, rather dramatically, yet another truth about the media business: It's deliciously unpredictable. Back in the 1980s when Ted Turner was trumpeting his idea of a twenty-four-hour global news service, most Americans were content to have their news spoon-fed to them in half-hour and hour increments at 6:00 and 11:00. The Big Three broadcasters—ABC, CBS, and NBC (Fox TV didn't yet exist)—handily dominated the airwaves. For weekly roundups and news analysis, we turned to *Time* and *Newsweek.* Ted's novel idea—that you could tune in to cable for the latest in news developments around the world—seemed so blue-sky as to be practically laughable. Cable TV was an also-ran compared to broadcast. Many people subscribed to cable just to improve TV reception.

Mike Jordan, Westinghouse's CEO, was similarly derided when he announced plans to buy CBS in 1995. At the time, Mike was sitting on top of a hodgepodge of industrial assets that included, among other things, a construction business that specialized in nuclear reactors. Westinghouse, with just a handful of TV and radio stations, knew next to nothing about the media business. It was also a lot smaller than CBS. Westinghouse had a market capitalization of about $4 billion; CBS was 50 percent larger, with a market value of nearly $6 billion. A lot of people thought Mike was out of his mind.

Appearances, of course, can be deceiving. Ted Turner, as we now know, was dead on the screws with his prescient vision of twenty-four-hour news. Ted's vision not only changed the world of news, it changed the world. Thanks to CNN, millions of Americans got their first real glimpse of the global village, and in the process it forced us all to expand our hearts and minds. As for Westinghouse-CBS, the only people who ate crow on that deal were Mike Jordan's detractors. By the time the merger was done, Mike had transformed Westinghouse into a sleek media powerhouse with one of the best brand names in news. Mike's successor, Mel Karmazin, subsequently sold CBS to Viacom for $34 billion, nearly six times what Mike paid for it.

Other big media gambles careened straight off a cliff. AT&T chairman Mike Armstrong spent more than $100 billion buying cable TV systems, with an eye on using them to offer AT&T-branded local phone service across the country. Four years later, with the job not even close to being done, Mike threw in the towel . . . and claimed victory. Mike wound up selling AT&T's cable assets to Comcast for a third less than what he paid for them. By then, AT&T had also piled on the debt. As this is being written, AT&T's stock price is trading at an historical low, and its once-vaunted credit rating has fallen to the point that its bonds are on the brink of becoming junk.

The jury is still out on the AOL–Time Warner merger. The merger was sharply criticized after the Internet boom went bust. Jerry Levin, Time Warner's former chairman, was eviscerated for paying what appeared, at least in hindsight, to be an exceptionally rich price for AOL. I don't know if Jerry paid too high a price, and, as I said, I would argue that nobody else does, either. There's a big difference between bad pricing and bad strategy. It will be a few years before any of us know for sure if Jerry paid too much. In any event the real question isn't whether Jerry overpaid— it's whether Time Warner is a better company for owning AOL. To my way of thinking the answer is clear: absolutely yes. Owning AOL-type assets in combination with traditional media assets is, on its face, a smart idea. Did Jerry overemphasize how quickly the two companies could meld and merge and realize benefits in the marketplace? Probably. But that doesn't mean the combination was a bad one for the long haul. Despite the jeers from Wall Street, I believe the AOL–Time Warner deal will prove to be enormously successful over time.

From a purely practical standpoint, of course, it doesn't matter if any of these deals *should* have been done. The fact is, they *were* done, and now they will be hard to undo, at least cost-efficiently. Witness AT&T: In buying TCI and MediaOne Group, AT&T took on billions of dollars in unrealized taxable gains that had piled up over the years. Since AT&T never intended to sell off its cable TV systems, all these taxable gains were largely viewed as a nonevent. And, in fact, it *was* a nonevent so long as AT&T stayed glued together as one company.

But now that Humpty Dumpty is coming apart, it's potentially a huge problem. Why? If and when the last chunk of AT&T is sold, all the taxable gains racked up (and carried forward) by AT&T over the years, including those arising from Mike's $100 billion shopping spree on cable, will have to be paid in full. The tax hit could approach $20 billion, which is more than what AT&T's entire long distance business was worth as of 2002. I'm not sure who is brave enough—or rich enough—to voluntarily take on decades of accumulated taxes like that. But only time will tell. Other big media mergers, for similar reasons, can't be easily—or inexpensively—dismantled. So we're basically stuck with them. The challenge going forward will be learning to live in the new consolidated, yet ever-changing, world we've created.

Samuel Goldwyn, the famous Hollywood producer, once said you should never make forecasts—especially about the future. At the risk of careening off a cliff myself, I'd like to at least take a stab at talking about the future of the media world. As AT&T's experience suggests, I think it's a good bet that some of the same companies that created seismic changes in the marketplace will, themselves, become acquisition targets. Though AT&T started out as an aggressive buyer of media properties, by the time it was all over AT&T was clearly in the selling mode.

AT&T isn't alone. Disney, which also owns ABC and 80 percent of ESPN, could easily become an acquisition target. Right after it purchased ABC, Disney was worth so much money that it was heavily fortified against unwanted suitors. (It was, as I've said, "Disneyfied" against intruders.) Since those heady times, however, Disney has given up so much of its value through mismanagement and other miscues that it is no longer secure. As this is being written, Disney's stock is at a five-year low, and a number of companies are circling. Disney would probably prosper under different management. The biggest question is whether Michael Eisner, Disney's current CEO, will do the right thing and permit Disney to be sold. Thanks to some longtime loyalists, Michael controls his board. He also likes his job a lot, so he may not be willing to take a smart deal, especially if it means he gets booted.

I will be watching along with the rest of the media world to see what happens with Vivendi Universal. As this is being written, Vivendi is still an odd collection of old-economy assets—such as water systems—and new-media assets, including USA Networks and Universal Pictures. The architect of Vivendi's dramatic transformation, Jean-Marie Messier, was recently asked to step down by his own board. It will fall to his successor to pick up the pieces. Mr. Messier used to take comfort in the fact that, thank God, they still have the utility assets. As should be apparent by now, that was a losing strategy. Vivendi needs to decide real fast what it wants to be—fish or fowl—then execute like mad. Vivendi needs to manage the old-economy assets well or manage the new-media assets well, because no management team can do both. Most companies don't have enough energy or know-how to pull off balancing acts like that. Those that try usually fail. Jimmy Ling's LTV Corp. embarked on a shopping spree in the late 1960s that would net him, over time, a hodgepodge of unrelated companies. By the time it was all over, LTV owned, among other things, a meat packing company, a steel company, a sporting goods company, and a commercial airline. Needless to say, LTV eventually imploded. I studied the LTV case when I was in business school. Vivendi could wind up as a business-school case study, as well.

Despite all the uncertainty created by consolidation, one thing is for sure: More big media deals are on the way. The only question is where, and in what time frame. Geographically, there's no telling where the next media gold rush might spring up. As economies around the globe shift, so do people's interests as well as their ability to partake of the commercial fruits that the media world can offer. Technology, which is always improving, only quickens the pace of change. James Murdoch (Rupert Murdoch's son) didn't decide to make his home in Hong Kong just because he likes the view. Hong Kong, after all, is now part of China, the biggest and potentially most lucrative untapped media market in the world. Once the Chinese market completely opens up—and the only question is when, not if—the expansion opportunities could be staggering. Other global hot spots, such as old Eastern Europe, are also compelling.

Will tomorrow's dealmakers be as creative as their storied predecessors? Maybe more so. James and Lachlan Murdoch are quickly moving up the ladder at News Corp. My short list of tomorrow's superstars also includes Jeff Bewkes, previously of HBO, the pay TV service owned by AOL Time Warner. Under Jeff's watchful eye, HBO turned into *The New York Times* of the cable world—a must-have for serious media buffs. Jeff has an eye for innovative programming and a stomach for pushing the edge. How else to explain *Six Feet Under, The Sopranos,* and *Sex and the City?* In 2002 Jeff was named chairman of the Entertainment and Networks Group at AOL Time Warner. I'm sure it won't be the last promotion he gets. Rich Bressler of Viacom is also one of the great ones. Rich, Viacom's chief financial officer, was right in the thick of things when Time Warner and Viacom were ratcheted up to the next level. So he understands, on a nuts-and-bolts level, how these media giants were put together, and how they need to be run. As this is being written, Rich is the de facto liason between Sumner Redstone and Mel Karmazin at Viacom. Even more impressive, Rich has so far lived to tell about it. Other up-and-comers include Steve Burke of Comcast, Matt Blank of Showtime, Anne Sweeney of Disney, and David Zaslav of NBC.

The person with the toughest and potentially most rewarding media job out there is Dick Parsons of AOL Time Warner. Dick was appointed chairman and CEO of the company following Jerry Levin's retirement in 2002. The company that Jerry handed over to Dick is huge and operationally challenging, to say the least. It's also a prime platform for validating the whole concept of convergence, as well as the AOL–Time Warner deal. The stakes are crushingly high. If Dick fails, he not only runs the risk of letting down his own company, he runs the risk of bringing down the entire media industry with him. AOL Time Warner is so bloody big that if it falters, so will the rest of the media world. Thousands of AOL Time Warner employees and millions of customers could also suffer. That is both the thrill and the terror of sitting atop a market leader like AOL Time Warner—the opportunity to affect positive change is matched only by the potential for unmitigated disaster.

I am confident that Dick will be enormously successful. Though some people criticized Dick, at least initially, because he didn't hail from the media world, I actually consider that to be one of his many strengths. Unlike so many other media CEOs, Dick didn't arrive at Time Warner with industry biases. When Jerry reached out to Dick in 1995, he was CEO of Dime Savings, a relatively small bank in New York City. During his six years as Jerry's No. 2, Dick showed a real gift for constituency building. That's no small feat in a company as large—and as territorial—as Time Warner. That talent will be even more important now that Time Warner is the size of Delaware.

Though he's not a dealmaker to the bone like Jerry, Dick has a mix of strategic vision, doggedness, and sensitivity like few others. His handling of Ted Turner was classic. By the time Jerry retired, unfortunately, his relationship with Ted had become quite strained. Ted had begun dumping on Jerry publicly and was making it clear he was extremely unhappy with the company's performance. People openly wondered if Ted was going to remain on the AOL Time Warner board. Right after he was appointed chairman, Dick reached out to Ted and asked him to stay on the board. Dick also made it crystal clear to everybody that he considered Ted's participation critical to the long-term success of the company. All in all, it was the kind of sensitive gesture you would expect from Dick, who has always had a great relationship with Ted. It was also incredibly smart, given that Ted owned about 10 percent of the company and still wielded a lot of influence in the media world.

If Dick uses his CEO power thoughtfully and wisely, as I know he will, he can not only leave a lasting impact on AOL Time Warner, he can, quite literally, change the world. How? By declaring his business and societal objectives loudly and clearly, then marching decisively to his own drumbeat, with only his shareholders' interests in mind. Given the business realities of living in a consolidated, albeit ever-changing, media world, having a thoughtful leader like Dick at the head of the table isn't just important—it's imperative. And the reason for that is simple: This is not the steel industry. Steel, no matter how cheap or abundant, doesn't change the world. But accessible, cheaper, and more diverse media do. That is the promise of the consolidated world we've created. It will be up to the next generation of leaders, such as Dick—and James, Lachlan, Jeff, Rich, Anne, Dave, and all the others—to deliver on that pledge.

As for me, I've pretty much reached the end of my dealmaking run. With any luck, I'll sell the YES network within a few years, then retire to indulge my passion for politics, my Colorado ranch, and Tuscany, though not necessarily in that order. Are any more deals in my future beyond that? As an admitted deal junkie, I would never say never to jumping back into the game. I love the thrill of the hunt, the rewards, and, yes, even the risks that are part and parcel of this grand game we call Dealmaking. (This book isn't called *The Biggest Game of All* for nothing, you know.) So let me hedge my bets by saying "maybe," and just leave it at that.

My aim in writing this book was to help readers understand and appreciate the larger impact of some of the most significant business deals of the past decade. Deals come and deals go. But as I hope is clear by now, there are lessons for us all in why they happen and how they happen. Likewise, there are lessons to be gleaned by taking a look at how dealmakers make decisions and interact behind the scenes. Sumner Redstone is a testament to the value of pure doggedness. Rupert Murdoch taught us the importance of keeping the bigger picture in mind. Jerry Levin's courage to follow his dream showed us the reward—and risk—of hewing to a vision. And Jack Welch? He left behind a credo that will be affecting managers up and down the line for generations. John Malone's ability to outthink the competition is an elegant testimony to the value of believing—in yourself, in your creativity, and in your intellect. Even the failures are instructive. Mike Armstrong showed us the danger of hubris and overreaching. So did Carly Fiorina, Bernie Ebbers, and a lot of others.

No matter how you happen to feel about any of the transactions I've discussed, the impact of these deals, as well as the men and women behind them, is undeniable. Considered in their totality, I think it's safe to say that they have fundamentally and forever altered the world we live in. And I'm not just referring to the competitive landscape. These transactions have profoundly influenced the manner in which we, as citizens and as consumers, shop, entertain, and inform ourselves. Even more important, perhaps, they've greatly affected the manner in which we interact with one another and, on a far more macro level, the world. Last but certainly not least, these transactions have created plenty of new opportunities—and pitfalls—for future dealmakers. And maybe, just maybe, a few old-timers as well.

INDEX